THE CATECHISM IN EXAMPLES

VOLUME II

HOPE: PRAYER

REV. D. CHISHOLM

SENSUS FIDELIUM PRESS

CONTENTS

PART I
THE VIRTUE OF HOPE

1. WHAT IS MEANT BY HOPE   3
   ST. FRANCIS DE SALES' WORDS OF
   CONSOLATION.   3
   HOME, SWEET HOME.   4
   ST. AUGUSTINE'S QUESTION.   5
   ST. JANE CHANTAL AT DEATH.   6

2. THE GRACE OF GOD THE CHIEF OBJECT OF
   OUR HOPE   7
   "GIVE ME BACK MY SON."   7

3. THE PARDON OF OUR SINS ANOTHER OBJECT OF
   OUR HOPE   10
   THE WIDOW'S CHILD.   10
   ST. BERNARD'S HOPE IN GOD.   11

4. THE KINGDOM OF HEAVEN THE INAL OBJECT OF
   OUR HOPE.   13
   "LOOK UP TO HEAVEN, MY CHILD."   13
   ST. LIDWINA'S CROWN.   15

5. ON PRESUMPTION   18
   QUINTUS DENIES HIS FAITH.   18
   PRINCE EUGENE AND THE AUSTRIAN
   GENERAL.   19
   DELAY OF CONFESSION.   20
   THE PRESUMPTUOUS MONK.   21

6. ON DIFFIDENCE IN OURSELVES   22
   PACCUS TEMPTED IN THE WILDERNESS.   22
   "BECAUSE I AM SO WEAK."   23
   ST. MARGARET IN PRISON.   23

7. ON DESPAIR   25
    THE TERRIBLE VISION.   25
    THE TERRIBLE END OF JUDAS.   26
    SATAN AND THE PIOUS MONK.   27

8. ON CONFIDENCE IN GOD   29
    RIPE FOR HEAVEN.   29
    THE DYING FATHER.   31
    IN THE ARMS OF JESUS.   32
    THE RESCUE OF THEODULUS.   33
    THE WOMAN HEALED OF THE ISSUE OF
    BLOOD.   33
    ST. FRANCIS DE SALES' CONFIDENCE IN GOD.   34
    ST. FRANCES DRIVES SATAN AWAY.   34
    ST. MARTIN OF NANTES.   35
    ST. BERNARD'S ADMONITION.   36

9. HOPE OUR CONSOLATION AT THE HOUR OF
    DEATH   37
    ST. PAUL'S WORDS OF ENCOURAGEMENT.   37
    ST. PHILIP NERI'S WORDS TO JESUS.   38
    ST. ROSE OF LIMA'S FEARS.   38
    "GOD IS FAITHFUL."   38

PART II

PRAYER

10. WHAT PRAYER IS   43
    ST. IGNATIUS AND THE CARRIER.   43
    THE POOR MAN'S PRAYER.   44

11. PRAYER IS ALL-POWERFUL WITH GOD   46
    LEGEND OF ST. SCHOLASTICA.   46

12. PRAYER, THE KEY OF HEAVEN   48
    THE TEMPEST CALMED.   48
    A SAINTLY MAN IN DANGER.   50

13. THE PRAYER OF THANKSGIVING   52
    KING ALPHONSUS AND THE BEGGAR.   52
    THE ABBOT SABBAS AND THE CAMEL-DRIVERS.   54

14. WE SHOULD PRAY WITH RESIGNATION   56
     A MOTHER'S RASH PRAYER GRANTED.   56
     THE BLIND MAN AT THE TOMB OF ST. THOMAS.   57
     ST. FRANCIS BORGIA'S PRAYER OF SUBMISSION.   58
     VI. WE SHOULD PRAY WITH CONFIDENCE.   59
     THE POOR WIDOW.   59
     THE ANGRY KING.   60
     "I SHALL NOT DIE TONIGHT."   61
     ST. ULRICH, BISHOP OF AUGSBOURG.   65

15. WE SHOULD PRAY ALWAYS   67
     ALWAYS PRAYING.   67
     THE IGNORANT WOMAN'S PRAYER.   68
     MORNING AND EVENING PRAYER.   69

16. WE SHOULD PRAY WITH PERSEVERANCE   70
     THE NEGRO BOY'S PRAYER.   70
     "HE ALWAYS SAID THE SAME WORDS."   71

17. WE SHOULD PRAY WITH GREAT DEVOTION   73
     WHY HE DID NOT GO STRAIGHT TO HEAVEN.   73
     ST. BERNARD'S VISION OF THE ANGELS.   74
     TWO MONKS AT PRAYER.   75
     HOW SATAN TEMPTS US AT OUR PRAYERS.   75

PART III
"OUR FATHER WHO ART IN HEAVEN"

18. GOD IS OUR FATHER BECAUSE HE CREATED US.   81
     THE SHEPHERD BOY OF THE MOUNTAINS.   81
     THE VETERAN SOLDIER AND HIS HEAVENLY
     FATHER.   83
     ST. HUGH OF GRENOBLE'S ANSWER TO HIS
     SERVANT.   84
     PAUL, THE LITTLE AFRICAN.   84
     THE STRANGER AND THE TWO LITTLE
     ORPHANS.   85
     THE POOR WIDOW'S OFFERING.   86

19. GOD IS OUR FATHER BY ADOPTION   88
     "FOR YOU ARE ALL THE CHILDREN OF GOD."   88
     THE ANGEL ON THE TOMBSTONE.   89
     MARY ANNE, THE LITTLE ORPHAN.   90

20. OUR HEAVENLY FATHER WATCHES OVER US   92
     AGNES, THE PIOUS HOUSEMAID.   92
     GERMAINE, THE LITTLE SHEPHERDESS   95

21. OF GOD'S PROVIDENCE   98
     THE SPIDER'S WEB.   98
     ST. PAUL, THE FIRST HERMIT, AND ST. ANTONY.   99
     ST. MAXIMUS AND ST. FELIX.   100
     "WHERE IS THE PROVIDENCE OF GOD?"   101
     "CAST THY CARE UPON THE LORD."   103

22. GOD CONSOLES US ON EARTH AND REWARDS US
     IN HEAVEN   106
     "OH, HOW GOOD IS DEAR PAPA!"   106

23. ALL MEN ARE OUR BRETHREN, FOR GOD IS THE
     FATHER OF ALL   109
     THE LAME MAN AND THE PRINCESS.   109

24. OUR CONDUCT SHOULD SHOW THAT WE ARE
     REALLY GOD'S CHILDREN   111
     "I KNOW YOU NOT."   111

PART IV
"HALLOWED BE THY NAME"

25. OF THE REVERENCE AND LOVE DUE TO GOD'S
     HOLY NAME   115
     THE VOICE OF GOD IN THE BURNING BUSH.   116
     GOD IS JEALOUS OF THE HONOR DUE TO HIS
     NAME.   117
     POPE PIUS V.'S ZEAL FOR THE GLORY OF GOD'S
     NAME.   118

26. HONOUR DUE TO THE HOLY NAME OF JESUS   120
     ST. PETER'S SPEECH BEFORE THE HIGH-PRIEST.   120
     ST. PAUL AND THE HOLY NAME OF JESUS.   121
     "JESUS OF NAZARETH, KING OF THE JEWS!"   121
     THE LITTLE BOY JULIAN.   122

27. WE SANCTIFY GOD'S NAME BY TEACHING
OTHERS TO KNOW GOD   124
ST. FRANCIS XAVIER PREACHES TO THE
CHILDREN.   124
AN ANGEL IN DISGUISE.   127
THE PRIEST ALPHONSUS.   128

28. THE MARTYRS BY THEIR DEATH GLORIFIED
GOD'S NAME   130
TITUS: A MARTYR STORY.   130

29. WE GLORIFY GOD'S NAME BY PRAYING FOR THE
CONVERSION OF SINNERS   136
"PRAY FOR THEM."   136
"COME WITH ME, AND I WILL TELL YOU."   137

30. GOD'S NAME IS SANCTIFIED BY OUR GOOD
EXAMPLE   140
THE MONK IN ALEXANDRIA.   140
THE GENERAL AND HIS GROOM.   141

31. ON AIDING THE WORK OF THE "PROPAGATION
OF THE FAITH."   143
"PLEASE BUY ME."   143
A POOR MAN WHO BUILT A GREAT CHURCH.   144

32. BY SINGING HOLY HYMNS WE GLORIFY
GOD'S NAME   146
THE MIDNIGHT HYMN.   146
ST. VINCENT AND THE MAHOMETAN PRINCESS.   147

PART V
"THY KINGDOM COME"

33. GOD THE KING OF OUR HEARTS.   151
THE HAPPY DEATH OF A CHILD OF MARY.   151
THE ANGEL OF THE HOUSEHOLD.   152

34. HEAVEN THE REWARD OF THOSE WHO SUFFER
PATIENTLY ON EARTH   156
THE TWO NOBLEMEN AND THE MONK.   156
"TAKE COURAGE."   157
DOROTHY, THE PIOUS CHILD.   159

35. OUR ONE GREAT DESIRE SHOULD BE TO GAIN
HEAVEN   163
THE LEGEND OF THE LITTLE SCHOLARS.   163
ST. TERESA AND HER BROTHER RODERICK.   166
THE LITTLE BOY CELSUS.   167
THE BOY-MARTYRS OF SPAIN.   169

36. THE KINGDOM OF GOD ON EARTH.   172
THE SLAVE OF THE SLAVES.   172
OUR LADY'S CHILD.   174
WHAT ST. CATHERINE SAW.   176

37. A HAPPY DEATH THE ENTRANCE INTO LIFE   178
ST. GERTRUDE'S HAPPY DEATH.   178
HEROIC FAITH OF A CHILD.   180

PART VI

"THY WILL BE DONE"

38. WHAT IS MEANT BY DOING THE WILL OF GOD?   185
"THY WILL BE DONE, O LORD."   185
NO CONSOLATION.   186
THE SUFFERINGS OF ST. VINCENT DE PAUL.   187
THE STATUE IN THE NICHE.   187
FLOWERS OF THE LORD'S PRAYER—"THY WILL
BE DONE."   188
ST. JOHN THE ABBOT'S DYING COUNSEL.   190

39. HOW THE SAINTS AND THE JUST OBEYED THE
WILL OF GOD   192
"BE MY FATHER, AND I WILL BE YOUR CHILD."   192
ST. EDMUND OF CANTERBURY IN HIS LAST
MOMENTS.   194

40. GOD KNOWS WHAT IS BEST FOR US   196
THE FAITH AND OBEDIENCE OF ABRAHAM.   196
AMONG THE ANGELS.   197
THE SCHOOLMASTER'S CHILDREN.   199

41. OUR PERFECTION CONSISTS IN DOING
GOD'S WILL   202
THE EMPEROR WHO WANTE TO BE A MONK.   202
HOW HE BECAME PERFECT.   204
THE PRIEST AND THE BEGGAR.   205

BLESSED CATHERINE OF GENOA: A SAINT IN
THE WORLD.   207

ST. JANE FRANCES RENOUNCES THE WORLD AT
THE CALL OF GOD.   208

42. ALL THINGS ARE ARRANGED FOR OUR GOOD   211
POISON IN A FLOWER.   211
"YOUR MONEY OR YOUR LIFE!"   212
"THANKS BE TO GOD."   214

43. "AS IT IS IN HEAVEN."   216
LITTLE BARTHOLOMEW'S PRAYER.   216

PART VII

"GIVE US THIS DAY OUR DAILY BREAD"

44. OUR DEPENDENCE ON GOD FOR EVERYTHING   221
THE BLESSED CURÉ OF ARS ON THIS PETITION.   221
THE BISHOP AND THE HUMBLE GARDENER.   222
A LITTLE CHILD'S FAITH.   223

45. GOD WILLS US TO LABOR FOR OUR DAILY BREAD.   225
ST. JOSEPH AND THE INFANT JESUS.   225
ST. PAUL LABOURS WITH HIS HANDS FOR HIS
SUPPORT.   226

46. THE FOOD OF OUR SOULS IS, FIRSTLY, THE HOLY
EUCHARIST   227
"I AM THE LIVING BREAD."   227
THE FOOD OF THE STRONG.   229
"GIVE HIM TO ME AGAIN."   230
A GREAT SINNER CHANGED INTO A GREAT
SAINT.   231

47. GOD'S HOLY GRACE IS ALSO THE FOOD OF
THE SOUL   233
THE BURDEN OF LIFE.   233

48. WE FEED OUR SOULS BY HEARING THE WORD
OF GOD   235
ST. PETER OF ALCANTARA AND THE NOBLE
LADY.   235
THE HERMIT AND HIS BASKETS.   237

49. WE FEED OUR SOULS ALSO BY READING GOOD
   BOOKS   239
   ST. JOHN COLUMBINO'S CONVERSION.   239
   HOW ST. IGNATIUS BECAME A SAINT.   240
   MY ABC AGAIN.   243

50. THE SUFFERINGS AND TRIALS OF THIS LIFE
   FEED THE SOUL   245
   THE SHEPHERD AND THE LAMB.   245

51. GOD'S CARE OF OUR TEMPORAL NEEDS   247
   HERMANN, THE PIOUS TAILOR.   247
   THE BREAD WHICH THE LORD SENT.   249
   HELP IN THE HOUR OF NEED.   252

52. THE HAPPINESS OF THOSE WHO "CAST THEIR
   CARE" UPON THE LORD   254
   THE EMPEROR AND THE MONK.   254
   THE PIOUS STUDENT   255

PART VIII
"FORGIVE US OUR TRESPASSES"

53. WHAT WE PRAY FOR IN THIS PETITION   259
   TOM, THE POOR INDIAN SLAVE.   259
   GOOD FOR EVIL.   261
   THE KING TAKES AN ACCOUNT OF HIS
   SERVANTS.   263

54. WE MUST PRAY FOR THOSE WHO HAVE
   INJURED US.   265
   OUR LORD'S ANSWER TO ST. ELIZABETH.   265

55. THE EXAMPLE OF JESUS CHRIST MAKES IT EASY
   TO FORGIVE   266
   ST. JOHN GUALBERT'S CONVERSION.   266
   THE CRUCIFIX IN THE HANDS OF ST. PHILIP
   NERI.   268
   "JESUS CHRIST DIED FOR YOU AND FOR HIM."   268

56. WE MUST FORGIVE IF WE DESIRE TO BE
   FORGIVEN   270
   ST. NICEPHORUS AND SAPRICIUS.   270
   THE FALSE FORGIVENESS.   274

ST. JOHN THE ALMS-GIVER AND A GREAT LORD.   275
THE NOBLE DUKE OF GUISE AND HIS ENEMY.   276

57. THE GREATER THE INJURY FORGIVEN, THE MORE
    CERTAIN GOD'S PARDON   277
    A CHRISTIAN'S NOBLE REVENGE.   277
    THE PRIEST AND THE SOLDIER.   279
    ST. JOHN THE ALMS-GIVER AND THE DEACON.   280

58. FORGIVING OTHERS IS OFTEN THE CAUSE OF
    TEMPORAL BLESSINGS.   282
    THE STATUE THAT DID NOT GET ANGRY.   282

59. GOD READILY FORGIVES THE PENITENT SINNER   284
    ST. MARY MAGDALEN.   284
    THE BRIGAND CHIEF.   287

PART IX
"LEAD US NOT INTO TEMPTATION"

60. THE MEANING OF THIS PETITION   293
    THE ABBOT AND THE YOUNG MONK.   293
    THE ABBOT THEODORE AND THE NOVICE.   294

61. "BLESSED IS THE MAN WHO ENDURETH
    TEMPTATION."   295
    A VOICE IN THE WILDERNESS.   295
    SEVEN CROWNS GAINED.   296
    A NOBLE ANSWER.   298
    BENIGNE DE FREMIOT'S GENEROUS ANSWER.   298
    EULOGIUS AND THE LEPER.   299
    THE VISION OF MOSES THE ANCHORITE.   301

62. WE MUST NOT EXPOSE OURSELVES TO
    TEMPTATION   302
    THE GOOD GIRL OF MILAN.   302
    THE BOY WHO FELL INTO THE WELL.   305
    THE LION IN THE MENAGERIE.   306
    ALIPIUS AT THE ROMAN SHOWS.   306
    SATAN'S COMPLAINT.   308
    "I'LL KEEP MY EYES SHUT."   309

63. TEMPTATION MUST BE RESISTED AT ONCE   311
    THE NEST OF VIPERS.   311

64. TEMPERATIONS ACCOMPANY US THROUGH LIFE   313
    DANGERS ON ALL SIDES.   313
    THE FISHERMAN AND THE LITTLE FISH.   314
    HOW SATAN TEMPTS THE JUST AT DEATH.   315

65. BAD COMPANY A GREAT CAUSE OF YIELDING TO TEMPTATION   316
    THE GARDENER AND HIS SON.   316
    THE LITTLE BOY OF PORTUGAL.   318

66. IN TEMPTATION WE MUST WATCH AND PRAY   320
    "WATCH AND PRAY."   320
    WHY HE FAILED.   321
    SISTER GRACE OF VALENCIA.   323

67. PRAYER TO OUR LADY POWERFUL IN TEMPTATION   325
    "COME WITH ME TO HEAVEN."   325
    THE HEROIC MOTHER.   326
    THE LITTLE BOY AND THE SERPENT.   327
    A HOLY HERMIT'S TEMPTATIONS.   328

68. HOW GREAT SHOULD BE OUR CONFIDENCE IN SAYING THIS PETITION   329
    THE FATHER'S PROMISE.   329
    THE WORDS KING DAVID SAID.   331
    "MY FATHER IS THE CAPTAIN."   332
    JESUS WALKING UPON THE WATERS.   334

69. WE SHOULD PRAY TO BE DELIVERED FROM THE SNARES OF SATAN   336
    ST. PERPETUA'S VISION.   336

70. PRAY TO BE DELIVERED FROM A SUDDEN AND UNPROVIDED DEATH   339
    THE DOUBLE VISION OF ST. FRANCIS.   339
    ST. BERNARD IN DANGER.   340
    A SAINT WHO WAS ALWAYS TREMBLING.   342

71. HOW WE SHOULD PRAY IN OUR SUFFERINGS AND TRIALS   343
    HAPPIER ON EARTH THAN IN HEAVEN.   343
    THE ANGELS ON THE HOUSE-TOP.   344

72. HOW GOD SOMETIMES DELIVERS US FROM
TEMPORAL EVILS 347
 HOW GOD SAVED A LITTLE BOY FORM DEATH. 347

73. "FROM EVERLASTING DEATH, O LORD, DELIVER
US." 349
 THE PIOUS SOLDIER ON THE BATTLE-FIELD. 349
 ST. ABRAHAM AND HIS NIECE. 351
 HOW A GREAT BARON BECAME A TRAPPIST. 354
 THE MAN WOUNDED BY A TIGER. 355
 THE GREAT EARTHQUAKE AT
CONSTANTINOPLE. 355

PART X
"HAIL MARY" (FIRST PART)

74. "HAIL MARY"—"O MARY, HOW SWEET IS THY
NAME!" 359
 THE SAINTS AND MARY'S HOLY NAME. 359
 THE NAME OF MARY BANISHES ALL SORROW. 360
 "AVE MARIA" ON THE LILY-LEAVES. 360
 MARY'S GENEROSITY 361
 ST. ALPHONSUS' LOVE FOR MARY'S NAME. 361
 "HAIL, BERNARD!" 361
 THE ANGELS AND OUR LADY'S NAME. 362
 ST. STEPHEN OF HUNGARY AND THE NAME OF
MARY. 363
 THE HOLY NAME OF MARY IN SUFFERINGS. 363
 IN THE NAME OF MARY. 363
 NEARLY LOST. 364
 THE "AVE MARIA" OF ST. FRANCIS DE SALES. 366

75. "HAIL MARY"—THE ANGELICAL SALUTATION 368
 A PROMISE OF OUR LADY TO ST. GERTRUDE. 368
 AN "AVE MARIA" OBTAINS PARDON OF OUR
FAULTS. 368
 THE LAY-BROTHER WHO KNEW ONLY THE
"HAIL MARY." 368
 THE VENERABLE ARMILLA. 369
 A LITTLE CHILD'S LOVE FOR MARY. 369
 THE LOVE OF ST. ALPHONSUS FOR THE "HAIL
MARY." 370

MARY DELIVERS A SINNER FROM THE SLAVERY OF SATAN.   370

OUR LADY'S BEAUTIFUL MANTLE.   371

THE VISIT TO OUR LADY'S CHURCH.   372

CONFIDENCE IN OUR LADY RECOMPENSED.   374

MARY PROTECTS HER CHILD IN DANGER.   375

THE PIOUS GENTLEMAN'S MISTAKE.   376

A DEVOUT WORKMAN.   378

76. "HAIL MARY"—"FULL OF GRACE."   380

RESTORED TO GRACE   380

77. "HAIL MARY"—"THE LORD IS WITH THEE."   382

OUR LADY AND ST. ELIZABETH OF HUNGARY.   382

78. "HAIL MARY"—"BLESSED ART THOU AMONGST WOMEN."   384

HOW JESUS REWARDS THOSE WHO HONOUR HIS MOTHER.   384

BLESSED ANDREW OF CITEAUX REWARDED BY OUR LADY.   386

THE OFFERING THAT PLEASES MARY BEST.   387

MARY DELIVERS A YOUNG MAN FROM PRISON.   387

79. "HAIL MARY"—"BLESSED IS THE FRUIT OF THY WOMB, JESUS."   389

THE BEGINNING OF ST. JOHN'S GOSPEL.   389

"HIS NAME WAS CALLED JESUS."   390

ST. PANTALEON WORKS MIRACLES IN THE NAME OF JESUS.   390

ST. HILARION AND THE DISCONSOLATE MOTHER.   390

ST. APOLLINARIUS, MARTYR.   392

PART XI

"HAIL MARY" (LAST PART)

80. "HOLY MARY, MOTHER OF GOD"—SHE IS ALSO OUR MOTHER   395

A VISION OF ST. MECHTILDES.   395

THE GREATNESS OF THE LOVE OF MARY.   396

BLESSED ANDREW OF CHIO.   396

"MY MOTHER MARY."   396

ST. HYACINTH, DEAR TO OUR LADY.   397

"O MARY! O MY MOTHER!" 397

ST. JOHN BERCHMANS' DYING COUNSEL. 398

BLESSED ALPHONSUS RODRIGUEZ OF THE
SOCIETY OF JESUS. 398

THE LOVE OF THE CHILD ST. BERNARD FOR
OUR LADY. 399

NESTORIUS THE HERETIC. 399

ST. ODILIO CURED BY OUR LADY. 400

81. "HOLY MARY, MOTHER OF GOD"—WE ARE ALSO
HER CHILDREN 401

ST. PHILIP NERI MIRACULOUSLY CURED. 401

THE VISION OF BLESSED MARY OF THE
ANGELS. 402

ST. STANISLAUS' LOVE FOR MARY. 402

ST. IGNATIUS CONSECRATES HIMSELF TO
MARY. 403

OUR LADY'S ANSWER TO ST. ALPHONSUS. 403

OUR LADY AND ST. ELIZABETH OF HUNGARY. 404

BLESSSED STANISLAUS OF CASMIR CONSOLED. 405

"I AM GOING TO HEAVEN." 405

ST. ALPHONSUS RODRIGUEZ AND OUR LADY. 406

THE SON OF ST. BRIDGET. 408

BLESSSED HERMANN JOSEPH, OUR LADY'S
CHILD. 409

OUR LADY'S LITTLE ORPHAN. 412

MUSA'S VISION OF OUR LADY. 413

82. "HOLY MARY, MOTHER OF GOD"—"PRAY FOR US
SINNERS NOW." 415

"O MARY, HELP ME, FOR I AM THINE." 415

AN UNEXPECTED GRACE. 416

THE EIGHTH SWORD. 418

83. "HOLY MARY, MOTHER OF GOD"—"PRAY FOR US
AT THE HOUR OF OUR DEATH." 420

"HOLY MARY, PRAY FOR HIM." 420

ADOLPHUS, THE PIOUS NOBLEMAN. 421

A CONVERSION AT THE ELEVENTH HOUR. 422

DELICIOUS FOOD ON A FILTHY PLATE. 424

84. "HOLY MARY, MOTHER OF GOD"—"AMEN."   426
    THE MUSIC OF HEAVEN.   426
    FATHER EUSEBIUS.   428
    OUR LADY INVITES HER CLIENT TO HEAVEN.   429

PART I

THE VIRTUE OF HOPE

1

WHAT IS MEANT BY HOPE

God has promised to give you, my child, the Kingdom of Heaven when you die, if you love and serve Him faithfully here on earth to the end of your life. He will keep His promise, because He is your Father, and because He is so good. This is why you say to Him in your prayers: "O my God, I hope in Thee."

ST. FRANCIS DE SALES' WORDS OF CONSOLATION.

One day a pious woman went to St. Francis de Sales, and told him she had suffered so much that she was almost losing courage, and was very miserable.

"I was once rich," she said, "but I lost all I possessed. Moreover, I am suffering much from a severe illness, and I have no one to feel pity for me or to say a kind word to me."

The Saint answered: "Your condition, my child, is one not to be pitied, but rather to be envied.

You are, in this world, the spouse of Jesus Crucified, and you know that those who are honored in this way on earth are chosen to be the eternal spouses of Jesus Glorified in Heaven.

"You are at present wearing the livery of your Royal Master, the cross, and the nails, and the thorns, and sharing with Him the gall and the vinegar; but have a little patience, and your Heavenly Father will exchange them, and give you in their place the white robe of glory, and a crown of everlasting splendor."

"O my Father," she replied, "your words console me. When shall that happy day come? When shall I hear His beloved voice calling me to enter His kingdom above?"

The desire of Heaven, and the remembrance of the reward to be given us there, make the few short hours of pain in this world pass quickly.

Catech. Historique, i. 493.

HOME, SWEET HOME.

During an epidemic of scarlet fever in the city of Paris, a priest was summoned to attend a man who was dying in one of the poorest localities of the city.

When he went into the hovel, he saw the man lying on some straw in a corner of the room, covered with a few rags and in the greatest poverty. There was no furniture in the room, not even a chair nor a table; everything had been sold at the beginning of his sickness to buy him some food. The only things the priest saw were a hatchet and two saws hanging on the wall.

"My child," said the priest to him, "take courage now: God has sent you this sickness as a great favor, for He is going to take you soon out of this weary world, where you are suffering so much from poverty and sickness, and will take you to Himself in Heaven, where you shall have no more sorrow."

"Sorrow, Father?" the dying man said, in a voice that could scarcely be heard; "I have no sorrow; I never had any. I have always lived in happiness and contentedness. I never knew what it was to hate anyone, nor to have envy; I always slept at night a calm, undisturbed sleep, because I labored hard all day. The tools you see there on the wall procured for me my daily bread, with which I was always perfectly contented; and I never envied the dainties I have seen others enjoy. I have been a poor man all my lifetime, but till now I have always enjoyed good health. If I get better, although I think that I may not, I will just resume my labor as before, till God's time comes, and I know that if I please Him now, He will take care of me during life—hasn't He promised that, Father?—and when the time comes for me to die, He will make me happy in Heaven. This has always been my hope."

"My child," said the priest, "you are indeed happy in having lived so much united to God. The happiness of Heaven will be a sufficient recompense for all you have done and suffered here below. Are you quite prepared to die, my child?"

"Yes, Father, I have been preparing since my childhood for the hour of my death; and now that it is near I feel happy, because I am confident in the mercy of God, that I am going home to my Father in Heaven." He died in these holy dispositions.

ST. AUGUSTINE'S QUESTION.

St. Augustine, who often spoke to the faithful under his charge of the joys of Heaven, one day said to them: "My brethren, if God came down here amongst us, and told us that He would grant each of us a hundred years more to live, or even a thousand, and that during these years we should have whatever our hearts could desire, but on condition that we should never see Him, or be with Him in Heaven, would any of you accept that offer?"

But the whole multitude with one voice cried out: "Never! May all earthly things perish; we desire God alone and Heaven."

O my child, let that also be your answer when Satan asks you to offend God. Think of Heaven, and you shall be able to persevere, and this will be your consolation and will confirm you in hope.

ST. JANE CHANTAL AT DEATH.

When her end seemed to be near, St. Jane Chantal asked her confessor to read to her the prayers for the departing soul. "O my God," she said from time to time, "how beautiful are these prayers!"

Suddenly she exclaimed: "O my Father, how terrible are the judgments of God!"

He asked her if she were afraid of her own judgment, which was so near.

"No, my Father," she replied, "I do not fear to meet Him Whom I have loved all my lifetime; but I assure you that I see now how terrible His judgments are, and how different from those of men."

Then her agony began. A crucifix was placed in one hand, and a lighted candle in the other. The Sisters were on their knees weeping and praying. Suddenly they heard her speak: "I must go now; Jesus, Jesus, Jesus."

Saying these words, she gently breathed her last, and went to meet her beloved Spouse in His heavenly kingdom.

THE GRACE OF GOD THE CHIEF OBJECT OF OUR HOPE

You cannot do any good towards your salvation without the help of God's grace. But with His grace you can do all things. He has promised to help you whenever you ask Him. This grace is the chief object of our hope.

"GIVE ME BACK MY SON."

In the city of Carthage there lived a young nobleman named Fulgentius. His learning and his great abilities raised him to the highest honors in the State, and everyone, from the Emperor to the humblest citizen, loved and esteemed him.

One day he took up a pious book to read. It was a sermon of St. Augustine on the vanities of the world and the shortness of life. When he had finished reading it, he began to think on what he had read.

"I have reached the highest honors that the world can give me." This is what he said to himself. "Everyone praises me and honors me, and, after all, of what use is it to me? I was not made for this. God sent me into this world to gain Heaven."

He at once took the resolution to throw at his feet all the honors and riches which he possessed, and go to some place where he would not be known, that he might, for the rest of his life, think only of "the one thing necessary."

So one morning he quietly left his home, and went to the monastery of which the great Faustus was Superior.

"I have come," said Fulgentius, "to ask you to admit me into your monastery, for now I want to live only for the salvation of my soul and to obtain a happy eternity."

Faustus, who knew him, answered: "Sir, the life we lead in this house is too severe for one who has been accustomed to the comforts of this world as you have been."

But Fulgentius was not to be repulsed; he asked the Superior to give him a short trial.

"Go away," said Faustus, in a voice which appeared harsh and repulsive. "Go and learn first to live in the world a life detached from its pleasures. How could it be possible for one who has been brought up in the midst of luxuries, and all kinds of comforts, to be able, all at once, to submit to the poverty we practice, to the coarse dress we wear, and to our fastings and watchings?"

Fulgentius, modestly casting his eyes upon the ground, answered: "My Father, He Who put into my heart the desire of serving Him can easily give me the help I stand in need of to overcome my natural weakness."

Faustus was touched by this beautiful answer, and admitted him on trial.

When the mother of Fulgentius heard of what her son had done, she ran to the monastery. "Give me back my son!" she cried out in tears—"give me back my son!"

Faustus tried to calm her, but in vain. For three days did that sorrowful mother stand at the gate of the monastery, weeping and calling on her son to return to her.

Fulgentius heard her. During the years he had lived in the world he had never before been separated from her. He loved her with an intense affection, and had never been known to disobey her. But he had not counted upon this trial; and as he heard the voice of her whom he so tenderly loved, and knew that her heart was bursting with grief, his own soul was plunged in the deepest sorrow.

Who can tell the conflict he had to sustain during these three days? Was ever a trial equal to his? But raising his eyes and hands to Heaven, he prayed for help. "O my God, help me to persevere."

God heard his prayer, and after the three days were ended a sweet peace filled his soul. His mother, seeing that her cries and prayers were unheeded, returned to her home, and Fulgentius remained faithful.

He afterwards became Bishop of Carthage, and was one of the greatest lights in the Church of God in the sixth century.

Grande Vies des Saints, Jan. 1.

THE PARDON OF OUR SINS
ANOTHER OBJECT OF OUR HOPE

God has promised to forgive us our sins if we be sorry for them. This, therefore, is another thing we "hope" for—pardon for our past sins.

THE WIDOW'S CHILD.

Some years ago, there was a poor widow who had an only son. She loved this son dearly, and spared no pains to instill into his heart the principles of virtue.

But when he grew up he began to go with wicked companions, and soon became the scandal of the neighborhood. He even sometimes struck his mother, and threatened to kill her.

This unhappy young man soon gave himself up to every crime, but the day of retribution came at last; he was arrested and cast into prison.

One day a stranger knocked at the prison door. The jailer came to see who it was, and learned to his surprise that it was the mother of this wicked young man.

"Ah!" said she, weeping, "I wish to see my son."

"What!" said the jailer in astonishment, "do you wish to see that wretch? Have you forgotten all that he has done to you?"

"Ah! I know it well," replied the widow, "but he is my son."

"Why!" cried the jailer, "he has robbed you of every penny you had."

"I know it," she replied; "but he is still my son."

"But has he not struck you and abused you, and even threatened to kill you?" said the jailer.

"That is quite true," was the answer; "but I am still his mother, and he is my son."

"But," again cried the jailer, "he has not only abused you and robbed you, but he has even shamefully abandoned you; such an unnatural son is not fit to live."

"Ah! but he is my child, and I am his mother." And the poor widow sobbed and wept, till at last the jailer was touched, and permitted her to enter the prison; and the fond mother threw her arms round the neck of that unnatural, ungrateful son, and pressed him again and again to her breaking heart.

Müller: *The Prodigal Son*, p. 272.

God loves us poor sinners even more than a mother loves her child. With what confidence, then, ought you to hope for pardon when you are sorry for offending Him!

ST. BERNARD'S HOPE IN GOD.

The great St. Bernard was lying on his bed sick. It seemed that already the hand of death was upon him. Satan, who had often tried to make him yield to sin, but in vain, tried now to make him fall into despair.

"You have never done any good," he whispered in his heart, "and you have offended God so much! How can you expect to obtain Heaven? Heaven is only for those who have served God faithfully, which you have not done."

St. Bernard knew that this was a temptation of the Evil One, and with his usual confidence in God he overcame it.

"I know," he said, "that I am most unworthy of God's grace, that I have sinned, and that I cannot of myself obtain the Kingdom of God. But Jesus Christ my Savior, by the merits of His sufferings and death, has purchased it for me, and has made over to me the right of obtaining it. It is a pure gift of God's liberality to me, and although I had no right to it, I now have full confidence of possessing it, for I am God's child, and Jesus died for me. So, begone, Satan!"

After this a holy calm filled his soul, and Satan tempted him no more.

Life of St. Bernard.

4

THE KINGDOM OF HEAVEN THE INAL OBJECT OF OUR HOPE.

J esus Christ tells His disciples that they must take up their cross if they desire to follow Him. What is it that gives the Christian courage to do this? It is the thought of the reward God has promised to give him in Heaven. It is this hope of Heaven, then, that gives you, my child, strength to bear your trials patiently.

"LOOK UP TO HEAVEN, MY CHILD."

Symphronian was the son of parents who were as illustrious for their piety as for their noble ancestry. Under their care he passed his youth in the practice of virtue, and everyone who saw him felt in his presence a supernatural awe, as if he were an angel of God.

He lived in the days of persecution, when so many martyrs shed their blood in testimony of their Faith.

He was seized, brought before the tribunal of Judge Heraclius, and commanded to adore the statues of the heathen gods. The judge as usual promised him great rewards and honors if he would obey, and threatened to put him to death, under the most awful torments, if he refused.

Symphronian answered that he was a Christian, and that the

Christian's hopes were not in this world, but in Heaven. "I do not fear your torments, neither do I esteem your honors. Our God has in Heaven greater and higher honors for those who are faithful to Him, as well as the most terrible punishments for those who disobey Him. Therefore, it is better for me to suffer now at your hands, and so come to my eternal King in Heaven, than to give my soul to Satan by obeying you."

The judge was surprised at these bold words of the young martyr, and again entreated him to obey him, promising at the same time to give him still greater honors.

"Do not imagine," said the holy martyr, "that any words of yours can force me to change my mind. The presents which you offer me are poison hid in honey, and your honors are as brittle as glass. Our riches are in Jesus Christ, and they shall endure forever; and the honors He confers on us are everlasting. This is the Christian's hope."

The judge, seeing that he was losing time, condemned him to be beheaded.

On his way to martyrdom he met his mother. She had heard of his being condemned to die, and she hastened to see him, and speak to him for the last time on earth.

As she saw the crowd coming along, and heard their shouts, and saw the axes that were so soon to immolate her beloved child, her motherly heart was pierced with grief.

But fearing lest the sight of her sorrow might influence him, she asked from God strength to bear the trial courageously. When the crowd drew near, and her eyes met those of her son, she cried out: "O Symphronian, my child, my dearest boy, look up to Heaven! think of God Who reigns there. Courage, then; do not be afraid to die, because your death will bring you to eternal life. The tyrant cannot take life from you; he will only give you one infinitely more happy in exchange for the short and weary life of this world. The way is indeed narrow and difficult, but it is short."

These words of his mother, spoken so earnestly, gave him new courage. He raised his eyes towards Heaven, to which she was pointing, and he seemed to see holy angels coming down to meet him with palms in their hands—the sign of victory.

When they came to the place of execution, they bound the martyr to the stake, and with one stroke of the sword severed his head from his body. His holy soul at the same instant joined the company of the angels who were witnesses of his martyrdom, and was led by them into the abode of everlasting joy.

Lives of the Saints, August 22.

ST. LIDWINA'S CROWN.

St. Lidwina was born in Holland about the end of the fourteenth century. When she was a little girl she was very beautiful. But God, Who foresaw that her beauty might be dangerous to her, took it from her, by permitting an accident to happen to her.

One day, when she was fifteen years old, she was walking on the ice which covered a pond not far from her father's house. Someone who was amusing himself by sliding, came against her with great force, and she fell heavily on the ice. When they took her home they discovered that some of her bones were broken, and that she had suffered other injuries. Remedies were applied, but without effect; from that day till the end of her life she was never able to stand upright, and could scarcely walk. The fresh color left her cheeks, and she became pale and thin.

When people saw the sad state to which she was now reduced, they said it was a great misfortune; but her Father in Heaven, Who loved her dearly, knew that this was one of the richest graces He could have given His beloved child.

Lidwina loved God. She had loved Him when she was in health, and now, when He had sent her this terrible affliction, she loved Him even more. She could not have had the courage to have asked Him to send her these sufferings, but since He had done so, she said from the bottom of her heart: "O my God, Thy holy will be done."

It would take a long time to tell all the consolation God gave her because she was so humble and resigned. Whenever God sends us a cross, He sends us also the grace to carry it. So Lidwina was very happy under her heavy cross.

One day she was brought by her angel guardian in spirit into Paradise. God wanted to show her what He would one day give her there if she would suffer her trials on earth patiently to the end.

She saw the Saints there in all their glory, each one according to the good works he had done on earth, and she heard the ravishing music of their canticles.

Some of the holy martyrs who had suffered the most terrible torments for the love of God spoke to her, and pointed out to her the bright crown of glory God had given them as their reward.

"Let our example," they said, "encourage you to suffer as we did, and be faithful unto death as we were. You have to suffer much from the afflictions with which God has visited you, but courage! they will soon be at an end, and then the crown of glory will be given you. Look at us now, how happy we are! where are now those sufferings we endured for the love of Jesus Christ? They are all past: they lasted only a few moments, then were over, and what did God give us in return for them? Look and see; behold the perfect happiness we enjoy in the Kingdom of our God, which will never be taken from us."

When the Saint returned to herself, the thought of this beautiful vision filled her with greater courage; she even desired Our Lord to send her greater afflictions on earth, that her glory might be greater in Heaven.

From the time she had that vision, everything in this world had no pleasure for her. "O my dear Father," she used to pray, "when will You come and take me home to Heaven?"

God was pleased to grant her another vision. She seemed to see one of the heavenly spirits at her side, with a beautiful crown of roses in his hand. But it did not seem quite finished: here and there there seemed to be a few roses wanting to make it complete.

The angel said to her: "This crown is for you, but I cannot give it to you till it is completed; you have yet to suffer a few things for the love of God, and when you have accomplished this it will be ready, and I will come again and give it to you."

She then earnestly prayed to God not to delay long, but to send her at once the trials He had ordained for her to suffer, that she might the sooner obtain her crown.

God heard her prayer. For some little time she had to endure most acute pains, which were augmented by the cruel treatment of some of those who attended her; but the thought that every moment was bringing her nearer to the glory she so much desired gave her courage.

At length the angel returned, according to his promise. In his hands he held the same crown, but this time it was finished. Not long after this she died, and her pure soul ascended at once to Heaven, where it was crowned with glory, in recompense for the trials and sufferings of this life borne so patiently for the love of God.

God is preparing a crown of glory for us also; but we cannot get it till we have won it by fulfilling our duty to God during our short time of trial on earth.

Life of St. Lidwina, April 16.

5

ON PRESUMPTION

Since we cannot do any good of ourselves towards our salvation, we must be sure not to trust to our own strength in our temptations, because if we do so, we are certain to fail. Not to put our trust in God, but to rely on our own strength, is called "presumption." It is one of the greatest sins against hope.

QUINTUS DENIES HIS FAITH.

About the beginning of the second century there came to Smyrna from Phrygia a man called Quintus. At that time there was a persecution of the Christians at Smyrna, and many of them were put to death by horrible tortures, because they would not deny their holy Faith.

When Quintus saw this, he thought he would like to be a martyr also, and so get to Heaven. He went, therefore, boldly to the judge, and said to him: "I am a Christian; put me to death."

The judge was astonished at his strange request, and thought he was a fool. "Let this foolish man," he said, "get what he wants. Take him, and throw him amongst the wild beasts, that they may devour him."

Quintus was very glad when he heard his sentence, and went

joyfully along with the soldiers towards the place where the wild beasts were kept.

But the poor man forgot to ask God to help him. No doubt if he had done so, God would have given him the martyr's crown, but because he trusted to himself, he came to a miserable end. For when he drew near the place, and saw the beasts, with their mouths wide open ready to devour him, and heard them roar so terribly, he began to tremble, and said to those who were leading him: "Stop! I do not want to be thrown in there!" "We will throw you in at once," they said, "unless you promise to sacrifice to the gods."

"Then I promise, if you only take me back again and spare my life."

They took him back to the judge; and when the judge ordered him to offer incense to the gods, he did it.

So Quintus denied his Faith because of his presumption, by trusting to himself rather than to God.

Vies des Saints Pct. Bolland., i. 618

PRINCE EUGENE AND THE AUSTRIAN GENERAL.

An Austrian General, who was as much renowned for his piety as for his bravery, had occasion one day to speak to a young nobleman called Eugene, who was living a gay, worldly life, neglecting prayer and the Sacraments, and yet was accustomed to say that he hoped to reach the Kingdom of Heaven when he died.

"My dear young Prince," he said to him with a fatherly tenderness, "you are trying to do what is altogether impossible. To think that you could reach Heaven without going to the Sacraments is a suggestion of the Evil One, that has already brought innumerable souls to ruin. To imagine that you could reach Heaven in this way is to believe that you could possess God in eternity without loving Him on earth. By refusing to do His holy will on earth, to pray to Him, to unite yourself to Him by receiving the holy Sacraments, and to love those things which He hates, is a certain sign of losing Him in eternity; it is to be guilty of one of the greatest sins that you could commit —that of presumption." Eugene did not at first care for this rebuke, but as he reflected on it he saw that it was indeed the truth. He changed his life, became a fervent Christian, and, by his example, led many others to do the same.

If anything should convince you of the great evil of this sin, it is the following example, which is only one out of many thousands that could be brought before you:

DELAY OF CONFESSION.

There was a young man who at first was very pious, but as he grew up and mingled with the world, fell away from this piety, and even committed great sins. In the midst of his evil life, he was continually heard to say: "I would not for all the world die without the Sacraments. Oh, that would be a terrible misfortune! But I am young yet, and I cannot, at present, make up my mind to go to Confession. There is plenty of time; God is good and merciful, and He will not permit me to die without being reconciled to Him."

But God is just as well as merciful. This young man became very ill. His mother, who had often spoken to him of making up his peace with God, now earnestly exhorted him to do so, as he was in very great danger of death.

He answered: "Yes, I must indeed change my life, but I will wait until I am well again."

"But you are in great danger of death," she said to him; "you must at once make up your peace with God, because you may never get better."

At last he allowed her to send for the priest; but it happened that he was absent at another sick-call when the messenger reached his house, so he had to wait till he returned. The priest then hastened to the house of the dying man. But it was too late; he had fallen into his agony, and died in despair, without making his confession, with the priest at his side.

Here is another terrible example of a great fall because of trusting in one's own strength instead of the grace of God.

THE PRESUMPTUOUS MONK.

There was a monk who lived in the desert in the days of St. Pachomius, the Abbot. This monk had a great desire to go forth into the world and publicly declare his faith, that he might die a martyr.

But before doing this he went to the Saint, to ask his prayers and to obtain his blessing.

"Do not go," said the Saint, "but return to your cell in the desert, for to do what you propose would be to tempt God, and, instead of dying for your faith, you would only deny it."

But the monk did not listen to these words, and left him, being determined to have his own way.

The following day, as he was passing through a forest, he met a band of barbarians, who seized him and brought him before their chief. When they saw that he was a Christian, they raised their swords to kill him, saying: "Renounce your Faith, else you are a dead man."

At first the young man showed some courage, but when he saw the sword about to fall on him, he cried out: "Spare me! I will renounce it." Then they allowed him to depart.

When he recovered from his fright and saw what he had done, he was filled with remorse and sorrow. He returned at once to the holy Abbot, and, with tears in his eyes, told him all.

"O my Father, what can I do now to repair the evil I have done? Can God ever pardon me?"

"Yes, my child," said the Abbot, in a kindly voice; "take courage, and humbly ask Him to forgive you, and most certainly He will do it. But let this be a lesson to you, for all time to come, never to rush into danger, for that is to be guilty of the sin of presumption."

6

ON DIFFIDENCE IN OURSELVES

My child, to escape the danger of falling into presumption we must have a great diffidence in ourselves; that means that of ourselves we cannot avoid evil or do good for Heaven without the help of God's grace.

PACCUS TEMPTED IN THE WILDERNESS.

Father Segneri relates that a young man named Paccus went into a wilderness to do penance for his sins.

After some years he was assaulted by great temptations. They were so great in the end that he thought it impossible to resist them any longer. And as he was often overcome by them, he began to despair of his salvation; he even thought of taking away his life.

He said to himself one day in his despair: "If I must in the end go to hell, it is better for me to go there now than to live on thus in sin, and so only increase my torments."

Another day he took a poisonous viper into his hands, and tried in every way he could to make it bite him. But the reptile did not hurt him in the least.

"O my God!" he cried, "there are so many people who do not wish to die, yet die, and I who wish for death so much, cannot die."

At that moment he heard a voice saying to him: "O foolish man, do you suppose that you can overcome temptations by your own strength? Pray to God for help, and He will give you grace to overcome them; but do not trust in your own strength."

These words gave him new courage. He began at once to pray most fervently, and soon lost all his fear. He ever afterwards led a very edifying life.

MÜLLER.

Do not imagine that because you are so little and so weak, Jesus, Who is so great, will not come to help you. No; He is your Father in Heaven, and you are His child, and He dearly loves you, so be not afraid.

"BECAUSE I AM SO WEAK."

We read of a pious woman who was so very poor that she used often to think how useless she was in the world, and used to wonder how the great God of Heaven could think of her, much less love her.

One day when these thoughts were in her mind, she heard over her a sweet voice which filled her heart with joy; it was the voice of Jesus Himself. "My child," He said, "I chose you to serve Me just because you are so weak; for knowing how worthless you are, you will take no glory to yourself, but will give it all to Me."

ST. MARGARET IN PRISON.

When St. Margaret, virgin and martyr, was in prison, having already suffered many cruel tortures for the Faith, she fervently besought Our Lord that He would be pleased to give her the grace of persevering to the end. While she was thus praying, she was seized with a trembling from head to foot, for the Devil appeared to her under the form of a terrible dragon, which rushed towards her as if about to devour her.

But the Saint, who had from her childhood given herself to God, strong in her confidence that He would never forsake her, made upon herself the sign of the cross, and asked Him to help her.

At the same instant the Devil fled in dismay, and the prison was filled with a bright light, and there came a voice out of the brightness which said to her distinctly: "O Margaret, servant of God, be full of joy, since you have overcome your enemies. The tyrant is filled with confusion, and the Devil is vanquished. Do not lose confidence in what you have yet to endure for the love of God, for your torments will soon come to an end, and your everlasting glory will soon begin."

The Saint was consoled by these words, and thanked her Heavenly Master for His infinite goodness to her. The next day she was brought forth to martyrdom, and thus entered gloriously into Heaven.

7

ON DESPAIR

If it is a great sin to trust in ourselves and not in God, it is also a great sin to think that God will not show us mercy, even when we may have grievously sinned. This sin is the sin of despair, another of the sins against hope.

THE TERRIBLE VISION.

Venerable Bede tells us that in his time there was a man who had once been very pious, but who had gradually fallen into a careless worldly life, and ended by being the scandal of the town in which he lived.

After a time he became ill. People who went to visit him, and saw how dangerous his illness was, told him it was time to think of preparing himself for the great passage into eternity.

"Oh! there will be plenty of time for that afterwards," he said. "I am too sick and weary at present to think of that. I will think about it when I get better."

But he did not get better; every day he became worse.

One day he seemed to see something terrible, for, turning to those who were in the room, he cried out in a voice which froze the blood in their veins: "Alas! I have deceived the world! I have deceived myself! I am lost forever!"

But they said to him: "Do not say these words; God is all-merciful, and offers pardon even to the greatest sinner."

"Yes; but it is too late for me. God put me into this world to serve Him, and I did not do it. I have not even one good work to offer Him. So I am lost! I am lost!"

"Oh! ask God for mercy," they cried. "Say, 'O Jesus, have mercy on me!'"

"No! no! it is too late! I have just seen Hell, and in it I saw Cain and Judas, and near them a place prepared for me. It is too late! I am lost!" They tried again to speak words of comfort to him, and of God's mercy, but all in vain; the poor man died in despair, because he would not ask for mercy.

From Venerable Bede.

My child, this example will show you how terrible is the end of those who have offended God, and who will not return to Him by repentance.

THE TERRIBLE END OF JUDAS.

Judas was one of our Blessed Lord's twelve Apostles. For three years he had been constantly in the company of Jesus Christ, and had, during that time, received from Him many special marks of His favor and love.

But the Devil tempted Judas, and he yielded to the temptation, which in the end led him to betray his loving Master into the hands of His enemies for a few pieces of silver.

When he saw that Jesus was condemned to die he was filled with the deepest remorse, and, running back to the chief priests, threw down at their feet the money they had given him, saying: "I have sinned in betraying innocent blood."

At that moment the grace of God was speaking to his heart, and urging him to repent of his crime. If he had done so he would have been forgiven, and would now be a Saint in Heaven. But he resisted the grace of God, and allowed despair to enter into his heart. He saw the greatness of the crime he had committed, and the sight filled him with so much horror that, forgetting the infinite mercy of God, and, thinking only of the terrible sin he had committed, he fell into despair, and, going out, hanged himself.

SATAN AND THE PIOUS MONK.

The Devil appeared once to Faverius, a disciple of St. Bruno, and monk of singular goodness, who was lying dangerously ill. After terrifying him in other ways, he began to remind him of all the sins he had ever committed, saying: "You committed all these sins."

The servant of God replied that it was quite true, but that he had already confessed them and received absolution from them, and therefore had every reason to trust that God had pardoned him.

"Confessed your sins! Confessed your sins!" replied the fiend. "You have not told all; you have not made a proper confession; you have not explained the circumstances of your sins; your confessions were all bad; they were all good for nothing; they will serve only to make your judgment heavier."

The holy monk, thus reminded of faults, shown to him by the fiend in that awful light, was greatly alarmed, and began to be filled with fear. He was so horror-stricken and full of dismay that he was on the point of falling headlong into the abyss of despair.

But the Blessed Virgin, ever the true Mother of mercy, who forsakes not such as are really devoted to her, appeared to him most opportunely at this terrible moment with the Divine Infant in her arms, and addressed him as follows: "Faverius, my child, why art thou afraid? Wherefore lose heart? Hope and be of good cheer, thou hast all but reached the port of Heaven. All thy sins have been forgiven thee by my most dear Child. Of this I give thee my assurance."

At these words the great anguish felt by the dying man at the thought of his sins gave place to a humble, confiding, peaceful sorrow, and shortly afterwards he breathed his last in great calm of soul.

Guide to Spiritual Life, p. 306.

8

ON CONFIDENCE IN GOD

God knows what is best for you, my child, for He is your Father. In sorrow and in joy, in sickness and in health, leave yourself in His hands. It is this confidence that is most pleasing to Him, because it is a sign that you hope in Him and love Him.

RIPE FOR HEAVEN.

There was once a man whom God visited with many and great trials. Scarcely had one trial passed before another one came upon him. But he was a good Christian, and knew that these sufferings were the gifts his Heavenly Father sent him, that he might gain a bright crown of glory hereafter. He had a wife and one child, a bright and beautiful boy, and in his quiet home, in their company, he found some consolation when the burden was heaviest.

It happened that a war broke out in the country where he dwelt, and he was obliged to take up arms against the enemy.

When the war was over and he returned to his native place, he found his once happy home in ruins, and learned that his wife and child had been put to death by the enemy.

This was for him the severest of all the trials that he had yet suffered, and his usual confidence in God seemed for a moment to forsake him in his great grief.

"O my God!" he cried out, "why hast Thou taken away from me the only things I prized in this world, my wife and my child? Why did the balls of the enemy spare me, when so many of my comrades were struck down by my side? Oh! why hast Thou preserved me from death to heap on me so great an affliction?"

And in the midst of his grief he besought Our Lord to take him out of this world, that he might not have to suffer more.

God consoled him in his grief. He seemed in his sleep to see a most beautiful angel coming near him, having in his hand three grains of seed. These he sowed in a field. Two of them grew up, and produced flowers of a magnificence and beauty far exceeding what he had ever seen before. But the third grain of seed did not spring up at all.

So he asked the angel: "Why is it that two of the seeds you sowed have produced such beautiful flowers, and the third one has not even sprung up?"

The angel answered: "Because it is not yet ready. Have patience; it will also appear."

Soon afterwards he saw it also coming forth from the ground, and the flowers it produced were still more beautiful.

When he awoke, he began to reflect on what he had seen. "O my God," he said, "it was wrong in me to murmur against Thy holy will as I have done. Pardon me, O my God; Thou art indeed a Father full of wisdom. Thou hast taken to Thyself those whom I loved, because Thou sawest that they were already ripe for Heaven, and Thou hast left me still a little time on earth to purify me, and prepare me for a still greater degree of glory in Paradise."

From that moment he complained no more. Afflictions still continued to come upon him, but he bore them all with an invincible patience, and his constant prayer was those words of the Scripture: "In Thee, O Lord, have I hoped; let me never be confounded."

SCHMIDT, *Rep. du Catéch.*, iv. 286.

THE DYING FATHER.

Not long ago a poor man, the father of a large family, was struck down by a dangerous illness. He felt the hand of death upon him, yet he was calm and happy.

His children were standing near his bed weeping, and praying to God that their dear father might not be taken away from them.

"My children," he said, "it is the will of God that I should leave you. With my dying lips I ask you to love and serve Him till He comes to take you to Himself. I have lived a long time in this world, and I can tell you that that alone can make you happy."

These words, spoken at intervals and in a low voice, told the children plainly that the end was indeed near. This made them weep still more. But the good man seemed to smile rather than weep, and to be full of joy rather than of sorrow.

Margaret, his oldest daughter, observed this, and said to him: "Ah! dearest father, how can you be so joyful while we are so sad? You have lived a hard and laborious life, and had many sorrows and trials, and now, even when death is at hand, and you are enduring so much pain, you seem not to feel it."

"My dear child," he answered, "long, long ago, when I was a little boy, my mother used to tell me what I have often told you all—those words of the Scripture: 'Keep the Lord always before thine eyes, and fear His holy name.' These few words gave me courage in my trials, and were my defense in the moment of danger, and now they are my greatest consolation. For they have led me to the gate of my heavenly home, and I die with the firm hope that they will lead me into the presence of Him Whom I have had always present in my heart. It is this that makes me so calm now and so resigned. And if you do as I have done, you also, at the hour of your death, shall be filled with the same blessed hope." This was the only legacy this poor man had to leave to his little ones, but it was of more value than the richest gift that the world could bestow.

Schmidt, Rep. du Catech., iv. 311.

My child, since God is your Father, and loves you so much, you should with the utmost confidence place yourself in His hands, and say to Him: "O my Father in Heaven, I am Thy child, do with me what Thou wilt."

IN THE ARMS OF JESUS.

In the year 1623, at the beginning of Lent, the Venerable Agnes of Jesus became very ill. She was at that time only twenty-one years old. The physicians who were called in did not seem to understand the nature of her malady, and gave her medicine which, instead of making her better, only made her suffer the more.

But Agnes never uttered one word of complaint; the only words she said were the following, which she repeated often every day: "O my God, O my sweet and amiable Jesus, mayest Thou be blessed a thousand and a thousand times."

When Easter Sunday came, God was pleased to reward the patience with which she had suffered the heavy crosses He had been pleased to send her, by permitting her angel guardian to appear to her.

"My child," said the angel, "are you happy in your sufferings?"

"Yes," she answered, "because it is the holy will of Him Whom I love with all my heart."

"But was it not also your own desire to suffer?" He has only done to you what you yourself asked Him to do."

Agnes answered: "My heart and my will are entirely united to Him: let Him dispose of me according to His Divine will; and if it should be His desire that I should suffer all my lifetime, and even to the Day of Judgment, I am ready to do so."

The angel answered: "Continue to love Jesus in this way, and be assured that He will never forsake you."

THE RESCUE OF THEODULUS.

Theodulus was the son of St. Nilus, and lived in the desert along with other holy solitaries. One day the Saracens fell upon them, and carried them away captive to be sold as slaves. Theodulus was taken to a town called Sabira, and exposed for sale in the market-place. He was surrounded by men with drawn swords, ready to kill him if he did not fetch the price they wanted.

When he had been thus standing for some time, and no one seemed desirous of buying him, they were preparing to put him to death. When he saw his danger he cried out piteously to the people to save his life by buying him, promising them that he would all his lifetime be the devoted slave of the one who would do so.

It happened at that moment that the Bishop of the place was passing by, and hearing his heart-rending cries, went and paid the money that was asked, and set him free. Theodulus threw himself at his feet, full of love and gratitude. From that moment he could not tear himself away from him, and never ceased to thank him for having saved his life.

Jesus has done more for you, my child; He has saved you from Hell, and He has paid for you a very great price. This should, then, make you love Him, and fill you with a great confidence in Him.

THE WOMAN HEALED OF THE ISSUE OF BLOOD.

When Our Lord was on earth, He went about amongst the people "doing good, and curing those who were sick."

One day it happened, as He went along, that He was surrounded by the multitudes; and there was among them a certain woman who was troubled with an issue of blood twelve years, who had bestowed all her substance on physicians, and could not be healed by any of them. She came behind Him and touched the hem of His garment, for she said within herself: "If I shall touch only His garment, I shall be healed." And immediately the issue of blood stopped.

And Jesus said: "Who is it that touched Me?" And all denying,

Peter and they that were with him said: "Master, the multitudes throng and press Thee, and dost Thou say, 'Who touched Me'?"

And Jesus said: "Somebody hath touched Me; for I know that virtue is gone out from Me."

And the woman, seeing that she was not hid, came trembling, and fell down before His feet, and declared before all the people for what cause she had touched Him, and how she was immediately healed.

But He said to her: "Daughter, thy faith hath made thee whole; go thy way in peace."

ST. FRANCIS DE SALES' CONFIDENCE IN GOD.

The great St. Francis de Sales tried to inspire those around him with that confidence in God that burned in his own breast.

One day a gentleman came to him in great distress. The thought of death, and of the judgments of God, had thrown him into the lowest depths of sadness and despondency, and he went to him for consolation.

"Alas! my friend," replied the Saint, "there is no torment so great as this one; I know it well, for I myself had to endure it for the space of six weeks, and I am well able from experience to speak on this matter. Let me tell you, then, that if anyone has the earnest desire to serve Our Lord, he should not always be tormented by the thought of death and judgment; or if we must need have some fear of them, let it be a fear mingled with confidence. God is Our Father, and His love for us is boundless; and has He not told us that those who hope in Him shall never be confounded? So, my child, keep before your mind what St. Paul says of those who love God: 'There is no condemnation to them that are in Christ Jesus.'"

ST. FRANCES DRIVES SATAN AWAY.

One day St. Frances of Rome was going to Holy Communion, when the Devil, envious of her happiness, said to her: "How can you, who are so full of venial sins, dare to receive the Immaculate Lamb of God?"

She instantly perceived that the enemy intended to deprive her of this great blessing, and she drove him away by spitting in his face. After this the Blessed Virgin appeared to her, and said: "My child, you have done well; your defects, instead of being an obstacle to your going to Communion, should, on the contrary, induce you to go more and more frequently, since in Holy Communion you find the remedy for all your miseries."

Thus was the confidence of St. Frances rewarded.

ST. MARTIN OF NANTES.

When St. Martin of Nantes was on his deathbed, he was calm and happy. He had spent a long life in the service of God, and now, like St. Paul, he waited to hear, from the Just Judge, the happy sentence that would place him forever in the enjoyment of his reward in Heaven.

Around his bed knelt the Fathers and Brothers of the monastery, weeping and praying.

While they were thus praying, there suddenly appeared in the room a troop of evil spirits, who came and surrounded the bed of the dying Saint. Those around him were seized with fear; he alone remained calm and tranquil.

"What do you want here?" he cried out to them. "Go away at once; Jesus Christ has redeemed me, and I cannot be lost along with you, because I have always placed in Him all my confidence." While he was saying these words, the evil spirits vanished, and he died in peace.

There is no more certain way of overcoming the temptation of despair at the hour of death than by being very devout to Our Blessed Lady during life, for those whom Our Lady loves and protects may confidently expect to be loved by her Divine Son.

ST. BERNARD'S ADMONITION.

"O you, whoever you may be, who are sailing on the tempestuous waters of this life's ocean, if you want to escape shipwreck, look up to the Star of the Sea; call on Mary. When the storm of temptations rises round you, and you are on the point of being dashed against the rocks of distress, look at the Star; call on Mary. When you are tossed about by the waves of ambition or pride, call on Mary. If anger, or avarice, or impure temptations try to draw you away from God, look up at the Star; call on Mary. If the greatness of the evil you have done troubles you, or if you are terrified at the thought of the judgment that is to come upon you, and if you are beginning to sink into the gulf of despair, think of Mary. In all dangers, in all difficulties, in all doubt, think of Mary, call on Mary."

9

HOPE OUR CONSOLATION AT THE HOUR OF DEATH

Hope, which has been our constant companion in life, and which has obtained for us so many graces from our Heavenly Father, will be our great consolation when the hour of our death comes, for has Our Divine Lord not solemnly promised that if we have served him during life He will after death grant us the eternal reward He has promised.

ST. PAUL'S WORDS OF ENCOURAGEMENT.

It was this thought that filled the soul of St. Paul with such confidence when his last hour had come. He said to his beloved Timothy: "The time of my dissolution is at hand. I have fought a good fight; I have finished my course; I have kept the Faith. As to the rest, there is laid up for me a crown of justice, which the Lord, the Just Judge, will render to me in that day, and not only to me, but to them also who love His coming" (2 Tim. iv. 6 et seq.).

ST. PHILIP NERI'S WORDS TO JESUS.

St. Philip Neri was not only a good Christian, but a great Saint. Every day of his life he tried to please God; and every day, too, by his good works, he was heaping up for himself great treasures for Heaven. Yet there was one thought that was always uppermost in his mind day and night. He thought that he might still be lost, because he might not persevere to the end. Every morning he used to say to Jesus: "O my Jesus, take care of me this day, and do not leave me to myself, for if Thou dost not watch over me, I may, like another Judas, betray Thee by falling into sin."

Again, he would frequently say: "O my Jesus, the wound in Thy Sacred Side was, indeed, very large, yet, if Thou leavest me to myself, I may make it still larger. If Thou dost not hold me up by Thy grace, I shall most certainly fall into sin."

St. Philip persevered unto the end, because he was always watching and praying; so it is only by constant watching and prayer, my child, that you will overcome temptation and obtain the grace of final perseverance.

ST. ROSE OF LIMA'S FEARS.

One day St. Rose was full of sadness as she thought that she might not persevere to the end, and that one day she might be condemned to Hell forever. In her distress Jesus appeared to her, and said: "Rose, My daughter, what makes you so sad, and why do you allow these thoughts to trouble you? Do you not know that I will never condemn to Hell any but those who wish to be condemned?" as if He had said: "If a person is condemned it is his own fault, for if he had only asked Me for perseverance he would have obtained it."

"GOD IS FAITHFUL."

When St. Jane de Chantal was troubled by thoughts of despair, she used to put them away at once. "God is faithful," she would say, "and

He has promised to give me the grace of perseverance if I only ask Him. It is my daily prayer to Him: why, then, should I be afraid?"

O my child, may God grant you the grace of perseverance, that, like His Saints who have persevered to the end, you may receive the crown of life.

PART II

PRAYER

10

WHAT PRAYER IS

Of all the duties we have to perform in this world towards God, there is none so important as that of prayer. It is, therefore, necessary for you, my child, to know how to pray well.

Prayer is the raising up of our minds and hearts to God.

ST. IGNATIUS AND THE CARRIER.

St. Ignatius and some of his companions being on a journey hired a poor man to carry their luggage, for they were traveling on foot. This man was very ignorant, and was, moreover, very impatient. He was also given to swearing and many other faults. The Fathers often spoke to him about this, and tried to correct him.

Whenever these holy men arrived at an inn, the first thing they did after hiring a room for themselves and their assistant was to kneel down at a little distance from each other, and spend a long time in prayer.

In the meantime the carrier generally slept upon a bench, or warmed himself by the fire.

But after some time the piety and reverence with which these men said their prayers made him think that they must indeed be very holy, and that it was because they were so holy that they were so cheerful in the midst of all their difficulties; so he made up his mind to pray also.

As soon as he saw them kneeling down, he went into a corner, and remained on his knees till they rose up. He had not done this often before a great change came over him. He soon gave up his old habits altogether, and became sober, patient, and obliging. The Fathers were glad to see this great change, and they knew that God had given him that grace because he had begun to say his prayers.

One day St. Ignatius asked him what prayers he said during the long time he spent on his knees.

The poor man answered: "I am very ignorant, and I do not know how to pray, but this is what I say to God when I see you praying. 'Lord, I am a poor ignorant man, and I do not know how to serve Thee; but these men who are praying so fervently must be great Saints. O my God, I have the desire to do for Thee all they are doing, and to say to Thee all they are saying.'"

St. Ignatius was much edified with this answer. He gave thanks to God for having given to the poor and the little ones of this world graces that the rich and the learned do not deserve to receive.

Heureuse Anne.

THE POOR MAN'S PRAYER.

In the village of Ars, not long ago, there lived a poor man who was very ignorant in the learning of the world, but was every day gaining great merit for Heaven by his simple faith.

Whenever that good man was going to his work or coming home from it, he was sure to be seen entering the church to adore his Divine Lord ever present in the holy tabernacle. He would leave his tools, his spade, hoe, and pickaxe at the door, and remain for hours together sitting or kneeling before the tabernacle.

The priest of the place, the Blessed Father J. M. Vianney, watched him with great delight. But what surprised him was, that although the man remained so long in the church, he never opened his lips, and kept his eyes fixed on the tabernacle all the time.

One day the priest said to him: "My good father, what do you say to Our Lord in those long visits you pay to Him every day?"

The poor man answered: "I say nothing to Him; I look at Him, and He looks at me."

Life of the Blessed Curé d'Ars.

You see, my child, prayer does not consist in saying a great many words, but in having your mind fixed on God, and that is not very difficult for a child of God.

11

PRAYER IS ALL-POWERFUL
WITH GOD

P rayer is all-powerful with God. Jesus Christ Himself continually asserted this truth during His life in this world. "Ask and you shall receive," He said. And this because we are the children of our Heavenly Father, who will always hear us, especially when we ask anything in the name of His beloved Son Jesus. The history of the Church and the lives of God's Saints in all ages have abundantly proved this.

LEGEND OF ST. SCHOLASTICA.

Scholastica was the sister of the Venerable Father Benedict, and had been consecrated to Almighty God from her very infancy. She was accustomed to visit her brother once a year. The man of God came down to meet her at a house belonging to the monastery, not far from the gate. The whole day was spent in singing the praises of God and in holy conversation, and at nightfall they took their repast together. On one occasion whilst they were at table, and it grew late as they conferred with each other on sacred subjects, the holy nun thus spoke to her brother: "I beseech thee stay with me tonight, and let us talk till morning on the joys of Heaven." He replied: "What is this thou sayest, sister? On no account may I remain out of the monastery."

The evening was so fair that not a cloud could be seen in the sky. When, therefore, the holy nun heard her brother's refusal, she clasped her hands together, and, resting them on the table, she hid her face in them, and made a prayer to that God Who is all-powerful. As soon as she raised her head from the table, there broke forth so great a storm of thunder and lightning and rain that neither St. Benedict, nor the brethren who were with him, could set foot outside the place where they were sitting.

The holy virgin had shed a flood of tears as she leaned her head upon the table, and the cloudless sky poured down the wished-for rain. The prayer was offered up, the rain fell in torrents; there was no interval; but so closely on each other were prayer and rain, that the storm came as soon as she raised her head. Then the man of God, seeing that it was impossible for him to reach his monastery amidst all this lightning, thunder, and rain, was sad, and said complainingly: "God forgive thee, sister! What hast thou done?" But she replied: "I asked of thee a favor, and thou wouldst not hear me; then I asked it of God, and He granted it to me. Go now, if thou canst, to the monastery, and leave me here." But it was not in his power to stir from the place, so that he who would not stay willingly had to stay unwillingly, and spent the whole night delighting his sister with discourses upon the spiritual life.

In the morning the holy woman returned to her convent, and the man of God to his monastery. Three days afterwards he was in his cell, and, raising his eyes upwards, he saw the soul of his sister going up to Heaven in the form of a dove. Full of joy at her being thus glorified, he thanked God in hymns of praise and gratitude, and told the brethren of her death. He straightway bade them go and bring her body to the monastery, which, having been done, he buried it in the tomb he had prepared for himself. Thus it was that, as their souls had ever been one in God, their bodies were united in the same grave.

12

PRAYER, THE KEY OF HEAVEN

My child, if you want to get into a house which is locked, you must, in the first place, procure the key, and when you have found the key, you go and open the door, and so enter into the house.

You desire to get into God's beautiful house, which is Heaven. Now, prayer is the key of Heaven. If you pray as you ought, you shall most certainly reach that happy place; if you do not pray, or pray carelessly, then you shall never enter Heaven. You see, therefore, how important it is to pray well.

THE TEMPEST CALMED.

It was a very stormy day; the wind was blowing, and the waves rose high, like great mountains on the face of the ocean.

While this tempest was raging outside, St. Francis of Paula was calmly saying his prayers in his little room. Suddenly he was disturbed in the midst of his prayers by the noise of people running in a great hurry to the place where he was. When they came to the door, they knocked very loudly.

St. Francis opened the door, and saw before him a number of people full of terror. They had come from the neighboring village, to tell him that there was a ship on the sea on the point of being lost, for the waves were tossing it about, and it seemed quite impossible for it to reach the harbor. They heard the people on the ship crying for help, and they could not help them, because they were too far away, and no boat could venture out on such a stormy sea.

"Come, holy Father," they all cried out together, "come at once. The people of the village sent us to ask you to come and help us, and to pray to God to save the ship and the people who are in it."

St. Francis at once said: "I will go with you." And they all went back together.

When the people saw the Saint coming, they ran to meet him. They had often felt the power of his holy prayers in their troubles and dangers, and they were sure that if he asked God to help them now He would certainly do it. So they cried out to him as soon as they were near him: "Help us, Father, help us!" and they pointed with their hands to the place where the ship was tossed about on the raging sea.

St. Francis made a sign to them to be silent. Then he went on his knees, and for a few moments prayed in secret to God. When the people saw him on his knees, they also knelt down and began to pray.

When he had finished his prayer he stood up. All the people looked at him to see what he would do. He raised up his hands to Heaven, and made the sign of the cross over the sea, and pronounced with a loud voice the holy Name, "Jesus."

As soon as he had uttered that blessed Name there arose a great calm, just as when Our Lord Himself stood up in the boat on the Sea of Galilee, and said: "Peace, be still." The ship, which a moment before had been on the point of sinking, lay calmly on the smooth waters of the sea, and the people who had been in the greatest danger of death were in an instant freed from it, and the vessel in a short time entered safely into the harbor.

Those who were in the ship were filled with astonishment at the sudden change which had taken place. When they came into the port, and heard from the people that they had been saved from a watery grave by the prayers of St. Francis, they all ran towards him to thank him.

But the holy man of God, pointing with his finger to Heaven, said to them: "Do not thank me, but rather thank the great God above, Who, by the power of the holy Name of His Son Jesus, has saved you from death."

Then the people who had been in the ship, and all the inhabitants of the village, fell down on their knees and gave thanks to God.

Like this ship, we are on a stormy sea. The world is the sea, and the temptations we meet with are the great winds that raise the storm. Of ourselves, we can never overcome these temptations, no more than the people in the ship could save themselves from death.

But God has given us the means of overcoming them, for when they come to trouble us, and when we are in the danger of falling into sin, if we invoke with devotion the holy Name of Jesus these temptations will at once go away, and there will be a great calm in our souls; then we will be able to reach the harbor in safety—the harbor which is the Kingdom of Heaven.

One of the greatest graces you should ask of God in prayer is that of perseverance. This is the "grace of graces"; this is the grace on which our salvation depends; and God has given us one means of infallibly obtaining it, and that is by praying for it continually till our last breath. This may truly be called the "Key of Heaven."

A SAINTLY MAN IN DANGER.

St. Francis of Assisi was one day preaching in Bologna. Amongst those who were listening to him was a young student called Rizzeri. The words of the Saint made so great an impression on his heart that he at once resolved to renounce the world that he might save his soul.

He kept his resolution faithfully, and made so much progress in piety that St. Francis considered him one of the holiest men of his Order. He appointed him the head of one of his houses, and finally made him Provincial.

But Satan was filled with anger, and assailed him with great temptations. He, for a time, overcame them with great courage; but so great did they become in the end that he was once on the point of yielding.

His historian tells us that in all likelihood he would not have persevered had not St. Francis come to his assistance, and by prayer obtained for him the grace of being faithful to the end.

13

THE PRAYER OF THANKSGIVING

The prayer of thanksgiving is the prayer by which we thank God for all that He has done for us. This is one of our first duties. To be ungrateful is accounted even in this world to be one of the worst of vices; and if we consider it an act of justice for a person to be grateful to us for a little favor we may have done him, how much greater is our obligation to show our gratitude to God, from Whom we have received our very beings and so many other spiritual and temporal graces.

KING ALPHONSUS AND THE BEGGAR.

There was once in Aragon a very pious King called Alphonsus. This King saw that the most of the young Princes who dwelt in his Palace were very worldly, and seldom, if ever, thought of prayer or of thanking God for the benefits they were daily receiving from Him.

One day he thought he would give them a lesson. He prepared a great banquet, and invited them all to come to it. As soon as they were assembled, he gave a sign to begin the meal. Not one of them thought of making the sign of the cross, or of asking a blessing on their food before they began. In the midst of the enjoyment of the feast the door of the hall suddenly opened, and a beggar came in. He was covered with rags, and his whole appearance showed that he belonged to the lowest class of society.

Without saying one word, or even asking permission, he sat down amongst the nobles, not far from the King, and began to eat and drink as if he had as much right to be there as the others had.

All the young nobles were full of indignation at such conduct, and looked towards the King, wondering why he did not at once give orders that the intruder should be cast forth from the hall. But the King sat there in silence.

When the beggar had eaten and drunk as much as he could, he rose up, and without as much as looking at the King, or thanking him for the food he had received, turned towards the door and disappeared.

As soon as he had gone out, a murmur of disgust broke forth among the guests. "What impertinence!" they cried out; "a miserable man like him to dare to come in here, and to eat and drink at the King's table, as if all belonged to him, and to go away without saying even one word of thanks!" And for some time they continued to speak in the same strain of what had just occurred.

At length the King rose up and said: "My friends, you are wondering among yourselves why I permitted that poor man to remain in the room, and you are indignant at his conduct. It was by my orders he came here. I wanted to give you a lesson. You speak of his impudence and his ingratitude and his rudeness. But you your-selves are as guilty as he, and even more so. Do you not daily receive from your Father in Heaven marks of His bounty and His love for you, and do you ever think of giving Him thanks? Let this be for you, then, a lesson. For the time to come, be grateful to Him, and never let a single day pass without thanking Him for the blessings He has bestowed upon you."

They bore the King's rebuke in silence, for they saw it was well deserved, and they profited by the lesson they received.

My child, perhaps you feel that you also have neglected to thank your Heavenly Father for the graces He has given you, but for the future you will be more careful. The more grateful you are, the more you will receive from Him.

THE ABBOT SABBAS AND THE CAMEL-DRIVERS.

There came one day to the monastery over which St. Sabbas ruled a number of camel-drivers who had lost their way in the desert. The abbot received them with his wonted kindness, and placed before them such food as his poverty could afford, consisting chiefly of herbs and roots which grew in his garden, at the same time expressing his regrets at having nothing better to offer them.

The wanderers were very grateful to him for his kindness, saying that although the meal was simple, it was abundant, and very welcome to men who were suffering from the pangs of hunger; and when they had refreshed themselves, and had the road pointed out to them, they resumed their journey.

On their return homewards they again passed near the monastery, and went to visit the abbot in his cell. As a thankoffering for the generosity he had shown them on their outward journey, they brought him a present of several cheeses and a large basket filled with dates.

The abbot after their departure summoned the religious to his cell, and having showed them the gifts the strangers had brought, and having praised their generosity, he said to them:

"Woe to us, my brethren! These people, who are barbarians, and as yet only pagans, far from forgetting the little kindness which we showed them, have shown their gratitude to us by these rich and abundant presents. How ashamed we should be—we who are the children of God, and who have received so many blessings, temporal and spiritual, from Him—at our little gratitude towards Him, and who, instead of pouring forth our prayers of thanksgiving, so often offend Him by breaking His Commandments!"

The religious listened with attention to this lesson of their abbot, and while partaking of the presents they had received, they did not forget to thank God, Who by the hands of these men had sent them to them.

My child, we would be unworthy of the name of children of God if we did not thank Our Father in Heaven for the blessings He is daily showering down upon us.

Blumen der Wüste.

14

WE SHOULD PRAY WITH RESIGNATION

When you ask anything from God, my child, you should always leave it to Him to grant it or to refuse it as He sees fit. God knows better than we do what is good for us.

A MOTHER'S RASH PRAYER GRANTED.

There was once a mother who had an only child, a boy for whom she had the greatest affection. It happened that the child became very ill. At first the mother did not think there was any danger; indeed, she thought it was impossible that anything could happen to her darling boy.

Some of the neighbors told her that the child was certainly dying, and began to console her by saying that her little boy would soon be an angel of God in Heaven.

These words frightened the poor mother. She now for the first time saw what others had seen long before, that her child was really dying, and she became almost beside herself with grief.

When the priest of the town was informed of what was taking place, he went to speak some words of the consolation to the afflicted mother.

Seeing that all he could say to her had no effect, he knelt down by the bedside of the dying boy and began to pray. "O my God," he said, "spare the life of this child, for the sake of the mother, if it be Thy most holy will."

When the mother heard him say these words she became very angry. "Why did you say that?" she said. "Do not say 'if it be His will,' but tell Him that He must make my boy better. Tell Him that He must not let my boy die."

God was pleased to listen to the rash prayer of the mother, and the child, contrary to all expectation, became well again. God wished to give us from this example a lesson, that it is best to submit ourselves to His holy will when we ask Him for anything.

As he began to grow up, and to mix with other companions, he began also to learn evil. Moreover his mother, who was too fond of him, never corrected him, and while others saw the faults and sins he was daily committing, she never saw any.

Time went on, and the boy became worse and worse. His mother was at length compelled to open her eyes, but it was too late. He commenced to abuse his mother, and for a long time she had to endure the most cruel treatment at his hands. She now saw how much better it would have been, both for him and for herself, had God taken him to Heaven in his baptismal innocence.

She tried over and over again to correct him, but it was now of no use. Instead of correcting himself, or even promising to do better, he sank deeper into crime, and at last the unfortunate mother had the grief to see him die a criminal on the scaffold, on account of a murder which he had committed.

Raineri: Homilies.

THE BLIND MAN AT THE TOMB OF ST. THOMAS.

Long ago, when the light of the true Faith was shining brightly in our land, a poor blind man was seen making a pilgrimage to the tomb of St. Thomas of Canterbury. He went there to ask through the prayers of the Saint the recovery of his sight. His prayer was granted, and he returned home cured.

When the first transports of joy were over, he remembered that in his prayer to the Saint he had omitted to add these words: "If it should be the will of God," or "if God should see that it would be useful for my salvation."

So he returned to the Saint's tomb, and said: "O great St. Thomas, I thank thee for the favor thou hast obtained for me from God. But if the use of my eyes should prove hurtful to me, or should endanger my eternal salvation, I humbly ask of thee to make me blind again."

At the same moment he once more lost the use of his eyes, and became blind as before. He spent the rest of his days in preparing for a happy death, and when that day came it found him ready.

Schmidt: Cath. Hist., i. 491.

ST. FRANCIS BORGIA'S PRAYER OF SUBMISSION.

St. Francis Borgia, before he became a religious, had been married to a lady who was in everything the model of a religious wife and mother.

But the time came when God was about to call Francis to a higher perfection. His wife became very ill, and the most skillful physicians pronounced her malady to be incurable. Francis, seeing that there was no hope for her cure in earthly remedies, had recourse to Him Who holds in His hands the lives of all men. By fastings, prayers, and many tears did he implore God to spare her to him, and to raise her up again from her bed of sickness.

One night, when he was praying with more than usual fervor, he heard a heavenly voice, which said: "Francis, I place in your hands the disposal of the life of your wife. If you ask Me to spare her to you I will do so, but if you desire Me to take her from you I will do this also."

These words filled the heart of the holy man with the greatest joy, and already tears of gratitude were filling his eyes. But the voice continued: "If you ask Me to make her well again, it will not be for her advantage nor for yours."

The Saint said: "O my God, who am I that I should ask Thee to do my will rather than that Thy will should be done? Far be it from me, O Lord, to do this. Let Thy most holy will, not mine, be done. If it is Thy most holy will to take away my wife from me, let it be done; and not only her, but myself also and my children."

This generous act of resignation was followed by the death of his wife. He wept for her, but his tears were not so much those of sorrow as of joy, to think that she whom he loved so tenderly was already with God Himself in Heaven, and that he would one day meet her there. Moreover, God, Who is never outdone in generosity, gave him such consolation in his bereavement that he felt even happier than before.

BOLLAND, xii. 249.

VI. WE SHOULD PRAY WITH CONFIDENCE.

My child, God is your Father and He loves you. Therefore, when you kneel to say your prayers to Him, you should do so with the confidence of a child who asks his father for something. It is the surest way of getting what you ask.

THE POOR WIDOW.

A poor widow one morning said to her little ones: "My children, I have nothing to give you today for your breakfast; there is no bread, nor flour, nor even an egg in the house. Go and ask God to come to your assistance, for He is rich and merciful, and has promised to help His children in their need."

One of the children, aged only six years, went out of the house, and seeing the door of a church open, entered and fell on his knees before the altar.

He looked around him to see if there was anyone near, but he saw no person; the church seemed to be empty.

Thinking himself alone, he spoke out aloud: "O my good Father Who art in Heaven, we poor children have nothing to eat today. There are five of us, and our mother has no bread to give us, nor flour, nor even an egg. O my God, give us something to eat, that we and our dear mother may not die of hunger. Oh, help us, for Thou art rich and powerful, and, besides, hast Thou not promised to do so?" When he had said this prayer, he rose up, and, hungry though he was, went to school for his morning lessons. On his return home, he was surprised to see on the table a great loaf of bread, a dish full of flour, and a basket full of eggs.

"O mamma," he cried out with great joy, "God has heard my prayer! Was it an angel who brought in all these nice things by the window?"

"No," said the mother, "but God heard your prayer, and has answered it in His own way. When you were kneeling at the foot of the altar, and when you thought you were alone, there happened to be a pious lady near you whom you did not see. She heard your prayer, and it is she who brought us all these good things. She was the angel whom God sent to help us. Let us kneel down and thank Him for His goodness to us; and during all your lifetime continue to ask Him for what you need, with the same confidence, and you will be sure to obtain it."

Catechisme de Persévérance, xii. 138.

THE ANGRY KING.

Louis XIV, King of France, had a special affection for one of his courtiers. Whatever this man asked was sure to be granted.

One day he went as usual to ask a favor from the King. But it happened that the King was angry at the time, and said to him in a passion: "You are always asking me for something. Are you ever going to stop?"

At these words the man hung down his head, and went away disappointed.

Sometimes our request may be refused by people in this world, even by those who love us, but God will never be angry with us, nor refuse us when we pray to Him; on the contrary, He is angry with us when we neglect to call upon Him in our needs.

"I SHALL NOT DIE TONIGHT."

During the terrible days which followed the change of religion in Scotland, the priests were either put to death for the Faith, or driven out of the country. Some few, indeed, remained at the risk of their lives, living secretly among the mountains, and going about from place to place in the night-time to minister to the wants of their flocks.

The faithful also, like their pastors, were either driven away to live as exiles in a foreign land, or dwelt in the fastnesses of their native mountains, where they were compelled to live, sometimes for many years without ever seeing a priest, or having it in their power to receive the Holy Sacraments. Yet their Faith burned brightly within them, and, above all, their confidence in the most holy Mother of God was unbounded; and even at the present day people recount many wonderful things which she accomplished in favor of her Scottish children. Of these, the following is a beautiful example, which will also show how powerful in the eyes of God is prayer offered up with confidence and perseverance.

It happened that one of the Bishops who were sent to preside over the Church in Scotland in those terrible times was one day walking on foot among the mountains. It was in the winter-time. He wore the dress of the common people, because to appear in that of a Bishop would have exposed him to certain death. Night came on whilst he was in the middle of a barren part of the country, and he had lost his way in the snow-covered roads.

When he had wandered for a considerable time, not knowing where he was, nor where he could obtain shelter for the night, but committing himself to the protection of God, Whose minister he was, he thought he perceived at some distance a light shining. He directed his steps towards the place, and saw that it proceeded from a very poor cottage near the entrance to a wood. Going to the door, he asked the people who dwelt in it if they could give him shelter for the night, as he had lost his way in the darkness.

The good people at once told him to enter, and welcomed him with the greatest kindness, made him sit down by the fire to warm his cold and weary limbs, while they prepared some food to refresh him. They did not know who their guest was, nor did the Bishop know who the people were who had so kindly entertained him. He cast his eyes around the little room to see if by chance he might discover any sign by which he might learn to what religion they belonged; but seeing no cross or pious picture on the walls, or any other thing of a religious nature, he came to the conclusion that they did not belong to the Faith.

After a short interval the simple meal was ready, and they invited the stranger to eat what they had placed before him. "It is true that we have only very simple food to give you, for we are very poor, and we are obliged to be content with the plainest fare." The Bishop said that they were quite mistaken in thus speaking of the food, which he found to be excellent, and, for a weary and hungry traveler as he was, to be delicious.

During the repast the conversation became less restrained, and each party was desirous to discover as much as possible about the other; but as in those days it was dangerous to confide in strangers, neither the people of the cottage nor the Bishop revealed much of their history.

As the conversation proceeded, the Bishop observed that although they all endeavored to be agreeable and attentive to him, there was a feeling of sadness and melancholy accompanying everything they said or did.

After a little time the Bishop ventured to observe: "My friends, you are indeed very kind to me, but you all appear to me to be very sad, as if some calamity had overtaken you."

"Alas! sir, it is only too true," said the mother of the family; "a deep sorrow does really oppress us. There, in that adjoining room, upon a poor bed of straw, lies my aged father at the very point of death. But what grieves us above all things else is that he persists in saying that he is not to die so soon, and obstinately refuses to listen to everything we can say to make him prepare himself to die."

"Would you permit me to see him?" asked the Bishop, full of surprise and emotion.

"Most willingly," said the other, with that confidence which arises in the soul that is suffering affliction, and she at once led him into the room where the old man lay.

The Bishop saw that the words of the woman were only too true, and that the old man was really dying. He was astonished that he had been able to exist until that time, seeing the emaciated condition to which he was reduced.

But no sooner had the Bishop, after a few words of sympathy, said to him that the hand of death was indeed upon him, than the old man all at once seemed to regain strength, and answered in a strong, firm voice, to the utter astonishment of the Bishop: "No, sir, I am not yet going to die."

"But, my good friend," said the Bishop, "we must all die, and we may die at any moment; but when people are old and infirm as you are, the hour of death cannot be far distant."

"I tell you, sir, again," said the dying man reverently, but with great energy, "I am not yet going to die; that is quite impossible."

The holy Bishop, seeing the imminent danger of death in which he lay, spoke to him more and more urgently on not delaying his preparation for his passage into eternity for a moment longer. But he always received the same answer: "I am not yet going to die."

"Would you be pleased to tell me what reason you have for speaking in this manner, you who even now are in the agonies of death?"

On hearing this question the old man fixed his dying eyes upon the Bishop, and seemed strangely moved. He said to him in a voice which could scarcely be heard: "Tell me, sir, perhaps you are a Catholic?"

"Yes," answered the Bishop, "I am a Catholic." "Ah, then, I will now tell you why I have said to you so often that I am not yet going to die."

With the utmost difficulty he raised himself in the bed to a sitting position, and seizing in his icy grasp the hand of the Bishop, spoke in a voice that showed the lively faith which burned in his soul: "I also am a Catholic. From the day of my first Communion until now I have never failed even for a single day to ask Our Blessed Lady for the grace of not dying without having a priest at my bedside to hear my confession, and give me the Last Sacraments, and do you think, sir, that my heavenly Mother will not hear me? That is impossible, quite impossible! So I am not going to die till some priest comes to visit me."

"My child," said the Bishop with deep emotion, "Our Lady has, indeed, heard your prayer and granted it, for I am not only a priest, but your Bishop. The Blessed Virgin herself must have permitted me to go astray in these wild places that I might be led hither to prepare you to die a happy death."

Then the Bishop opened his cloak, and showed the old man the cross which he wore upon his breast.

At the sight of it the dying man raised up his eyes to Heaven, and exclaimed: "O my dearest Mother Mary, from my inmost heart I thank thee!"

Then, turning towards the Bishop, he said: "My lord, be pleased to hear my confession, for now I know that I am going to die."

The Bishop did as he requested, and gave him the Last Sacraments. A few minutes afterwards he placidly expired in the Bishop's arms. And who can for a moment doubt but that he is now in Heaven, praising her who during life had been his protectress and his joy in death.

My child, if you pray with the same confidence and perseverance as did that good old man, you also shall one day die happily as he did, and reign for all eternity in Heaven with Jesus and Mary, His most Holy Mother.

Annie de Marie.

ST. ULRICH, BISHOP OF AUGSBOURG.

In the year 955 an immense army of the Huns marched into Germany, and penetrated even as far as the Black Forest, devastating the whole land with fire and sword, and spreading wild dismay in every place.

Nothing could escape the fury of these savage men, who, mounted as they were on fleet horses, seemed to fly over the plains, slaying the people or making them prisoners.

In course of time they reached the gates of Augsbourg, the see of the saintly Bishop Ulrich. The town, being but slenderly fortified, seemed to promise to fall an easy prey to the invaders, and the inhabitants fell into despair.

"Alas!" they cried out at the thought of the terrible destruction which seemed to be inevitable, "we are lost. A cruel death and the destruction of our city is the fate that awaits us."

But the Bishop did not allow himself to yield to the general despondency. He besought the people to take courage, and to put their confidence in God. He ordered public prayers to be offered up throughout the city to move God to have pity on them, and save them from the swords of the Huns.

The enemy, as was anticipated, attacked the city in overwhelming numbers, but the inhabitants, having regained courage from the Bishop's words, flew to arms, and vigorously drove them back. St. Ulrich, clad in his pontifical vestments, stood in the midst of them with his hands raised up to Heaven, and this gave them fresh courage to withstand the attack. Moreover, they had all, with the greatest fervor and devotion, received Holy Communion before going forth to the combat, and this inflamed them with the heroic resolution to save their city and their people, or die in their defense.

The Huns, who had hitherto found little opposition in their victorious career, did not expect to meet the resistance they now encountered. They were repulsed in the first attack, and had retired from the walls to prepare for another and more powerful onset. But just as they were about to renew the assault they perceived an immense and well-organized army, under the command of the Emperor Otho, hastening to attack them in their rear. Seeing themselves thus situated, they dared not begin the attack on the city, but concentrated their forces to meet the army of the enemy on the plains behind them.

But here their undisciplined hordes could not withstand the attack of the well-trained soldiers of the Emperor. On August 10, 955, a terrible and bloody battle was fought on the banks of the Lech, and Otto succeeded in gaining a glorious victory, completely destroying the forces of the enemy.

Thus, by the prayers of the holy Bishop Ulrich and of the devout people of Augsbourg, their city was saved from imminent destruction.

History of the Middle Ages.

15

WE SHOULD PRAY ALWAYS

Jesus Christ tells us to pray always. This is very easy, even for those who have to work all day long, as the following examples will show you:

ALWAYS PRAYING.

One day the holy Abbot Lucius was visited in his desert home by some monks, who had come from a great distance to see him.

After the first salutations were over, Lucius said to them: "My brethren, tell me with what kind of work do you occupy yourselves when you are at home?"

"We do not do any work at all," they replied; "we pray without ceasing, according to the advice of the Apostle."

"And do you never eat?" inquired the Abbot.

"Yes," they answered, "we take our meals every day."

"And who prays for you when you are eating?"

They did not know what answer to give to this question.

Then the Abbot said to them: "My brethren, you must work as well as pray. I also try to pray always, but I work at the same time. Before I begin to work I ask the assistance of God, then I dip into the water the leaves with which I make my baskets, and while I am doing this I say to God this prayer: 'Have mercy on me, O my God, and according to Thy great mercy blot out my iniquities.' Is not that a prayer?"

They all answered that it was.

"Then," continued the Abbot, "when I have labored in this way till evening, and have been praying all the time with my lips or in my heart, I sell the work which I have made, and with the money I receive for it I am able to support some poor people who come to me for an alms, and with the rest I provide for my own wants. Then those who have received a little in charity from me pray for me while I eat and sleep. This, then, is the way in which I fulfill that precept of praying always."

The strangers returned to their homes edified by the lesson they had that day received—a lesson they also put in practice for the rest of their lives.

Catechisme de Persévérance, xii. 115.

You, also, my child, can pray always by doing all your work to please God, and by raising up your heart from time to time to Him in Heaven.

THE IGNORANT WOMAN'S PRAYER.

There was once a poor woman who could not read, but who was very good and pleasing to God. She lived in the attic of a house in a very small room, and was employed by a certain community of nuns to sweep the convent and the schools which were attached to it.

The whole day was spent in this kind of work; but while she was working she used often to think of God, and say some short prayers to Him. She used also to think often in her mind how good God had been to her, and of the blessings He had given her during her whole lifetime, and thanked Him for them.

Whenever she saw the nuns going to the chapel to their prayers, she would say to herself: "What a happiness it must be for these Sisters to say such long and such beautiful prayers, and to think so much about God! As for me, I cannot say long prayers, and I cannot always be thinking of God. I must be content with very short ones, because I cannot read as they can. But I go on sweeping and cleaning because it is God's will."

This poor woman was very pleasing to God, and her short prayers were like darts of love, which reached up to God and drew Him down from Heaven to dwell in her soul.

Now, at the day of God's judgment, we shall see that God was perhaps more pleased with her short prayers than even with the prayers of the holy Sisters which she called so beautiful.

It is not only in temptation that you must pray if you desire to persevere, but at other times, particularly in the morning and at night. It is this frequent prayer that keeps us, as it were, chained to Heaven, our true home.

MORNING AND EVENING PRAYER.

Gothold, one of the most learned men of his age, was most careful never to omit his morning and evening prayers, and to say them with great devotion.

"If you say your morning and evening prayers," he used to say, "you will be God's true child, and a faithful disciple of Jesus Christ all the days of your life. The prayer in the morning will procure for you the graces needful to you during the course of the day, and the prayer at night those you need during the night; so that these prayers, regularly said, become, as it were, a continual chain uniting you to God from the beginning of your life until the end of it."

This will be consoling for you, my child, if you always say your morning and evening prayers devoutly.

16

WE SHOULD PRAY WITH
PERSEVERANCE

You must not be disappointed if God does not at once give you what you ask, but continue to ask it till He grants it. This is called Perseverance in Prayer.

THE NEGRO BOY'S PRAYER.

There was once a young negro who had been stolen by some sailors from his father's home, and taken by them into a distant country far away from the land of his birth.

In the country to which he had been brought there were some Catholic missionaries who had gone to preach the Gospel to the poor savages who dwelt there. Among others who received the gift of the Faith was this little negro. At his baptism he received the name of Thomas.

One day, as one of the priests was passing near the house where the negro boy dwelt, he heard him saying the following words: "O my dear Jesus, I thank Thee with my whole heart for having sent into my country a great ship, and in that great ship some wicked men, who stole me from my home, and brought me into this place, where I have been able to know and love Thee. And now, dear Jesus, I have another great favor to ask of Thee. Oh, be pleased to send another great ship into my country, with more bad men in it, that they may bring my father and mother here, so that they may also learn to know and love Thee."

Some days after this the same priest saw the little negro standing on the shore, looking far away over the sea.

"Thomas, my child, what are you looking at so earnestly?" said the priest.

"I am looking to see if Jesus has heard my prayer," said the boy. "I asked Him to send my dear parents here that they may become Christians, and I want to see if the ship is coming."

For about two years did that little boy go down day after day to look for his parents, but they never came. Still he continued his prayer, for he knew that God had promised to hear the prayers of those who pray to Him with confidence and perseverance.

One day the priest saw the boy running towards him singing joyfully, and his face all radiant with smiles.

"Well, Thomas," said the priest to him, "what makes you so happy today?"

"O my dear Father, Jesus has heard my prayer at last! My father and mother have come; they are in the big ship that has just come to land. Oh, how kind it was of Jesus to hear my prayer and send them to me!"

"HE ALWAYS SAID THE SAME WORDS."

There was in a certain town in Spain a little boy, who was the only son of a widow, and she was very poor. She had to send her boy to work very early in the morning, and so his education was neglected. But she taught him to love God, and to be good, and everybody loved him. He had a very bad memory, and no one could teach him his prayers even. If they succeeded in making him learn the Lord's Prayer and Hail Mary, he would just as soon forget them again.

But there was one prayer he did learn, a very short prayer—it was this: "O my God, I believe in Thee; O my God, I hope in Thee; O my

God, I love Thee;" and this prayer he was saying all day long. Every day when his work was done he would go into the church where he knew the good God dwelt, or to the poor little room where his mother stayed, and there in a quiet corner he would kneel down and remain on his knees for a long time.

People used to wonder what he did all the time, because they knew he could not learn even the "Our Father." Still, there he knelt, with his hands clasped together; and when in the church, his eyes would be fixed on the tabernacle all the time.

One day the priest hid himself behind a pillar of the church near where the poor little boy used to kneel, to watch him to see if he said anything. The boy soon came in, and without looking about him, knelt down and joined his hands and fixed his eyes upon the altar.

The priest then heard him say for a whole hour and more the little prayer over and over again: "O my God, I believe in Thee; O my God, I hope in Thee; O my God, I love Thee."

He did not live long, but his death was the death of the Saints. His last words were: "O my God, I love Thee." He is now with God in Heaven, and will be forever happy there.

17

WE SHOULD PRAY WITH GREAT DEVOTION

M y child, when you say your prayers you must be careful to keep away all distractions; if you are careless at your prayers, or say them with willful distractions, God will be displeased with you.

WHY HE DID NOT GO STRAIGHT TO HEAVEN.

St. Severinus, Archbishop of Cologne, was so holy that God granted many miracles through his intercession.

One day, soon after his death, the Saint appeared in a vision to a priest. He seemed to be in great suffering, and marks of sadness were upon his face.

The priest said to him: "My Father, how is it that you are so sad and in a state of suffering? You were so holy that I was sure you had entered the happiness of Heaven as soon as you had left this world."

"It is true," replied the Saint, "God in His infinite goodness has given me the great grace of dying well, and I am to reign with Him eternally in Heaven. But, alas!" he continued, "I am not there yet; I am suffering in the purifying flames of purgatory." The priest asked him what he had done to keep him, even for a time, out of Heaven.

"I am suffering these terrible torments," replied the Bishop, "because, when I was alive, I sometimes said my prayers hurriedly and with distractions. I was so much taken up with the duties the Emperor required of me that I would sometimes put off my prayers, or say them without devotion. It was my own fault, and God is now punishing me for it."

He asked the priest to intercede for him, and then suddenly disappeared, leaving him filled with a great fear of God's judgments.

From St. Peter Damian.

ST. BERNARD'S VISION OF THE ANGELS.

While St. Bernard was in the church one night at matins, he had a vision, in which God made known to him the manner in which the religious were saying their prayers. He saw the angel guardians of the monks standing near them with pens in their hands. Some of these angels wrote in letters of gold, and others in letters of silver. Some were writing with common ink, and others with water, while a few stood sorrowfully, and did not write anything at all in their books.

As the Saint was gazing in wonder at the vision, and pondering in his mind what it signified, an angel said to him: "The religious whose guardian angels are writing in letters of gold are those who say their prayers with great attention, and are full of Divine love. Those whose angels are writing in silver letters love God well, and pray with great attention, but are less fervent and less perfect than the others.

Those whose guardian angels are writing with ink have, indeed, a certain desire to please God, but there is not much fervor in their souls; while those whose angels are writing with water are honoring God only with their lips; their hearts are far from Him, and are full of distractions. Those beside whom the angels are standing with sad countenances, and are writing nothing in their books, have already lost the grace of God, and their prayers are only a mockery of Him."

The holy man made known to them in the morning what he had

seen. Those who were fervent were encouraged to persevere, and those who had become negligent were aroused to serve God more faithfully.

TWO MONKS AT PRAYER.

We read in the Life of St. Macarius that one day he saw in a vision two monks who were saying their prayers. They were both very fervent, and seemed to keep themselves always in the presence of God, not only when they were on their knees, but also when they were at their work.

The Saint saw coming from the lips of one of them, from time to time, as it were, flames of fire, which appeared to fly up towards Heaven; while from the mouth of the other flames came forth as from a furnace, also reaching up to Heaven.

The Saint knew from this vision that both these monks loved God; but he saw that the first one had many distractions, and that he was often thinking of other things, so that his prayer was not continual, whereas the other one, whose heart was entirely detached from the things of the world, was able to send up to God a constant fire of prayer.

Be very fervent, then, my child, when you say your prayers, because the more fervently you pray, the more abundant graces you will receive, and the easier will it be for you to obtain the gift of final perseverance.

HOW SATAN TEMPTS US AT OUR PRAYERS.

God was pleased once to show St. Macarius in a vision how Satan tempts us when we are saying our prayers.

In the middle of the night he heard someone knock at the door of his cell and say: "Rise, O Macarius, and let us go along with the brethren to midnight prayers."

But the Saint, by a revelation from Heaven, knew that it was Satan who had come again to trouble him; so he answered: "O lying spirit, what have you to do in the assembly of the Saints?"

"And do you not know," replied Satan, "that your solitaries never go to the church for prayer without me and my companions going along with them? Come and see for yourself what we do there."

St. Macarius prayed to God to enlighten him, that he might not be deceived by the enemy of souls; then, rising up, he went to the church, where the brethren were already assembled.

Now, it was the custom for the religious to sit while one who was appointed read the Psalms and the Sacred Scriptures. As soon as they were seated, the holy Abbot saw an army of wicked spirits enter, and, running about with great swiftness, endeavor to distract the religious during their prayers. He saw some of them trying to close the eyes of a few of the brethren, so as to make them fall asleep; others appeared to stand before them as it were in the act of building houses or of preparing for a journey, and in various other forms, as if to try to make them think on these things.

The Saint also saw how the religious acted under these temptations. Some of them drove the wicked spirits away as soon as they came near, so that they could not reach them. Others willfully permitted the thoughts to remain in their minds, and so he beheld the devils trample on them as a sign that they had gained a victory over them.

On seeing these things, St. Macarius burst into tears, and cried out: "O my God, see how Satan lays snares for our ruin. Oh! let him hear Thy powerful voice and feel the effects of Thy anger, since Thou seest how he tries to fill the hearts of Thy servants with these vain and worldly thoughts."

When the prayers were ended, and the solitaries were about to leave the church, he called them one by one to his side, and asked them if such and such thoughts had not come before their minds during the time of prayer. Each one was obliged to acknowledge that he had been tempted with the very thoughts the Abbot mentioned to him. Then he related to them his vision, and they saw more clearly than ever that there is no time Satan is so busy with his temptations as the time of prayer, and that those who keep their hearts united to God easily keep him back, and that he rejoices whenever he is able to fill our minds with worldly things, because he has gained a great victory over us.

PART III

"OUR FATHER WHO ART IN HEAVEN"

18

GOD IS OUR FATHER BECAUSE HE CREATED US.

God is our Father, my child, and we are His children, because He created us and made us what we are. His Kingdom in Heaven will be also our Kingdom, if we live in this world as His children ought to live in deed and in truth. This is what you should always keep in mind when you say the "Our Father."

THE SHEPHERD BOY OF THE MOUNTAINS.

A little boy was tending a flock of sheep on a lonely mountain. A priest who was traveling in the neighborhood saw him, and, being struck with his devout and recollected appearance, turned aside to speak to him.

"My child," he said, "I am sure you must feel very lonely all day here by yourself."

"Oh no, Father," said the boy, "I am not at all lonely; I am always busy."

"And what is it you do which keeps you so busy?" rejoined the priest.

"I will tell you, Father: I have a beautiful prayer that I say, and it keeps me occupied all the day." "It must surely be a very long prayer, my child, since it takes you all day to say it."

"No, Father; on the contrary, it is very short, and yet I can never reach the end of it; it is so beautiful, so sweet, that it makes my heart full of joy."

"And what is that beautiful prayer which is so short and yet so long?" asked the priest.

"It is the 'Our Father,'" said the child; "but when I say the first words of it, 'Our Father Who art in Heaven,' I come to a full stop, and can get no farther."

"Why not?" asked the priest.

"Because I cannot help crying," replied the child, "when I think of those words. 'Is it possible,' I say to myself, 'that I can call God my Father—God Who is so great and so powerful, Who made the beautiful sky and the bright sun, and these lofty mountains, and all the universe?' And yet I know that it is quite true, and that He allows me, a poor shepherd-boy, to call Him by that sweet name of Father, while He on His part loves and cherishes me as if I were His only child. When I think of all this, I begin to weep, and cannot get on with my prayer."

Then, turning round and pointing with his finger over the valley, he continued: "Father, do you see there below, between those two trees far away behind the third hill, that little village with only a few houses? Well, it is there where I live, and my father is the poorest man in it. But just think that I can call God my Father as truly, and be as much loved by Him, as if I were the greatest gentleman in the city. I am a child of God just as much as he is."

The priest, who could with difficulty hide his emotion, said to the boy: "My child, do as you have been doing, and God will bless you and love you."

So the good Father continued his journey, praising God Who has hidden the mysteries of His goodness from the wise ones of this world, and has revealed them to His chosen little ones.

Catholic Anecdotes.

THE VETERAN SOLDIER AND HIS HEAVENLY FATHER.

The following legend is related on reliable authority, and shows the excellence of that prayer which Jesus Christ Himself has taught us:

An old soldier, renowned for his bravery on the battlefield, but not less so for his simple piety, desired to spend the evening of his days amongst the monks of St. Benedict. He had never acquired any learning in his youth, and knew only his prayers, which he devoutly said many times a day, particularly that prayer which Jesus Christ Himself taught His Apostles when He said to them: "Thus, therefore, shall you pray: 'Our Father Who art in Heaven.'" And during the time that the religious were in church singing the psalms of the Holy Office, he recited over and over again this beautiful prayer.

But as time went on, on seeing that all the brethren of that holy house were more learned than himself, he became discouraged. Satan tempted him with the thought that this abode of peace was not the place in which God desired him to dwell, and he made up his mind to return to the world, and work out his salvation in a more obscure and humble life.

As these thoughts were passing through his mind, God vouchsafed to grant him a vision for his own consolation and our instruction. He saw standing before him a venerable man, whose countenance was full of sweetness, and encouraging; it was St. Benedict himself. He held in his hand a garment of the greatest beauty, richly embroidered with gold, and adorned with the most precious gems, which were arranged in such a manner as to form the two first words of the Lord's Prayer, "Our Father."

The holy old man gazed upon the robe with inexpressible admiration; such magnificence he had never seen before; but he was surprised that no other words were to be found upon it but only the two first words of his beloved prayer, "Our Father."

The holy patriarch, seeming to divine his thoughts, said to him: "My son, it will be your work to finish this robe which you are preparing for yourself by reciting so often the 'Our Father' with devotion. Do not go away from this house; it is the place in which God desires you to remain. Continue till the day of your death to repeat that same prayer, which is the best of all prayers, then this garment will be completed, and you shall be vested in it at the gate of Paradise, and wear it throughout all eternity as a testimony of your love for your Heavenly Father."

Schouppe: Instruc. Religieuse, ii. 196.

ST. HUGH OF GRENOBLE'S ANSWER TO HIS SERVANT.

Surius relates in his "Life of St. Hugh" of Grenoble, that it was his custom very often during the day to say the Lord's Prayer. One time he became very ill, and lay in his bed without being able to sleep. He spent those silent dreary hours of the night in saying over and over again the Lord's Prayer, according to his custom.

His servant, who spent the night along with him, hearing him continually saying this prayer, said to him: "You surely, my Father, must become very weary repeating this prayer so often."

St. Hugh answered: "No; on the contrary, I feel more and more refreshed the oftener I say it."

Surius: Life of St. Hugh.

PAUL, THE LITTLE AFRICAN.

Two missionary Fathers returned home to France after laboring for many years on the African missions. They brought with them several little boys whom they had bought in the slave-market, that they might be instructed in the Christian religion, and that afterwards, when they returned to their native land, they might teach their fellow-countrymen to believe in the one true and only God.

It was difficult at first to make them understand anything; but as they were gentle and diligent, they soon began to know what was said to them.

The Fathers often spoke to them of the great God Whose home is in Heaven. "My children," they said, "God, Who made this great world, made you also. He made you to be His own children on earth, and if you love and obey Him here, He will take you to Heaven when you die, and you will be forever happy with Him there." One of the boys, whose name was Paul, was often heard saying to himself: "Oh, how good God has been to me! Am I really the child of that God Who made this great world? Yes, I am, because every day I speak to Him, and call Him Father—'Our Father Who art in Heaven.'" This thought seemed to fill the boy with great happiness.

One day he was telling the Fathers how cruelly he had been treated by his former masters. "Oh," he cried out, "what a difference there is between God and my masters at home! They were always striking me and maltreating me, and I was always miserable; but since I became God's child, I have been always happy; no one ever strikes me now."

The Fathers were also full of joy at seeing him so grateful. He seemed to be always thinking of God, and trying to show his gratitude to Him in every way he could.

My child, God has given you the same and even greater favors, and are you grateful to Him for them? or may He not have to complain of you as He had to do of some others when He said: "If I am your Father, where is My honor?"

THE STRANGER AND THE TWO LITTLE ORPHANS.

One beautiful evening in the summer-time a carriage drove up to a village inn. The last rays of the setting sun were visible on the fleecy clouds, and on the vane of an antiquated church which stood on the opposite side of the way. A stranger stepped out, looked about him for a few minutes, and then directed his steps to the church. He opened the gate of the graveyard surrounding the sacred edifice, and walked around it.

While he was reading the various inscriptions on the tombstones, his attention was drawn by the sobs of two ragged children, who sat weeping on a newly-made grave. A piece of hard bread was between them. The stranger inquired into the cause of their distress. The little boy began to tell him that his sister was naughty, and would not eat the piece of bread which he had begged for her. She here interrupted her brother, and told the gentleman that she had some bread yesterday, but her brother had eaten none since the day before, and she wanted him to eat this.

The boy told the stranger that about a year ago his father left the village, went to sea, and that in a storm he was drowned. "And poor mother cried so hard and said that she must soon die too, and that we must love each other, and that God would be our Father. She called us to her bedside, kissed us both, and then died. Can you tell us, sir, where our Heavenly Father can be found?"

After listening to this sorrowful tale, the stranger, with emotion, exclaimed: "Come with me, my children; God will be your Father. He has, without any doubt, sent me here this day to befriend you."

He took them to the inn, and had them provided for until he returned home, whither they were taken, fed, clothed, and instructed; and the stranger, in his declining years, had the happiness of seeing them pious, useful, and honorable members of society. His kindness was rewarded a hundredfold even in this life.

Ave Maria, vol. 32.

THE POOR WIDOW'S OFFERING.

A certain priest was once collecting money to build a church. A widow dressed in the poorest clothing went to him, and offered him a crown-piece. "My child," the priest said to her, "I cannot accept from you such a great sum, for you are poor and stand in need of it for your own support."

"Father," she replied, "I am not poor, for am I not the daughter of the King of Heaven, Who is infinitely rich, and the heiress of His own kingdom, which will never end?"

The priest accepted the offering, and blessed God for having granted the gift of true wisdom to the poor and lowly, while the rich and the great ones of this world live without thought of the eternity for which they were made.

The thought of the eternity of God should make you happy, my child, and cause you to be good. For is not that Eternal God your Father? and has He not promised to take you to Heaven to be eternally with Him if you are only His true child in this world?

19

GOD IS OUR FATHER BY ADOPTION

God is our Father, not only because He created us, but because He has adopted us as His own children. By bestowing on you, my child, the Sacrament of Baptism, He has made you His own child, and heir to the Kingdom of Heaven. "He hath not done in like manner to every nation," says holy David in the Scriptures, "and His judgments He hath not made manifest to them." How grateful, therefore, you should be to Him, for this great mark of His love for you!

"FOR YOU ARE ALL THE CHILDREN OF GOD."

St. Paul the Apostle, in his letter to the Galatians, wrote: "For you are all the children of God by faith in Christ Jesus; for as many of you as have been baptized in Christ have put on Christ. You are all one in Christ Jesus.

"When the fullness of time was come, God sent His Son, made of a woman, made under the law: that He might redeem them that were under the law, that we might receive the adoption of sons. And because you are sons, God hath sent the Spirit of His Son into your heart, crying: 'Abba, Father.' Therefore, now he is not a servant, but a son, and if a son, an heir through God."

THE ANGEL ON THE TOMBSTONE.

A little boy was one day crying bitterly over a newly-made grave in the cemetery. They had just laid the remains of his father in their last resting-place by the side of his mother, and he was left alone to the mercy of strangers.

"Alas!" he cried, "I have no father or mother now; both are lying here in the cold, cold grave. Never shall I again see the sweet smile of my dear mother, nor feel the affectionate pressure of my father's hand, which used to be my greatest reward when I was good and obedient; never again shall I hear any more of those beautiful lessons they taught me—their lips are closed forever. There is no one now to love me as my good parents did. Ah! but it is hard, hard to have neither a father nor mother."

Thus did the poor child lament as his tears fell fast on his parents' grave. Raising up his head, his eyes chanced to fall upon a tombstone near him. On it was engraved the figure of a beautiful angel, who with one hand pointed up to Heaven, while in the other he held a scroll, on which was written the words: "Our Father Who art in Heaven."

His tears ceased to flow as he read these words, and, raising his eyes towards Heaven, he said: "O my God, how is it that I have so soon forgotten You? You still remain my Father. I have not lost You. You took away my earthly father from me, and now You are going to take his place. My father, when he was living, loved me much, but Your love for me is greater still. Then, dear Father in Heaven, do not abandon me, a poor homeless orphan all alone in the world."

Thus the orphan prayed. He was consoled, and even happy in his bereavement, and his Heavenly Father did take care of him. He did not, indeed, become a rich man; but, what is infinitely better, he lived in the peace of a good conscience, and when in after-life he was tempted to sadness, he thought of the angel on the tombstone pointing upwards, and of the words engraved on the scroll: "Our Father Who art in Heaven."

SCHMIDT.

MARY ANNE, THE LITTLE ORPHAN.

Mary Anne was the daughter of poor but pious parents. She loved them with the tenderest affection, and their love for her—their only child—can only be understood by a father or mother who has but one child to love.

The girl was pious like her parents, and her daily prayer to God was that they might be long spared to watch over her, and teach her how to please Him.

Scarcely had she reached her eleventh year when she tasted her first great sorrow. Her mother died. Not long afterwards her father also became sick, and the thought that he too might be taken from her sent a pang through her heart as if it had been pierced by a two-edged sword.

"O my God, my God," she cried, "spare my father!"

As time went on her father became worse, and even she, young as she was, could see that he was fast sinking into the grave. Still she prayed, and hoped against hope that God would not take him away.

Day and night she sat by his bedside and nursed him with affectionate tenderness. She watched his every motion, and noted even every look of his eye. One day he lifted up his arms, and, throwing them round her neck, he drew her close to him, and whispered in her ear: "O my child, I must leave you; I am dying; it is the will of God. But if you are a good girl, and love Him as I have so often told you to do, He will be a Father to you, and will protect you and watch over you, and provide for you far better than I could do had I been spared to you."

He could say no more. The poor child lay sobbing on her father's breast, as if her heart would break, but her father heard her not; he was dead.

Mary Anne was inconsolable when she saw he was no more, and she wondered why God, Who had so solemnly promised to hear the prayers of His children, had not granted hers; and she had prayed, too, so fervently.

But, remembering her dying father's last words, she took courage, and raising up her hands to Heaven, she said: "O my God, why should I grieve at what Thou hast done? Thou hast freed my dear father from his suffering here, and hast given Him Heaven in exchange. I have no one now on earth to care for me. O my God, be Thou henceforth my Father, and I promise—yes, O my God, I promise faithfully—to be Thy dutiful and loving daughter."

When she had said this prayer, she felt a kind of secret joy in her heart, which told her that her prayer had been heard and answered.

As Mary Anne was pious and diligent, she very soon got sufficient employment from some kind neighbors, and thus her present wants were supplied. When she was sixteen years old she obtained an excellent situation in a good and wealthy family. She was fond of work, and was never idle; and was modest, faithful, gentle to her fellow-servants, and obedient to her master. Often was she heard to repeat half aloud to herself: "I have no father or mother on earth, but if I am good, God will be my Father and provide for me." They were her dear father's last words, and she loved to remember them.

Every year, when her master paid her her wages, he always added a good large sum as a present; for he knew she deserved it, and that she would not misspend it; and after many years of faithful service he told her that as long as she lived she was to consider herself as one of his family, and that she would never want for anything. He kept his word; and thus did God provide for His dear child, who had lovingly entrusted herself to His care. So will our Heavenly Father do to us if we cast our care affectionately upon Him.

Catchisme de Persévérance.

20

OUR HEAVENLY FATHER WATCHES OVER US

My child, it would be impossible to number the favors our Heavenly Father has bestowed on us His adopted children. He does not, indeed, grant to all of us the same favors, nor in the same degree, but He bestows on each of us what He considers best, and what He Himself chooses. It will only be in eternity that we will be able to understand all this.

AGNES, THE PIOUS HOUSEMAID.

A gentleman who possessed a large mansion in the country had a young girl named Agnes, who served as waiting-maid in his family.

She was very different from the other servants of the house, who were indeed very diligent when the eye of their mistress was upon them, but were often negligent when they thought that no one was looking at them. Agnes always did her work with promptitude, exactness, and diligence, whether her mistress was present or not.

This diligence on the part of Agnes was soon observed, not only by her superiors, but even by strangers.

One day a doctor happened to call, and among other things

Agnes's diligence and prompt obedience became the topic of conversation.

"I would like very much," said the doctor, "to see this maid of whom you speak, for I have heard so much about her. I am sure she must have some secret motive for acting in this manner. Do you think it is because she wishes to be praised for it, or to obtain a better position in your household?"

"Oh no," replied the master of the house, "that certainly is not her motive, for whatever we say to her in praise or in blame seems not to have any influence on her conduct; she is as ready to perform the humblest work in the house as the more important, and on all occasions does what she is told to do without the slightest murmur."

"What you tell me," replied the doctor, "makes me still more eager to see her and speak to her. I will avail myself of the first opportunity of doing so."

That same evening he met Agnes in one of the rooms of the house, with a brush in her hand, arranging the apartment with the greatest care. She was weeping. The doctor suddenly entered, and, perceiving this, said to her:

"My little girl, what is the matter with you? Why are you weeping? Has anyone been unkind to you, or has some affliction befallen you?" Agnes, thus taken unawares, did not answer him, but hung down her head. The doctor in the gentlest manner urged her to confide in him, and tell him what was the cause of her tears.

Encouraged by his kind words, she replied that, far from being sad, she was very happy; that the other servants of the house were good to her, and that her master and mistress treated her with much more kindness than she deserved; that she was weeping, not through sorrow, but rather through joy and happiness.

"It is indeed a pleasure to hear all this," said the doctor, "but would you let me into your secret, my child, and tell me how you are always so happy and contented?"

Agnes hesitated a little, but in a few moments answered: "Sir, if it will be of any interest to you to hear from a poor maid like me the reason of this, I will tell it to you. Before I came here I happened to hear an instruction on the love of God. The priest who gave us the instruction told us how good God is, in allowing us to call Him Our Father, and to love Him, and how happy those are who do love Him. When I heard this I thought in my own mind that I would like very much to love God perfectly, and I began to wonder how I could do it, for I was only a poor girl, and had to go to work to get my livelihood, and had no time to say long prayers, like some pious people whom I knew.

"Just as these thoughts were passing through my mind, the Father said in his instruction to us these words, which I have kept in my mind ever since: 'My children, it is easy for you all to love God. Do exactly, carefully, and punctually, the work which you have to do day by day, and while you are doing it think that it is God Who sent you to do it. If you do this, you really love God with your whole heart.' So, sir, when I am sweeping the floor, as you saw me doing just now, or whatever else I do, I think in my own mind that it was God who sent me to do it, and that he is looking at me to see how I do it. So I try to do it carefully, that I may please Him; and I know that God is pleased with me when I do this, and so I am always happy."

"But I saw you weeping; why those tears?" asked the doctor.

"Sir, I cannot keep from weeping when I think that I, who am only a poor servant-girl, am permitted to love God as much as those great Saints who were so holy, and that He Who is so great not only thinks of me, but even loves me. O sir, since God is so good, how could I not try to love Him with my whole heart!"

The doctor went home that night with thoughts in his mind very different from what he had been accustomed to. He had that day learned a great lesson which he never learned before, a lesson of more importance than all the others he had ever received, and that lesson he learned from a poor servant-maid.

We will also, like the doctor, learn a lesson from this story; and since we can so easily love God, we will take the resolution to do it as Agnes did. We will do everything as if God had sent us to do it, and as if we saw Him looking at us to see how we are doing it.

Letters Ed.

GERMAINE, THE LITTLE SHEPHERDESS

God has promised to be our Father in a special manner when those whom He has given us to be our parents in this world neglect us. This He showed in the care He took of Germaine, the little shepherdess of Languedoc, who lived in the sixteenth century.

One day the grave-digger of the village of Pibrac, near Toulouse, was opening a grave; all at once he came upon a coffin which he did not expect to find there, and, to his astonishment, it looked as if it had been recently buried. Through curiosity he opened it, and saw that it contained the body of a little girl, quite entire, looking as if she were in a calm sleep. The grave-clothes were clean and white, and the flowers which covered the little corpse as fresh as if they had been newly culled.

The news of this wonderful discovery soon reached the village, and the people all ran to the place to see it for themselves.

"Who can this be?" they said one to the other. "We never knew of anyone who had been buried here."

Among the crowd whom curiosity was bringing to the spot was a very old woman. She could not walk fast because of her great age, and thus she was amongst the last to reach the grave.

When she got near enough to see the body, she began to tremble. "Oh, I know who that is!" she cried out. "I know her by that mark on her neck and by her paralyzed hand. That is Germaine, the pious shepherdess, of whom you have so often heard me speak. I was one of those who prepared her for her grave: it was I who put all around her those ears of wheat which you see quite fresh, for she died in the harvest-time, and that crown of wild flowers on her head, which looks as fair as when I placed it there many, many years ago. O my God, this is indeed wonderful!"

The story of the old woman and the miraculous preservation of the child's body made the people inquire into her history, and this is what they found out about her.

Her parents were very poor people, and from the time of her birth she was afflicted with sufferings. Her little body was covered over with running sores, and she never had the use of her right hand. When she was quite an infant her mother died, and her father married again. The woman whom he brought home as his wife could not endure the sight of little Germaine, because of her deformity, and used to shut her up in an outhouse all night, and would never allow her to go near her own children, lest she might infect them with her disease.

When she was able to take care of the sheep, her cruel step-mother would send her away in the morning to the fields, and bade her never return till night came on. Then, as soon as she did return, she threw her some hard crusts of bread, and sent her to pass the night in the cold dark stable, with no fire to warm her, or anyone to say to her even one kind word. Her father, too, could not bear to see her, and, not wishing to displease his wife, left her to suffer all this harsh treatment without interfering.

But her Heavenly Father did not forget that she was His child, and in proportion as her own father neglected her, He loved her; and He filled her soul with every consolation all the day long.

In the morning, when she heard the bell ring for Mass, she used to plant her shepherd's crook in the midst of her flock, and thus leave them there under God's care till she returned from Mass. During the day she would gather around her the poor children, little like herself, and speak to them of God, and of His holy love which inflamed her whole soul. The crusts of bread which her hard-hearted stepmother gave her as her allowance of food she shared among these little ones, and she was never so happy as when she had none left for herself.

Then, when she was left alone, and when her little companions had gone home, she loved to kneel down under the trees and say her prayers, for nothing gave her so much consolation as these loving conversations with her own dear Father in Heaven.

At night, when she returned home with her flock, she had often to endure the cruel blows, and still more cruel words, of her step-mother; and she was always glad when the time came for her to lie down on her hard bed of straw, that she might be alone with God, Whom she loved so well.

One morning in the autumn of the year 1601 Germaine did not appear at the usual time, and her father went to the place where she slept to see what was the matter. He found her lying as if asleep, with a beautiful smile upon her lips, but quite motionless. She was dead; and her innocent soul was safe in Heaven, resting on the bosom of the Father Who had never forsaken her.

Now, it happened that during that night two religious were traveling towards Pibrac. Overtaken by the darkness, they lay down under the shadow of an old castle to rest until the morning. Suddenly they perceived a company of angels proceeding in the direction of the place to which they themselves were going; and as they were wondering in their own minds what this could mean, they saw them returning again, and in their midst, crowned with beautiful flowers and clad in white garments, walked a young maiden. The vision soon disappeared, and they knew that some great Saint had just entered Heaven.

When they reached Pibrac they told the people what they had seen on the way, and inquired if any great and holy person had died that night. It was noised abroad that the poor little Germaine had been found dead, and then the people knew that it was her happy soul that the religious saw the angels conducting into Paradise.

So they took the body and buried it with reverence in the place where it was found. For a time the story of her life and death was on the lips of everyone; but as years went past she was forgotten, until God in His own good time was pleased to glorify on earth the memory of the dear little child who had loved Him so much.

21

OF GOD'S PROVIDENCE

You often hear, my child, about the providence of God. This means that God has for each one of His children a fatherly care, and watches over them with great love. Everything that happens to us is for our good, although sometimes we may not perceive it. St. Paul says: "To those who love God all things are heaped together unto good."

THE SPIDER'S WEB.

While the persecution of Decius was at its height, St. Felix of Nola was one of those whom the persecutors of the Church were most anxious to arrest; but God, Who desired to make use of His servant, to exhort His children on earth, and to encourage them in their trials, hid him from his enemies who pursued him.

One day, while he was standing on the public square of the city instructing and exhorting the faithful, those who were sent to look for him came near him, but their eyes were shut as they passed him, and they hastened onwards. Someone having told them that they had just passed him on the street, they retraced their steps, and Felix, who saw them returning, fled from the place, and concealed himself in an opening of a wall not far distant. As there was no door to conceal him, he would undoubtedly have been captured had not God caused a spider to weave its web over the opening.

The soldiers who were in pursuit having come to the place, and finding it covered with a web, thick and unbroken, thought that it would be folly to imagine that anyone could enter the house without breaking the web, which could not possibly be made in so short a time, and they passed by, and hastened onward to look for him elsewhere.

But God's providence with regard to St. Felix did not end here; for, having retired from Nola to live in a deserted cave far away from any dwelling, he was miraculously fed for six months, when at last peace was restored to the Church, and he was able to return to the city.

Life of St. Felix of Nola.

ST. PAUL, THE FIRST HERMIT, AND ST. ANTONY.

St. Paul, who is distinguished by the title of "the First Hermit," desirous of escaping from the persecutions of Decius, fled into the desert of Upper Thebaid, and dwelt there in solitude with God. Until the fifty-third year of his age—that is to say, during thirty years—he supported himself on the wild herbs that grew in the desert and with the fruit of the palm-trees; but from that time God Himself, in a miraculous way, undertook the temporal care of His servant. Every day He sent a crow with half a loaf of bread, which he laid at the feet of the holy man. This he did for the long period of sixty years.

Now, at the end of that time it happened that St. Antony, also a hermit in a desert at some distance, received an order from God to go forth in search of the "Father of the Hermits," that he might receive his blessing before he died. The two Saints at once recognized each other as if they had known each other for years, and saluted one another by their names; and while they were sitting together speaking of heavenly things and of the happiness of having left all things to follow Christ, a crow appeared before them. It carried in its beak this time not a half-loaf, as it usually brought, but a whole one; and as St. Antony, who knew nothing of the wonderful goodness of God in furnishing His servant with food for so many years past, expressed his astonishment at what he saw, St. Paul said to him: "During the last sixty years God Himself has provided for me each day my daily support. Today, because you are with me, He has sent a double portion. Oh, my brother, let us together bless Him and glorify Him for His infinite goodness in thus taking care of those who serve Him."

Life of St. Paul, First Hermit.

ST. MAXIMUS AND ST. FELIX.

St. Felix, who had been ordained priest by Maximus, Bishop of Nola, was put in prison, and loaded with chains during the persecution of the Emperor Decius.

One night an angel from Heaven entered the prison, and, having awakened him from sleep, told him to go into the desert where Maximus had retired, and where he was suffering from cold and hunger, and to give him all the help he needed.

At first Felix thought that it was only a dream; but the angel having commanded him to rise, he obeyed, and immediately the chains that bound him fell to the ground, and the gates of the prison were opened, and he found himself free. Then, through ways entirely unknown to him, under the guidance of the angel, he reached the desert, and even the very place where Maximus was. He found him lying on the ground, almost without movement and without life, and appeared to be at the point of death. Felix raised up the good Bishop from the ground, and tried to restore heat to his limbs. Then, seeing he had nothing to eat, he wondered where he could procure some food. Looking around him, he saw hanging on a thorn-bush a large bunch of juicy grapes. Taking it, he pressed it, and poured the juice on the parched lips of Maximus, who immediately regained consciousness. Smiling sweetly on Felix, he said to him: "You have been long in coming to visit me, my child. It is now a long time since God promised me that He would send you to assist me, and I was awaiting your coming with impatience, that you might bear me back to the midst of my poor flock, which I never should have left."

Then Felix, raising the old man upon his shoulders, set out for Nola, where his flock received him with delight and with great veneration and love.

Life of St. Felix of Nola.

"WHERE IS THE PROVIDENCE OF GOD?"

Father Beauregard had just concluded one of his beautiful sermons on Divine Providence, at which a large audience had assisted, as always happened when he was announced to preach.

He had scarcely returned to his house, when a man, quite unknown to him, followed him, and asked to be permitted to speak to him for a few moments.

"Most willingly, my friend," replied the venerable preacher, at the same time placing a chair near him, and asking him to sit down.

"Sir," began the stranger, "you preached a magnificent sermon— no one could have done better; and you spoke in strong terms of the trust we should place in the Providence of God. Now, I do not give credit to what you said on this matter, because I do not believe that there is a Providence."

The priest answered: "What are these words you have just uttered? How can you for a moment doubt of the Providence of God and of the watchful care He has over us?"

"No, sir," said the other; "for me there is no Providence. Hear me, and judge for yourself. I am a carpenter by trade; I have a wife and three little children; we are honest, simple-living people, and have never done wrong to anyone."

"I believe this without any difficulty," said the good Father; "but in what way is all this connected with your disbelief in Providence?"

"If you listen to me, I will tell you. I have a sum of money to pay on the thirtieth day of this month, and I cannot pay it, for I have not the means of doing so. I asked many of those who used to call me their friend, but they would not come to my assistance; and my relatives are as poor as I am, so they could not help me. I came at length to the determination of ending my miserable life by drowning myself in the river."

"But how did it come to pass," interrupted the priest, "that, with these awful thoughts in your mind, you found yourself present at my sermon?"

"Oh, sir, I had no intention of going to hear you preach; it was all by chance. As I happened to pass near the church, I saw a large multitude of people going in. I asked one of them the cause of it. He told me, in answer, that they were assembling to hear a great preacher. I went in along with the people from simple curiosity to hear what he had to say. I heard you preach, and I felt interested, and remained till you had finished. All that you said was indeed very beautiful and interesting; but, sir, in reflecting on my bygone life, and seeing therein nothing with which I could reproach myself, I could not make up my mind to act as you suggested, nor even to believe in the existence of a Providence."

"My dear friend, listen to me. You tell me you went into the church, as it were, by chance, without any serious reason for doing so, and that you heard me discourse on the Providence of God, and you have come to visit me, and have exposed to me your difficulties and your escape from the terrible death you had foolishly intended to inflict upon yourself. Is that in itself not a proof of God's providence over you?"

The man seemed much struck with this observation, and after a moment's silence he replied: "Yes, sir; what you say is, indeed, true; but that will not enable me to meet my liabilities on the thirtieth of this month."

Father Beauregard was much moved by this recital of the poor man's story, and felt keenly the condition to which poverty had reduced him in soul and body. He also thought for a few moments in silence, and then suddenly exclaimed: "Hear me. I believe that you are, indeed, the unfortunate man you have described yourself to be, and that these misfortunes have fallen upon you without any fault on your part, and that you do not intend to deceive me. How much money would you need to meet the bills which will then be due? I am not rich, but perhaps I might be able to assist you a little."

"Oh, sir, how kind of you! One hundred crowns would enable me to pay all I am due."

Father Beauregard arose, and, opening his desk, drew forth a sum of money. "Here is exactly the amount you need," said he; "of myself I could not have possibly given you so much, but a few days ago, after having been present at my sermon on Almsgiving, the good Princess — sent me this money, with the request that I would spend it on some work of charity or mercy which I thought deserving. Take it, and I am sure in future that you will have confidence in the providence of our Heavenly Father."

We can imagine the feelings of gratitude with which the man accepted the gift. From that moment his life was one of great piety, and he never afterwards was heard to complain against the Providence of God.

BILLECOQ: De la relig. chrét

"CAST THY CARE UPON THE LORD."

It is recorded in the "Annals of the Order of St. Francis" that one of the brethren in the monastery of Perousa was one time sent by his Superior to a distant house of their Order, to bring thither a young novice of great piety, and endowed by God with great talents, whom the continual visits of his relatives and their affection for him placed in the imminent danger of losing his vocation. When they had traversed a considerable part of the journey, they found themselves, when evening came, in a deserted part of the country, where they could not find a place of shelter for the night. Already fatigued and hungry, they found it impossible to proceed any farther, especially as the darkness hid from view the path they had hitherto followed; and they resigned themselves to the necessity of passing the night in the open air. The novice, as yet unaccustomed to the austerities of the Order, began to complain of their hard lot; but the elder religious endeavored to comfort him by reminding him that they were the children of our "Father in Heaven," and that He would take care of them. "Do not fear the terrors of the night, for He has sent His angels to guide us in all our ways."

He then took him by the hand, and they continued to walk onwards together, but without knowing whither they were going.

Suddenly they saw coming towards them a young man, who, having saluted them respectfully, offered to be their guide, and to procure for them shelter for the night. They joyfully accepted his invitation, and followed him till he brought them to a hut formed of branches, in the midst of an extensive plain. A good fire was burning near, and on a table within the hut was an abundance of bread and wine. Surprised at their unexpected good fortune, the good brothers could not find words to express sufficiently their gratitude to their kind host for his hospitality.

"My Fathers," said the young man, "warm your limbs at the fire and partake of this little refreshment, while I go to prepare supper for you."

In a very short time he returned, bearing on a plate a magnificent fish. It was during the holy time of Advent, and this dish was well suited to the season. The religious sat down at the table and partook of the food he had brought, which they found better than they had ever before eaten. The young man's conversation and his edifying conduct during the meal afforded them great pleasure.

When the repast was ended, and when they had said grace fervently for this unexpected refreshment, the young man led them to a little room, where two straw mattresses had been laid on the ground.

"These are your beds, my Fathers," he said; "they are not, indeed, very comfortable, but they are such as your rule prescribes. Rest here in peace, and tomorrow morning I will see you again."

They soon fell asleep, and slept comfortably till the morning light began to shine over them. The young man came according to his promise, and, having partaken of some food, he conducted them on their journey till they arrived at an open country. Here, after pointing out the way, he bade them adieu, asking them, as the angel did Tobias, to thank God for the mercy He had shown them.

The two religious turned towards him to thank him for his kindness to them, but he was nowhere to be seen; he had suddenly disappeared. Then they knew that it was indeed an angel of the Lord who had been sent to help them in their need, and, falling prostrate on the ground, they thanked their Heavenly Father for His care of them, and wherever they went they recounted this marvel of His goodness and power.

Chronic. Minorum, P. Mark.

22

GOD CONSOLES US ON EARTH AND REWARDS US IN HEAVEN

My child, our Heavenly Father gives His children when they are in this world consolations in their trials, to encourage them to bear them patiently; but it is when these trials are ended that He bestows on them the magnificent rewards He has prepared for them in His kingdom above, and which He has promised to give them if they persevere to the end.

"OH, HOW GOOD IS DEAR PAPA!"

A gentleman lived with his wife and family in a comfortable house in one of our great cities. His occupation frequently led him away from home, but he always returned as soon as possible to the bosom of his family, where he found his chief comfort and happiness.

On one occasion his absence was longer than usual, and his wife and little ones were inconsolable. They did, indeed, from time to time receive letters from him which contained expressions of his great love for them all; but this was far from filling the void caused by his long absence.

One day, about two months after his departure from home, a large box arrived at his house in town, addressed to his children.

With great eagerness they opened the box to see what it contained, and, to their intense delight, they found a large number of presents of every description sent them by their kind papa. One by one they were unpacked, and each one as it appeared seemed to give them fresh delight.

"Oh, how good is dear papa!" cried out Elizabeth, the eldest child. "Although he is so far away from us, he has not forgotten us, but has sent us all such delightful presents. He has taken care, too, to send each one of us just what he knew would please us best."

Their mother, who had been quietly looking on, enjoying their happiness, saw a letter lying at the bottom of the box, which the children, in their excitement, had overlooked. She took it up, and, after reading it to herself, she said to them: "Here is a letter from your father."

"Oh, mamma, what does he say in the letter? Tell us!" they all cried out at once.

The mother read aloud the letter. It was as follows:

"'My Dear Children,—Although I am far away from you, I have not forgotten you; I have been thinking about you all every day since I came here, and I have been collecting all these presents which I now send you, because I know they will please you, and make you think of me. But I have far more beautiful things for you which I cannot now send you; but if you are good and obedient children, I will someday come for you, and bring you here to enjoy them, and to live with me in this beautiful place. I need not try to explain the beauty of the delightful things I am preparing for you here, because you would never be able to understand it; you will only understand this when you come here and see them. So try and be good till I return.'"

The children were overjoyed at the good news contained in the letter, and began to say among themselves: "I wonder if it will be a long time before he comes for us. I hope he may come soon; oh, won't we be glad when we see dear, good papa!"

The mother here said: "You see, my dear children, how much papa loves you, and how he thinks of you, and how his whole desire is to make you happy; but your Heavenly Father loves you infinitely more, and is continually occupied in taking care of you and in trying to make you happy. It is quite true you cannot see Him just now, no more than you can see dear papa, who is so far away; but He shows you that He does not forget you, for He sends you beautiful presents every day. Is it not for you that the sun shines in the heavens, and that the earth produces its fruits? and does not the Holy Scripture tell us that the presents He is going to give us in Heaven, if we are good and faithful to Him on earth, far surpass our comprehension—'That eye hath not seen, nor ear heard, neither hath it entered into the heart of man what things God hath prepared for them that love Him'? Oh, my dearest children, be good now, and obey God, your Father in Heaven, and He will soon come for you, and take you all to His happy home above."

The children listened attentively, and Elizabeth, ever ready to speak, answered: "Yes, mamma, we will all of us, I am sure, do that, not only because He is to make us happy in Heaven, but because He is so good in Himself, for that is why we all love good papa so much. We love him not because he sent us all these presents to-day, nor because he has promised to give us more, but just because he is so good. Oh, yes, dear papa is so good."

Schmidt.

23

ALL MEN ARE OUR BRETHREN, FOR GOD IS THE FATHER OF ALL

Since God is our Father, and we are all brethren, we must pray not for ourselves only, but for all others, and love them as we love ourselves.

THE LAME MAN AND THE PRINCESS.

The Princess Galitzin was one day passing over a bridge in St. Petersburg, when she saw an old man sitting there, asking alms from those who were going by.

She gave him some money in value about sixpence, and then continued on her way. The poor old man, who was also lame, no sooner received the money than he ran as fast as his feeble limbs would carry him to a blind man who sat a short distance off, and gave him the half of what she had given him.

The Princess, who saw this act of charity, was very much moved. She sent for the lame man to whom she had given the alms, and said to him: "Who is that poor old man with whom you have shared the alms? Is he your father or your brother?"

"He is not related to me by blood," the old man replied, "but he is my brother in Jesus Christ. In our younger days we served together in the army, and now in our old age we are brothers in misfortune. He is, indeed, more to be pitied than I am, because he cannot see; is it not therefore just that I should help him, and beg for him as well as for myself?" The Princess was moved to tears at the poor man's generous conduct, and gave him a gold piece, promising at the same time not to forget him. She afterwards told one of her friends that she had never in all her life experienced so much pleasure as when she gave that alms.

24

OUR CONDUCT SHOULD SHOW THAT WE ARE REALLY GOD'S CHILDREN

M y child, it is not sufficient for us to be the children of God in name only; if we desire to enter Heaven, we must, while in this world, lead the lives of those whom He has thus highly honored, otherwise He will cast us away from Him forever in eternity.

"I KNOW YOU NOT."

We read in the lives of the Saints that in a certain monastery the religious had fallen away from the fervor prescribed by their rule, and were leading worldly lives.

One year, when the festival of their holy founder came round, they went to the church to sing the Divine Office.

When they came to a certain part of it, they said, as usual, this prayer: "Pray for us, O holy Father." But immediately a voice was heard, as if coming from Heaven, saying: "Call me not your Father, for you are no longer my children: you neither follow the path I have traced out for you, nor the example which I have given you. I know you not."

Might not our Heavenly Father reproach us in the same words when we, in our daily prayers, say to Him, "Our Father Who art in

Heaven"? Might He not say to us as the Saint said to these religious: "Call me no longer your Father, for you do not obey my commandments, nor follow my example. You ought rather to call yourselves the children of Satan, for it is him you obey, and his maxims you follow"?

Catchisme de Persévérance.

PART IV

"HALLOWED BE THY NAME"

25

OF THE REVERENCE AND LOVE DUE TO GOD'S HOLY NAME

"In the Name of the Father, and of the Son, and of the Holy Ghost." My child, these are the words by which you always begin and end your prayers, and which you make use of at many other times.

You also often say this prayer in honor of the most Holy Trinity: "Glory be to the Father, and to the Son, and to the Holy Ghost." And, again, when you assist at Benediction, you say this beautiful ejaculation: "Blessed be God; blessed be His holy Name."

In the prayer which Jesus Christ has taught us, the words of the first petition are: "Hallowed be Thy Name." By these words we pray that God may be known, loved, and served by all His creatures, and that His holy Name may be loved and revered by everyone.

In the Old Law, God required from His people a great reverence and intense respect for His holy Name, and punished with the utmost severity those who dared to pronounce it irreverently or "to take it in vain."

THE VOICE OF GOD IN THE BURNING BUSH.

When God gave the Commandments to Moses, He declared the importance He attached to the honor to be given to His holy Name in these words: "Thou shalt not take the Name of the Lord thy God in vain; for the Lord will not hold him guiltless that shall take the Name of the Lord his God in vain" (Exod. xx. 7).

On the occasion when Moses was chosen to be the deliverer of the people of Israel from the hands of their oppressors, "the Lord appeared to him in a flame of fire out of the midst of a bush," says the Scriptures, "and he saw that the bush was on fire, and was not burnt.

"And Moses said: 'I will go and see this great sight, why the bush is not burnt.'

"And when the Lord saw that he went forward to see, He called to him out of the midst of the bush, and said: 'Moses, Moses.'

"And he answered: 'Here I am.'

"And He said: 'Come not nigh hither, put off the shoes from thy feet: for the place whereon thou standest is holy ground.'

"And He said: 'I am the God of thy father, the God of Abraham, the God of Isaac, and the God of Jacob.'

"Moses hid his face, for he durst not look at God.

"And the Lord said to him: 'I have seen the affliction of my people in Egypt, and I have heard their cry because of the rigor of them that are over the works: and knowing their sorrow, I am come down to deliver them out of the hands of the Egyptians, and to bring them out of that land, into a land that floweth with milk and honey. . . . For the cry of the children of Israel is come unto Me; and I have seen their affliction wherewith they are oppressed by the Egyptians. But come, I will send thee to Pharaoh, that thou mayest bring forth My people, the children of Israel, out of Egypt.'

"And Moses said to God: 'Who am I that I should go to Pharaoh, and should bring forth the children of Israel out of Egypt?'

"And He said unto him: 'I will be with thee; and this thou shalt have for a sign, that I have sent thee: when thou shalt have brought my people out of Egypt, thou shalt offer sacrifice to God upon this mountain.'

"Moses said to God: 'Lo, I shall go to the children of Israel, and say to them: "The God of your fathers hath sent me to you." If they should say to me, "What is His Name?" what shall I say to them?'

"God said to Moses: 'I AM WHO AM.' He said: 'Thus shalt thou say to the children of Israel: "He Who is hath sent me to you."'

"And God said again to Moses: 'Thus shalt thou say to the children of Israel: "The Lord God of your fathers, the God of Abraham, the God of Isaac, and the God of Jacob, hath sent me to you." This is my Name for ever, and this is My memorial unto all generations.'"

Exodus iii. 2 et seq.

GOD IS JEALOUS OF THE HONOR DUE TO HIS NAME.

Again we read in the Old Testament the words of God to the people of the Jews, commanding them to use His holy Name with the most profound devotion:

"And the Lord spoke to Moses, saying: 'I am the Lord that appeared to Abraham, to Isaac, and to Jacob, by the Name of God Almighty; and my Name Adonai I did not show them.

"'Thou shalt not swear falsely by My Name, nor profane the Name of thy God: I am the Lord.

"'Blessed be the Name of the Lord from henceforth, now and forever; from the rising of the sun to the going down of the same the Name of the Lord is worthy of praise.'"

Then we read of the severe judgments He threatens against those who do not give due honor to His holy Name:

"'If thou wilt not fear His terrible and glorious Name, that is the Lord thy God, the Lord shall increase thy plagues, and the plagues of thy seed: plagues great and lasting, infirmities grievous and perpetual.

"'They profaned My holy Name by the abominations which they committed; for which reason I consumed them in My wrath.'"

The Sacred Scriptures in many examples tell us how faithfully the just in the Old Law honored the Name of God.

David said: "I will sing to the Lord Who hath given me good things; I will sing to the Name of the Lord, the Most High." "Blessed be the Name of the Lord from henceforth, now and forever. Kings of the earth and all people, princes and all judges of the earth, young men and maidens, let the old with the younger praise the Name of the Lord, for His Name alone is exalted. Bring to the Lord glory and honor; bring to the Lord glory to His Name. Oh, magnify the Lord with me, and let us extol His Name together."

My child, you hear many people, old and young, who have constantly the Name of God and the most sacred Name of Jesus on their lips, not to praise His Name, but to revile it; they use the sacred Names as bywords almost in every sentence, without sense or meaning. What a terrible punishment awaits those who do this!

Whenever you hear God's Name thus profaned, you should do what many of the Saints were accustomed to do when they heard the Name of God taken in vain—you should raise up your heart to God, and make Him some little reparation, saying: "Hallowed be Thy Name," or "Blessed be God: blessed be His holy Name," or "Blessed be the Name of the Lord, from henceforth, now and forever."

POPE PIUS V.'S ZEAL FOR THE GLORY OF GOD'S NAME.

Some of the friends of the great Pontiff, Pius V., once advised him that, since he had grown old and infirm, he should take greater care of his health, and give himself some little repose, after having spent so long a life in the service of God.

"Ah, my friends," was his reply, "if it is the duty of every child of God to sanctify His holy Name, how much more is it my duty! God did not place me upon the Chair of St. Peter for my own sake, or for my own personal honor or glory, but solely for the advancement of His kingdom on earth. Therefore it is my first and only duty to glorify His holy Name, and, as long as I am left on earth, to labor that it may be honored and glorified by all His creatures."

Lohn. Bibl., iii, 510.

26

HONOUR DUE TO THE HOLY NAME OF JESUS

ST. PETER'S SPEECH BEFORE THE HIGH-PRIEST.

W hen the chief priests and the Sadducees were informed of the great miracle St. Peter wrought upon the lame man at the gate of the Temple, and that a great multitude of the people had been converted, they were filled with consternation.

"And as they [St. Peter and St. John] were speaking to the people, the priests and the officer of the Temple and the Sadducees came upon them, and they laid hands upon them and put them in hold till the next day: for it was now evening.

"And it came to pass on the morrow, that their princes and ancients and scribes were gathered together in Jerusalem, and setting them in the midst they asked: 'By what power, or by what name, have you done this?'

"Then Peter, filled with the Holy Ghost, said to them: 'Ye princes of the people and ancients, hear: of the man this day are examined concerning the good deed done to the infirm man, by what means he hath been made whole, be it known to you all, and to all the people of Israel, that by the Name of Our Lord Jesus Christ of Nazareth, Whom you crucified, Whom God hath raised from the dead, even by

Him this man standeth before you whole. Neither is there salvation in any other; for there is no other name under Heaven given to men whereby we must be saved."

Acts of the Apostles iv. 1 et seq.

ST. PAUL AND THE HOLY NAME OF JESUS.

"Let this mind be in you which was also in Christ Jesus, Who being in the form of God thought it not robbery to be equal with God: but emptied Himself taking the form of a servant, being made in the likeness of men, and in habit found as a man.

"He humbled Himself, becoming obedient unto death, even to the death of the cross. For which cause God also hath exalted Him, and hath given Him a Name which is above all names; that in the name of Jesus every knee should bow of those that are in Heaven, on earth, and under the earth; and that every tongue should confess that the Lord Jesus Christ is in the glory of God the Father."

Philippians ii. 5-12.

"JESUS OF NAZARETH, KING OF THE JEWS!"

St. Edmund of Canterbury had a pious mother, who taught him from his earliest childhood a great love and reverence for God's holy Name.

One day, as he was walking with some of his school companions, he heard them speak with irreverence of the holy Name of God. He at once left them, and walked home by himself.

On the way the Holy Child Jesus appeared to him under the form of a most lovely little boy, and, looking on him with great affection, saluted him in these words: "Good day, My own beloved companion."

On hearing the strange voice, St. Edmund looked to see who it was; but not knowing Him, he did not return the salutation.

The Holy Child said: "Do you not know Me, Edmund?"

Edmund answered: "No, I never saw You before. You must surely have mistaken me for someone else."

"What!" said the Divine Child, "is it possible that you do not recognize Me? I am at your side all day long; I am with you at school, with you in your home and wherever you go. Look on My face and see what is written there."

Edmund looked, as he had been told to do, and saw written on His forehead these words: "Jesus of Nazareth, King of the Jews." "That is my Name," said the Heavenly Child.

When Edmund saw who his visitor was, he fell with his face on the ground.

But Jesus raised him up, saying: "My beloved child, continue to have a great respect and love for My holy Name; let it ever be engraved on your heart; and when at night you retire to rest, trace it upon your forehead; it will preserve you and all who do the same from a sudden and unprovided death." Saying these words, and having blessed the boy, Jesus disappeared from his sight, leaving him filled with great joy and happiness.

Petits Bollandists, Nov. 16.

THE LITTLE BOY JULIAN.

In the days of St. Ephrem there lived a pious scholar whose name was Julian. St. Ephrem was his teacher, and he loved the boy because he was so good and gentle. There was one thing that the Saint had to find fault with: the boy did not take good care of his books. In many places the words were entirely blotted out, and it seemed as if some of them had been eaten away.

One day the Saint took up the book to look at it, and he saw that it was at those places where the Name of Jesus had been written that the book was thus destroyed. "My child," he said to him, "why is it that you have rubbed out everywhere in your book the holy Name of Jesus?"

The humble boy immediately answered: "My dear Father, I love

Jesus, my beloved Savior, with all my heart; and whenever I see His holy Name in my book, I remember how Mary Magdalen, who was a great sinner, kissed the feet of Jesus, and how He forgave her all her sins. I cannot see Jesus nor kiss His sacred feet as she did, but I often see His blessed Name in my book, and I kiss over and over again the place where it is written, asking Him at the same time to pardon me my sins, and telling Him that I love Him with all my heart, and that I long for the time when I may see Him in Heaven."

St. Ephrem answered with a smile, saying: "My dear child, may God in His mercy hear your prayer, and grant you what you so earnestly ask of Him! but for the time to come try to take better care of your books."

27

WE SANCTIFY GOD'S NAME BY TEACHING OTHERS TO KNOW GOD

A ll those who instruct the ignorant, or teach others to know God, are sanctifying His holy Name and great will be their reward in Heaven.

ST. FRANCIS XAVIER PREACHES TO THE CHILDREN.

When St. Francis Xavier arrived in India, he found the people of that country living in a state of the grossest idolatry. They did not know the true God, but worshipped the idols their own hands had made.

St. Francis burned with zeal to bring them to the knowledge of the God Who made them, and for this end he prayed and labored during the whole of his life.

Early every morning he offered up the holy sacrifice of the Mass, to obtain grace for himself and for them. Then he would go from house to house, comforting those who were sick, begging alms for those who were in want, and showing the greatest charity to all. It was by this means that he hoped to obtain their conversion.

One day, after the scorching heat had passed, and the people began to come forth from their dwellings to enjoy the cool breeze of the evening, children might be seen here and there playing in groups before the doors of the houses, or along the streets of the city.

Presently the sound of a bell was heard, and as he who rang it came near, many of the people recognized the stranger priest, whose days were spent in ministering to the wants of the afflicted and the sick. Some were acquainted with him, from his having come to their houses to beg alms for the poor of Christ. To others he was unknown; but his dress was of an unusual appearance, and they stood to listen. The little children left their play and listened too.

Then in a loud voice he cried out: "Fathers and mothers of families, I have a message for you; send me your children, and I will teach them that which will make them obedient and dutiful. If you have slaves, send them also to me, and I will tell them that which will make them serve you faithfully. For you also I have good tidings of great joy, but send me now your little ones."

Then, turning to the children who, attracted by his kind and gentle manner, had gathered round him, he said: "Come, my children —come with me, and I will tell you of One Who loves you dearly, though you know Him not; One Who has prepared for you in His own beautiful country a home of joy and happiness, such as you have never dreamed of. Come, and I will tell you about the journey thither; and I will tell you also stories about this same kind Lord— how He at one time was a child as young as you, of what He did and said, and of all He suffered to purchase for you that happy home of which I speak." The children looked at him in wonder; and then, assured by his gentle looks and his loving words, they followed him in crowds, some clinging close to him, holding by his cassock, or striving to reach his hand. Others, again, clapped their little hands, and called to their young companions as they passed along the streets to come and join their company and hear the beautiful things the Father had to tell them.

Thus he led them to the church, where he talked to them of God Who had created them, and of Heaven, for which He had made them. He told them that, although it was He Who made the thunder roar, and the waves of the great ocean run mountains high, and though He could, and would, punish them if they did wrong, yet He was a God of such tender love and pity that He had consented for their sakes to become a little child like themselves.

Then he showed them in that holy place in which they were assembled how they should bow the knee, and join their hands in prayer to Him, Who, although in every place, was present in a special manner there; and, kneeling down, he taught them to pray, and prayed with them to their Father in Heaven, begging that His holy Name might be hallowed in them, and that He might reign in their young hearts.

Then, turning to Mary, the Mother of Jesus, he begged her to adopt these little ones as her children, and obtain for them grace to become the dutiful children of her Divine Son.

The prayer ended, instructed by the Saint, they bowed two and two before God's altar and left the church in silence. It was sufficient to look at their little faces, wearing, as they did, a look of modesty and piety, to see that the work of grace was already begun in their hearts.

Day by day, after his usual visits to the sick, St. Francis, bell in hand, passed through the streets. In a very short time he did not require to speak at all. At the first sound of the bell the children, who had been anxiously looking for him, ran to meet him; and the hours they spent in the church became the happiest of their lives.

Little by little there came a great change over them: no quarreling or angry words were heard; they became gentle, modest, and devout, trying who would most resemble the Holy Child of Whom the Father spoke; and thus in their own sweet way they taught a lesson to all around them.

Their parents, too, could not but be thankful to one who had made their children so patient and obedient, and wondered by what means he had wrought so great a change in them. And when, soon afterwards, he began to preach in the public thoroughfares, they flocked to hear the holy man of whom their children had talked so much, and who had so completely gained the confidence of their young hearts.

In a short time a great change came over that city. The people, like their children, became pious and devout, and where iniquity and sin had abounded the holy Name of God was known and loved.

Life of St. Francis Xavier.

AN ANGEL IN DISGUISE.

A priest was once walking through one of the great thoroughfares of Paris, when he was met by a little boy who asked him for an alms. "Oh, Father," he said, "give me one little halfpenny to buy some bread, for I am very hungry."

The priest was pleased with the boy's appearance, and the modest way in which he had made his request, so he gave him what he wanted.

When he had given him the halfpenny, he said: "Can you say your prayers, my boy?"

"Yes, Father."

"Let me hear you say them. If you can say them well, I will give you ten times as much."

The child at once began, and without making a mistake said the Lord's Prayer, the Hail Mary, the Creed, and the Acts of Faith, Hope, and Charity.

The priest then put some questions to him on the principal truths of our holy Faith, and the boy answered them all without hesitation, so that the servant of God was astonished at the beautiful and correct answers he gave.

"Who was it that taught you all these things?" he asked.

"It is a young gentleman who comes every day from a distance to the poor lane in which we live, and teaches us our Catechism. He gathers all the boys into one place, and makes us say our prayers, and tells us about these things."

"And do you not know who the gentleman is, or where he comes from?" inquired the priest.

"No, Father; he never told us. But he comes every day in all kinds of weather, in winter and in summer, and sometimes his clothes are covered with mud; but he never yet told us his name.

"Oh, Father," continued the boy, "he must be an angel; he never gets angry, although we often amuse ourselves when he is speaking, and although he has sometimes to tell us over and over again the same things. He also brings little presents with him, which he gives to us when we are good, and when we remember the things he has told us."

The priest then gave the boy the additional money he had promised. He also made inquiries about the young gentleman who was in secret doing so much good, and discovered that he belonged to one of the highest families in the capital.

Catéch. en Exemples, 1555.

THE PRIEST ALPHONSUS.

A very holy priest, by name Alphonsus, belonging to the Order of St. Francis, had spent many years of his life among the Indians, teaching them the Christian religion.

But being now an old man, he took the resolution of spending the rest of his life in preparing himself for a happy death. He therefore went into a solitary place, and began to think only of God and of the world to come.

He had not been many days in his solitude when, as he knelt before his crucifix, he seemed to hear the voice of Our Lord lovingly reproaching him.

"How is it, my child," said the voice that spoke to him—"how is it that, while there are so many poor souls who do not know Me, and who cannot yet call Me Father, you come here that you may think only of yourself?"

The kind heart of Alphonsus was moved by these words. "O my God," he cried out, "if I am yet necessary for Thy people, I do not refuse to labor. I will return to my poor Indians and continue to preach to them Thy most holy Name."

God then renewed to him the promise He had made, that those who would instruct many unto justice would shine as the stars in Heaven for all eternity.

Alphonsus that same day returned to his labor with even more zeal than before to make God's holy Name known amongst men, that they might one day go to praise Him in Heaven.

Lokn. Bibl.

28

THE MARTYRS BY THEIR DEATH GLORIFIED GOD'S NAME

The holy martyrs glorified the holy Name of God by sacrificing their very lives in testimony of their faith in Him and for His Name's sake. It was their glory to declare before the world that there was no God but the one true God, and that they feared not to die, since their death would tend to His honor and glory.

TITUS: A MARTYR STORY.

In the history of Japan it is related that a certain Christian, whose name was Titus, and his wife, who was called Mary, had three children—two sons and a daughter—whom from their earliest infancy they trained up to serve God.

They lived in the days of persecution, when those who remained faithful to their religion had to suffer many torments, and were often put to death.

Now, it happened that the Prince who ruled over that kingdom hated the very name of Christian, and had issued a decree that the severest penalties were to be enforced against those who professed the Christian Faith.

He was soon informed that Titus and his whole family were

Christians, and that they refused to renounce their religion; so he commanded Titus to be sent for, and resolved in his own mind either to gain him over to idolatry or to put him to death.

When Titus was brought before him, he said to him: "You know that a decree has been published in this kingdom for everyone to profess the religion which I profess, and to adore the gods which I adore, and that those who refuse to obey this command are to be put to death."

Titus answered: "Sire, I know that such is your command; but there is a King in Heaven Who is your master as well as mine, and Whose decrees we are both bound to obey. Now, it is His command that we worship and serve Him alone; Him, therefore, will I obey, and nothing—not even that death with which you threaten me—shall ever cause me or mine to be wanting in our duty towards Him."

The Emperor became very angry when he heard these words, and said: "Go home for the present; in a little time we shall see how vain and empty is all this boasting."

Next morning at break of day a messenger was sent from the palace. "The Emperor has sent me," he said, "to summon your youngest son before his tribunal, because yesterday you did not obey his commands; and if you still refuse, your son shall certainly be condemned to die a cruel death."

The poor father's heart sank within him when he heard this message. "Oh, my boy," he cried out, "what will become of you? I know the tyrant will show you no mercy. How will you be able to remain faithful amidst the tortures he is sure to inflict upon you? Oh, my child, my child!"

But the boy said: "Fear not, my father; you have often told me that God made me to serve Him in this world, and that if I persevere faithfully to the end, He will take me to Himself in Heaven. Oh, how I desire that time to come! My sufferings here will be short, and then— happiness with God forever."

At these words tears flowed down the old man's cheeks. Embracing him tenderly, he said: "Go, my son, in the Name of Jesus Christ. I commit you to His care. Fight bravely, and fear not to die for

His sake. We shall soon meet again in that kingdom where there is no separation."

Two days after this the Emperor sent other messengers to Titus to tell him that his son had been put to death because he had refused to renounce his Faith; and that if he himself still refused to submit to the royal commands, his only daughter was to go along with them to the judge to suffer the same fate as her brother.

The poor father felt this affliction more than the former one, but he would not yield. "No, my God," he exclaimed; "dearly as I love my darling child, I love Thee still more, and willingly will I sacrifice even her rather than be unfaithful to Thee. Go, dearest," he said to his daughter; "do not be afraid of the short sufferings which will procure for you eternal happiness. God will protect and sustain you."

The child was taken before the Emperor, and commanded to adore the heathen gods. She refused, and he ordered her to suffer the same punishment as had been inflicted on her brother.

Not many days after this another order was sent to Titus. "Come, now, and offer sacrifice to our gods," said the messenger. "Be no longer obstinate. You have already lost two of your children, and if you refuse now to obey, I have orders to take Simon, your only surviving son, before the Emperor, who will treat him as he treated the others."

The afflicted father knelt down before the image of Our Savior crucified, and prayed for strength to support this new trial. He thought of Abraham, who had been ordered to sacrifice his only child whom he loved, and how he had submitted without murmuring to the Divine will. Could he himself do otherwise? "O Father in Heaven," he prayed, "Thou knowest how I have loved my children, and how I have already sacrificed two of them for Thee. Yet Thou dost require one more offering. Take him, then, O Lord! May Thy adorable will be done! may Thy holy Name be forever blessed!"

Then, turning to his son, and embracing him for the last time, he said: "My own dear boy, you know what has become of your sister and of your younger brother: they have laid down their lives rather than prove unfaithful to their God; they are now safe with Him in His kingdom, and are now beckoning on you also to go and join them. Go, then, my boy, and show yourself to be a worthy child of God; be not afraid of death, for it will bring you to eternal life. Your brother and your sister did not fear the tyrant, neither will you; I know it. Go, then, my son—go and act manfully, as becomes a child of your Father in Heaven."

Simon answered: "My father, I have often said to God that I would rather die than offend Him. Now is the time for me to prove the sincerity of these words. Nothing could give me greater joy than this news that I am to be a martyr of Jesus Christ."

Having said this, he fell on his knees at his father's feet. "Give me your blessing, dearest father," he said, "and pray for me." Having received it, he rose up and joyfully resigned himself into the hands of those who had been sent to take him.

Titus, thus deprived of all his children, turned for consolation to his wife. Like himself, she was a faithful servant of God, and although it had cost her maternal heart many a pang to resign her children to their cruel death, she did not hesitate for a moment. Like the mother of the Maccabees, she had encouraged them to die, and now she supported her husband in his grief. "They are God's children," she said to him. "He has only lent them to us for a time, and now He wants to take them home. Let us resign them willingly to Him. In a little time He will give them all back to us again in Heaven."

Not long after these events, a messenger was again seen approaching the house of Titus. "Simon your son has suffered the punishment of his disobedience," said he, "and I am come to tell you that if you still persist in your obstinacy, I have orders to bring your wife before the Emperor, that she may also die."

Titus, firm as a rock, made this answer: "You have taken from me my little ones; now you come to take away their mother. There is one favor I ask of you, and that is that you take me also, that my blood may be mingled with theirs."

God alone knew the grief which filled the hearts of this saintly couple as they bade each other adieu; but they had the consolation of knowing that their separation would be for a short time, and that they would soon see each other again in Paradise.

The servants in the house wept bitterly as they saw their beloved mistress led away. She alone was joyful and happy, and spoke to them of the happiness she felt at being chosen to die for her God.

Again another messenger was sent to Titus. "Your wife has been beheaded," he said, "because she would not obey the royal decrees; I am come to summon you also to share the same punishment."

"Thanks be to God!" cried out the holy man, as he raised his hands and eyes to Heaven. "I have suffered death already four times, in the persons of my wife and little ones; willingly will I die a fifth time that I may go and be with them again."

He was then conducted to the palace.

There was a look of triumph on his countenance as he stood before the Emperor. With a voice full of emotion he besought him to command him to be executed without delay, that he might be the sooner with those he loved.

The tyrant was astonished at these words; but instead of complying with his request, he tried every means he could think of to shake his constancy. But promises and threats were alike unheeded. "My duty in this world," he said, "is to serve and obey my God, in sorrow as in joy, in adversity as in prosperity, and never while I live will I be unfaithful."

Suddenly the countenance of the Emperor changed. "Titus," he said in a tone of mildness, "your heroic fidelity to your God deserves to be rewarded, even in this world." Then, turning to one of the officers standing near him, he whispered something into his ear. The officer instantly disappeared, and in a few moments returned, leading in Mary and her three children safe and unhurt.

A cry of joy burst forth from the bewildered Titus, as he flew to embrace them. "O my wife, my dearest little ones, do I really behold you again? O my God, eternal thanks be to Thy goodness for thus restoring them to me again even in this world!"

The spectators of this scene were moved to tears; even the Emperor himself had to make great efforts to conceal his emotion.

"Titus," he said, "you told me that you were the servant of the God of Heaven; now you have proved it. Return to your home, take your wife and your children with you, and let no one from this time henceforth molest you in the practice of that religion which has made of you so many heroes."

That happy family, once more united, returned home, and, thanking God for His great mercy to them, they continued to the end of their lives in their fidelity to Him, and died as they had lived— faithful servants of the King of Heaven.

Their example should encourage us to be faithful to God in our trials as they were in theirs, for we also are His children and His servants, and it is our duty to obey Him and to serve Him faithfully. In Heaven throughout eternity we shall be rewarded for our fidelity to God, and there also shall we meet those who loved God on earth, and whom we also loved, never to be separated again.

29

WE GLORIFY GOD'S NAME BY PRAYING FOR THE CONVERSION OF SINNERS

P ray, my child, for the conversion of sinners. There is great joy in Heaven when the angels see even one sinner doing penance. How great, then, will be the reward God will give to you, if by your prayers you have been the means of sending many there to glorify the holy Name of God for all eternity!

"PRAY FOR THEM."

In the days when the heresy of the Albigenses was bringing ruin to many thousands of souls, the most holy Mother of God appeared in a vision to a holy virgin whose name was Lutgarde, who dwelt in a convent in France. Her countenance was sad, and she was clad in garments of sorrow.

When the Saint saw her, she said: "O most holy Mother of God, how is it that thou, who art all fair and beautiful, art now plunged in sadness and sorrow?"

The Blessed Virgin answered: "It is the sins of these people who crucify over again my own beloved Son that make me so sad, because His anger is about to fall on the world on account of their iniquities; and the punishments He will inflict upon them will be terrible.

Wherefore I have come to you, to ask you to intercede for them, that they may not perish, but that they may be converted and glorify Him eternally in Heaven."

She then told her to pray for them, and to perform acts of penance for them for the space of seven years. This the pious virgin accomplished with great courage and perseverance.

After that time Our Lord Himself appeared to her, and asked her to undertake another similar penance for the conversion of Catholics who had turned away from Him and were living in the state of sin. To encourage her in this work of mercy, He appeared to her covered with wounds, and His sacred blood flowing from them. "Behold, My child, how I present Myself before My eternal Father in behalf of poor sinners. I desire also that you pray and suffer something to obtain their conversion, and that they may yet come to glorify His Name in Heaven."

From that moment her heart became so full of compassion for sinners that she prayed and wept for them as long as she lived. "O my Jesus," would she sometimes say in the excess of her love for them, "either forgive them or blot my name out of the Book of Life."

It was revealed to one of the Saints that by her prayers and good works Lutgarde saved from eternal death an immense number of souls who had been living in sin; they are now in Heaven with God, praising Him and loving Him there.

Life of St. Lutgarde.

"COME WITH ME, AND I WILL TELL YOU."

Monsieur de Berg, a physician of great reputation, was summoned to visit a sick person who dwelt at a considerable distance from his house. To reach him he had to pass through a thick forest. Evening was coming on, and in the darkness which soon followed he lost his way.

For about an hour he wandered hither and thither without being able to find an outlet from the wood. Suddenly a terrible voice fell upon his ears: "Stop! stop! otherwise you are a dead man."

At the same moment a man of terrible appearance, and disguised, leaped forward from behind a thick bush, and, with a pistol in his hand, which he aimed at the breast of the doctor, cried out: "Your money or your life!"

Without any hesitation, the doctor at once took out his purse, opened it, and, presenting the robber with the only silver piece it contained, calmly said to him: "Take this; it is all I have. But, my dear friend, I beseech you to cease to lead this kind of life, for in the end it will infallibly bring you to the scaffold. Remember, also, that it was for your sake that Our Divine Savior died upon the cross. So I entreat you to think of all this, and take the resolution to save your soul."

Seven years afterwards it happened that Monsieur de Berg undertook a long journey. One day he entered a town where a fair was being held, and, for his diversion, went to the market-place to see the sale of horses which was there taking place. As he was standing in the middle of the crowd, he felt a hand gently touch him on the shoulder. He instantly turned round, and perceived standing at his side a man, who respectfully saluted him, and said: "Do you not recognize me?"

Monsieur de Berg having replied that he had no recollection of ever having seen him, the other asked him to come to his house, and he would inform him who he was. He accompanied him to a beautiful little villa, which they entered. In a room, neatly furnished, sat a lady of gentle appearance, with a little child on her knees. The doctor cast his eyes around him, more and more astonished at this incident, and wondering what could have caused the gentleman to bring him, an entire stranger, into his house.

This astonishment was increased when the other, throwing himself down at his feet, and bursting into tears, said: "What return can I make to you, excellent sir, for all that you have done for me? It is to you alone that I owe all my present happiness. Never shall I forget you or your kindness to me.

"You may remember that about seven years ago, while you were passing through a certain wood, a man rushed upon you from a thicket, and, with a pistol in his hand, threatened to kill you unless you gave up your purse to him. I am that man. Often did the simple words you then addressed to me recur to my mind; I yet remember them well. These words, uttered in a tone of kindness—I may even say affection—were to me like a bright star indicating the path on which I should walk in my future life. I could find no rest till I had renounced my evil course and become a fervent disciple of that Divine Savior of whom you spoke to me. May God reward you, my kindest and best benefactor, for having been the cause of my return to the way of virtue."

Monsieur de Berg was filled with emotion as he listened to the recital of this narrative. He stretched forth his hand, and took within it that of the man he had gained to God, and as long as he and his estimable wife lived, they were among the doctor's most devoted friends.

My child, you see from this example how a kind word may at times produce great fruit, and bring wandering souls back to a state of grace. You will certainly, in your lifetime, have many occasions of performing similar good works, and in doing them you will be sanctifying God's Holy Name.

Rep. du Catéch., iii. 238.

30

GOD'S NAME IS SANCTIFIED BY OUR GOOD EXAMPLE

Y ou can also contribute to the glory of God's holy Name by giving good example, which will move people to become good; also, by giving to God all the glory of your good works.

THE MONK IN ALEXANDRIA.

A very holy man left his cell in the desert to assist at the death of a friend of his youth who dwelt in Alexandria, and who wished to see him before he died.

The most of the inhabitants of that city were pagans, who hated the Christian religion. As soon, therefore, as he entered, they knew by his dress that he was a Christian hermit, and began to mock him. Some carried their hatred so far as to strike him, and abuse him in many other ways.

But the good man passed on without uttering a word of complaint, and bore all patiently for the love of God.

Some of them cried after him in mockery: "Did Jesus Christ ever work a miracle?"

A man who was passing, and who was a Christian, said: "Yes, Jesus Christ did work many miracles; but even if He had not wrought any, the conduct of this holy man is enough to prove the truth of the Christian religion. What greater miracle could you desire to see? You have insulted and abused this good man because he is a disciple of Jesus Christ, and yet he has borne it all without a murmur; and in the midst of all your cruel words he has never uttered a word of reproach."

These words silenced the people: they were ashamed of what they had done. And some of them, touched by the meekness of the good monk, were led to believe in God, and to renounce forever the errors of paganism.

THE GENERAL AND HIS GROOM.

There was once a famous General who had gained many victories, but had, in every country which he conquered, left marks of ruin and devastation behind him.

But it happened that in a certain battle he was defeated, and had to fly from the field, covered with wounds, and forsaken by all except his faithful groom. In their flight they came to a great forest, and, as they were both exhausted, they sat down under a wide-spreading tree to seek a little rest.

Not far from the place where they had halted there lived a hermit —a very old man with hair as white as snow. When he saw the two strangers, and heard their sad story, he was moved with compassion, and brought them into his own humble dwelling, and attended as well as he could to their wants.

When the groom saw that his master was likely to die from the wounds he had received, he began to weep. "How shall I ever get to Heaven? My whole life has been spent in taking care of my master's horse, and that is all I have done. Oh no! I can never hope to see Heaven, because I have never done anything great enough to merit it."

Then, turning to his master, he said: "But you, my dear master, you will certainly get there, for you have done so many great things; you have gained so many victories, and done so many other brave deeds which men have praised so much. Ah, I wish I had done some great things, that I might get to Heaven with you." The hermit, who was a witness of this scene, said to the General: "My son, what was the end you proposed to yourself in all these great exploits?"

"It was that I might acquire great renown, and that people might speak of me, and that my name might become famous in the history of my country."

"Was that, then, the end you proposed in all the ruin you heaped upon so many countries, and the grief with which you filled so many homes?

"And you, my child," he said, speaking to the groom, "why did you attend so carefully to your master's horse?"

"I had no other end in view than to perform it well because it was my duty, and because God had placed me in that humble state of life."

The hermit then said to the General: "Your groom has, in his humble condition, done more for God and for Heaven than you have, because in all you did, even in those great actions which have made your name famous, it was the glory of your own name you sought for; but your servant did all for the glory of God, and because it was His blessed will; therefore he will be rewarded by God. But, as you have already received your reward on earth, you cannot expect to receive it above."

Rep. de Catech., iii. 282.

31

ON AIDING THE WORK OF THE "PROPAGATION OF THE FAITH."

You cannot, perhaps, go and preach the Gospel as these great missionaries do, of whom you read so often, but you have it in your power to help them. By the little alms given for the Propagation of the Faith, or for the Society of the Holy Childhood, many people have been rescued from paganism and brought to know God.

"PLEASE BUY ME."

A missionary was one day passing through one of the slave-markets of Africa. There were many children there for sale. Amongst them was a little girl who had been stolen from her parents by some cruel men who had brought her into the market to be sold.

When she saw the missionary coming near, she thought he was going to buy her; so she looked up into his face with her sad eyes, to see if he was likely to be a kind master if he bought her, for she thought he was a slave-owner.

When she saw the look of kindness that shone in his eyes, so different from that of all the others she had been accustomed to see, she cried out: "Oh, kind sir, will you buy me? Please buy me."

The good priest looked at her for a moment, and a tear came into his eye, but still he did not offer to buy her.

"Oh, do not leave me—do not leave me! I will be a good slave to you; I will work hard for you. Do not leave me," and the poor child burst into tears because she saw him turn away his head.

She cried out again: "Have you not something to buy me with?"

But the missionary had nothing; he had spent all he had in buying food for the poor children he had already purchased, and he had nothing left. So he shook his head sadly and turned away.

Then the poor child knew that she would fall into the hands of someone else who would not be so kind to her.

Such was the case. A man came towards her, and, after looking at her for some time, bought her from her master. She went away with him to be beaten and treated as a brute beast till death would put an end to her sufferings.

The priest went away very sad. "Oh," he said, "if all the Catholic children at home would only join the Society of the Holy Childhood, how many poor children could I rescue from slavery, and teach to love God!"

My child, if you cannot become a member of the Society of the Holy Childhood, you can at least lay aside for the Propagation of the Faith some of those pennies, which you are accustomed to spend in buying what is of no real use to you: in this way you will glorify God by being the means of others coming to know Him.

A POOR MAN WHO BUILT A GREAT CHURCH.

There was in one of the missions of China an old man who had to labor from morning to night to obtain his livelihood. He was poor in the eyes of the world, but rich in God's eyes, because he was most attentive to all his religious duties.

One day he went to the priest and said: "Father, will you build a church in our village? for our chapel is only a poor hut, and is not good enough for the worship of God."

The Father answered: "It has long been my most earnest desire to raise up a church which would be more worthy of God; but as I have no money, I am obliged to be content with the humble church which we built long ago."

"But, Father, I will build you a church."

The priest, who had known him for many years, and knew that he was a poor man, said: "I know, my child, your great piety and your zeal, and when it is possible for me to begin this great work, I am sure you will contribute a little out of your poverty."

"But, Father," he continued, "I want to pay for the whole myself."

The priest looked into the good man's face, and replied: "I do not for an instant doubt your wish to give all you have in the world to help in this holy work; but do you not know that it would take more than two thousand crowns to build a church large enough for all our people?"

"I know that," he answered, "and I would not have come here to trouble you if I had not already that sum in hand. Here it is." And he laid down the money on the table before the priest.

The surprise of the good Father was indeed great when he saw the poor man count out the money, but it was greater still when he told him how he had been able to amass such a large sum.

"It is now forty years ago," he said, "since I first thought of this, and I said to myself, 'What a great joy it would be to me in my old age if I could raise up to the glory of God's holy Name a splendid church in my native village!' So I laid aside every farthing I could spare, and lived with the greatest frugality and used only the poorest clothing, that I might have this happiness before I died." The missionary accepted the generous gift, and the church was built. The old man had the happiness of seeing it completed, and then God took him to Himself in Heaven, to reward him there for the glory he had given His holy Name on earth.

MÜLLER: *The Mass*, p. 616.

32

BY SINGING HOLY HYMNS WE GLORIFY GOD'S NAME

By singing sacred hymns we glorify God's holy Name. St. Paul exhorts us to perform this work of piety. "Be ye filled with the Holy Ghost," he says, "speaking to yourselves in psalms and hymns and spiritual canticles, singing and making melody in your heart to God."

THE MIDNIGHT HYMN.

The holy Bishop Gerardius, who lived at the beginning of the eleventh century, being on a journey, was passing the night in the house of a simple countryman, situated by the wayside.

After retiring to rest, he was awakened from his sleep by the sound of someone singing. He listened for a short time, and heard the words of a simple hymn sung to a melody of surpassing sweetness.

He called his servant, and asked him who it was that was singing so sweetly the praises of God at such a late hour.

The servant, on his return, told him that it was a poor girl appointed to attend to the night-work of the house, who was filling up the lonely hours by singing hymns of praise to God.

The Bishop was touched by the piety of the child, and said: "Oh, how happy are those who begin in this world the employment which must forever occupy them in Heaven! How much happier are they than the great ones of the world, who forget God altogether, and who never think of praising Him!"

The next morning the Bishop sent for the young girl, and exhorted her to persevere in this holy practice. "Sing the praises of God, my child; it is the surest means of sweetening the labors of this weary life, and of securing for yourself the endless joys of Heaven."

CHINANI.

ST. VINCENT AND THE MAHOMETAN PRINCESS.

St. Vincent de Paul was ordained to the priesthood on September 23, 1600.

Five years afterwards, as he was returning home by sea from Marseilles, to which place he had gone on some important business, the ship in which he sailed was attacked by pirates, and all on board were made prisoners. They were taken to Tunis and sold as slaves. Vincent was also captured and sold with them.

It happened that the man who bought him had at one time been a Christian, but had renounced his Faith and had become a Mahometan. This man took him home to his farm, which was situated on a hot and desert mountain, where he employed him to till the ground.

Now, one of his master's wives, who was a Turkish woman, used to go often into the fields where Vincent worked. There was something about him so different from the other slaves that she felt a particular interest in him. She used to put many questions to him about the law of the Christians and their manner of life.

One day she asked him to sing. "Sing me some of the hymns which contain the praises of your God," she said.

Vincent did as she requested him, and sang for her one of the psalms, the canticle "Hail, Holy Queen!" and some of the other hymns in praise of God and His Saints.

The woman listened in rapture. "Oh, what beautiful hymns!" she cried out; and during all that day she could think of nothing else.

When her husband came home at night she said to him: "How wrong it was in you to renounce the Christian Faith! That good man Vincent, who labors in the fields, has today spoken of it to me, and has sung some of the hymns by which the Christians worship their God. Certainly, I think that the God of the Christians is worthy of being served and loved, and ought never to be abandoned in the way you have done."

These words, instead of making the man angry, led him to reflect on the great sin he had committed, and he resolved to renounce his evil life, to begin again to serve God. Next morning he went to Vincent, and made known to him his intention. After considering how this could best be done, it was agreed that they should secretly fly from that place, since it would be impossible for him to profess his Faith there, and to return to France, where he would be free to do this without danger.

Ten months, however, passed before they succeeded in making their escape. Placing themselves under the protection of the God of Heaven, and of her who is called the "Star of the Sea," they embarked in a little boat, and after a prosperous voyage, arrived in France on June 28, 1606.

In this way did God in His providence restore Vincent to his native land and to his friends, who had long mourned for him as dead.

PART V

"THY KINGDOM COME"

33

GOD THE KING OF OUR HEARTS.

When we say "Thy kingdom come," we pray that God may come and reign in the hearts of all by His grace in this world, and bring us all hereafter to His heavenly kingdom.

My child, God has already come into your heart to reign there; He came into it by baptism. It is sin only that will make Him leave it. Oh, keep away from sin, that He may always dwell there!

THE HAPPY DEATH OF A CHILD OF MARY.

Not long ago there was a little girl who had just made her first Communion. The priest was full of joy, because he saw how carefully she had prepared herself for it and how full of devotion she had been on that happy morning.

"My dear child," he one day said to her, as he saw her kneeling devoutly before the altar, "I am sure that Our Lord loves you very much, and that He is at this moment dwelling in your heart. But, my child, you are young yet, and perhaps you may one day banish Him from your heart by committing a mortal sin." "Oh, my Father," she replied, "be not afraid. I would never be guilty of such an awful crime. Ah no! I would rather die than do anything to offend my dear Jesus, Whom I love so well."

The good priest looked with affection on the innocent face of the child. The fervor that shone in her eyes told him that she was sincere in what she said. But, alas! his experience had shown him how often good resolutions like these were broken.

"Yes, my child," the priest said, "I know you would like to be good all your lifetime, and that you would rather die than commit even one sin. Well, then, ask our Blessed Lady to obtain this grace for you."

As soon as she went home, the girl knelt down before an image of the Blessed Virgin, and said to her: "O my dearest Mother in Heaven, ask thy Divine Son Jesus to give me the grace never to commit a mortal sin; ask Him to take me out of this life rather than permit me to fall into sin."

Not many days afterwards a little sore began to appear on her cheek. At first no one thought that it would be of any consequence, but it soon grew into a great swelling, and, in the end, showed itself to be a cancer, which in a short time ate away one side of her face.

The sufferings this caused her to endure were very great, but she bore them all without a word of complaint.

"My Father," she said to the priest who attended her, "our Blessed Lady has heard my prayer; I am going to die. She is going to take me out of this world at once, that I may not fall into sin, and so I shall be in Heaven forever with God."

Very soon afterwards the pious child died. She is now happy in God's kingdom along with those holy souls to whom He promised it. "Blessed are the clean of heart, for they shall see God."

Catch. en Examples.

THE ANGEL OF THE HOUSEHOLD.

Mr. B—— was a well-to-do merchant in one of our large cities. In his youth a pious mother had taught him his duty to God, but when he grew up, the turmoil of the world had blotted out from his mind those early impressions of religion. He still retained the Faith, but did not practice it; and for many years he had entirely neglected his religious duties.

He had only one child—a little girl—and although he was so indifferent himself, he was anxious to see his child grow up piously. Therefore, he sent her regularly from her earliest years to holy Mass and Sunday-school, for he knew that this was the only way of instilling into her mind the knowledge of God and of her duties towards Him. Mary (for such was the little girl's name) was gentle and obedient: she did not gaze about in the chapel like many others, but listened attentively, and tried to remember all the priest said, and afterwards, when at home or at school, or wherever she was, she tried to put into practice what she had been told there.

When she was eight years old, towards the end of the summertime, her father became very ill. The doctor was sent for, and from the time of his first visit, when he saw the nature of the disease, he did not entertain much hope of his recovery. In one of his visits he found his patient much weaker. He thought he could not delay any longer in making known to the family the danger he was in, and privately told Mrs. B—— that he was dying fast, that no human skill could save him, and that her only hope was in Him Who holds in His hands the lives of all His creatures.

Little Mary overheard these words, and, young as she was, she understood what they meant. Long and bitterly did the poor child weep, for she loved her dear papa so much; but what made her more sorrowful still was the thought that he had not been for many years to the Sacraments, and she was afraid that he might die without being reconciled to God, for she saw that no one had the courage to tell him that he was dying.

"Oh, if I could only go and tell him myself!" she said.

Suddenly a thought seemed to have entered into her mind. "Yes; I will go and tell him. I am sure he will listen to me," and she hastily dried up her tears and went to her father's room.

When he saw her looking so sad, and her eyes red with weeping, and her cheeks yet wet with the tears she had shed, he asked her:

"What ails you, child?"

"Oh, my own dear papa," she sobbed out, "you are going to die and leave me."

"What has put that into your head, darling?" he said. "I am not going to die yet; I will soon get better." "No, papa; you are not going to get better. I heard the doctor tell mamma today that you could not get better." Here the child burst out into a fresh flood of tears. Her father did not speak.

"Oh, papa," she continued, "I am so sorry to think that you are going to die, for if you die I will never, never see you again."

"Why not, darling?"

"Because you have not been to Confession for a very long time, and the priest has often told us at instructions that it is a great sin not to go to Confession; and if a person dies in great sins, he cannot go to Heaven."

The father said nothing, but a strange feeling came over him, and he began to shed tears—perhaps it was the thought of being separated from his little Mary that made him weep.

"Oh, father," said the child in her own endearing way, "won't you go to Confession if I get the priest to come? I am sure you will, and then when you die you will go to Heaven, and when I die I will go to Heaven, too, and then I will see you again, and then we will be so happy. Won't we, papa?" and she laid her little head upon his face.

The dying man kissed her, and said: "My own darling, go and get the priest at once. Yes, I will go to Confession; I will delay no longer. Oh, my child, if I do get better, what a different life you will see me live; and if I die, I will hope in God's mercy for Heaven." Then, raising his eyes, he said: "O my God, blessed be Thy holy Name for having given me this dear child—this little angel to guide me back to Thee." The priest came and gave him the last Sacraments, which he received with edifying devotion. Then, sending for his daughter, he said to the priest: "Father, do you see this little child? It is to her I owe my conversion; if it had not been for her, I would have died in my sins, and would have been lost forever. It was she that made me send for you."

The priest took the child by the hand and said: "You see, my dear child, what a blessing you have brought to your dying father because you were so diligent in learning your Catechism, and so attentive to the instructions which were given. You have been the means under God of saving your good father's soul. If you had not gone to Sunday-school, or if you had been inattentive, you probably would not have yet known much about God or anything about the necessity of Confession, and your father might never have got the grace of repentance. Yes, my friends," he added, speaking to those around him, "a truly pious child, like this one, is the greatest treasure of a household."

Next morning Mr. B—— died. There was great sorrow in that house, and much weeping; but they wept now as those do who hope.

Noël: Cat. de Rodes.

34

HEAVEN THE REWARD OF THOSE
WHO SUFFER PATIENTLY ON EARTH

To reach the Kingdom of Heaven, my child, you must bear with patience the trials of this short life. The reward that God will give for each one of them is far greater than any human mind can imagine.

THE TWO NOBLEMEN AND THE MONK.

Two noblemen went to visit a certain monastery. As they were going the round of the cells, they chanced to enter that of a venerable monk, whose hair was white as snow. His countenance was joyous as that of an angel, and his whole person calm and gentle beyond what can be described.

At seeing this they were amazed. They said one to the other: "How can a man who wears such a coarse garment, and who lives the austere life of a monk, be so cheerful, and always smiling?"

"Tell me, Father," said one of them, "have you ever during the course of your life had any affliction or sadness of heart?"

The holy man replied: "Yes; many a time have temptations to sadness come upon me; but, thanks be to God, He has given me a remedy, which in an instant changes sorrow into gladness, and affliction into great joy."

Saying these words, he pointed to the window of his cell: "You have but to go over there to that window, and you will at once see what gives me my strength and joy."

The two men went to the window, but they found nothing save a rough wall, that hindered them from seeing anything, and even nearly cut off all view of the sky.

"We can see nothing that can possibly give you any comfort; on the contrary, that dreary wall is of itself enough to fill you with melancholy."

"Look a little closer," said the monk, "and you will see something most comforting." They looked again. "We see nothing from this window. A few inches of the blue sky through a chink in the roughly built wall is all that can be seen."

"That is just what gives me comfort," said the monk. "When melancholy comes upon me, I have only to look at that little portion of the sky, and immediately the thought of the eternal joys that are to come gives me comfort, and the clouds of sadness melt into sunshine of consolation and peace. I then pray to my Father in Heaven to hasten the time when, in that happy kingdom, I may find eternal rest."

As he said these words, tears came to his eyes—tears of joy. The two noblemen also wept, but these tears filled their souls with an emotion they never felt before. "Yes," they said one to the other, "if we want to find true joy, it is only in serving God here, and looking forward to the joyous reward of Heaven, which God has promised to those that do so."

Rossign: De Vita Æterna.

"TAKE COURAGE."

There was once a young man of noble birth and possessing much wealth, in whose heart God had placed a great desire of gaining Heaven.

At the same time, remembering what Our Lord had said about the difficulty of a rich man entering the Kingdom of Heaven, he resolved to leave to someone else all his great possessions, and become a humble monk in a Franciscan monastery.

He began his new life with great fervor. But as time went on, his devotion began to fade away.

His first fervor had almost entirely disappeared, and every one of the duties of the monastic life became a burden to him.

"It was very foolish of me," he said to himself one day, "to leave the world as I have done. I am sure it would have been easier for me to reach Heaven by living a good life in the world than here, where everything is so difficult. I cannot any longer perform these works of penance, so I will return to the world, and live in it as I did before."

On the night he had fixed for leaving the monastery he happened to pass before an altar, in which the Blessed Sacrament was reserved. Falling on his knees, he bowed down in lowly adoration. As he was saying his prayers, God, Who had pity on the weakness of His child, allowed him to see a wonderful sight to encourage him.

He saw a beautiful procession, which passed before him. It seemed to be going from earth towards Heaven. All those who were in it were clothed in magnificent garments, and their faces beamed with heavenly joy. Among the number were two who seemed to surpass the rest in beauty and glory, and who seemed to be leading in triumph to God's kingdom a young man as beautiful as themselves.

This glorious vision filled the monk with great joy, and he cried out to one of the blessed spirits in the procession: "Tell me, I pray thee, O spirit of God, who are these bright souls I see, and whence they come."

The one to whom he spoke answered: "We are those who, when on earth, had left all things to follow Christ, and are now in heavenly glory. The two whom you see more bright and beautiful than the others are St. Francis of Assisi and St. Antony of Padua; and we have been sent by Our Father above to conduct to Heaven with all this magnificent pomp of Paradise the soul of that young monk who has just died."

The vision then disappeared; but the heart of the religious was now filled with such a burning desire of one day obtaining the same glory that he at once returned to his cell. All his former dislike for the severity of the religious life suddenly disappeared, and his first fervor returned.

Sweet to him now were mortifications and strict obedience; in a word, the religious life, which had hitherto seemed so hard to him, became all at once easy and pleasant, and to his dying day he remained faithful.

Chron. of St. Francis.

DOROTHY, THE PIOUS CHILD.

Many of the stories you have read in this little book have been about the martyrs who died for their Faith. But you have little or no chance of dying as they did, yet you have also to fight the good fight in your station of life if you want to be with the martyrs in Heaven. The following story will show you how you can do this.

There was once a pious widow who did not enjoy much worldly wealth, but possessed that which is so much more precious, the one true Faith. God gave her a little daughter, and she called her Dorothy; because she wanted her to grow up under the protection of that great Saint, to whom she had a special devotion.

But when Dorothy grew up to be a big girl, she began to show signs of thoughtlessness, and many a time did her poor mother weep over the faults of her dear child. She was fond of play, and would forget her prayers and her lessons to run about with her companions, although her mother told her not to do so.

Yet the child had a kind heart, and she often wept when she saw that she had made her good mother sad by her bad behavior and disobedience.

When she was ten years old, her mother, although she was poor, sent her to a convent to live for a time under the care of the pious Sisters, who, she knew, would watch over her, and teach her to grow up piously. God only knows the great sacrifices she made in doing this, but she was well rewarded for what she did.

Dorothy remained in the convent for two years, after which time she returned to her mother's house. But what a change had come over her during these two years! People who knew her before she went to the convent could not believe she was the same child. She who had been so disobedient and idle, was now an example to all her companions, and to those, even, who were older, by her gentleness, patience, obedience, and piety, although she was only a little more than twelve years old. She was never angry, always pleasant, and found her greatest delight in helping others. Some people said she was a hypocrite, and others, who were jealous of the praise people gave her, said some very harsh things about her. But Dorothy bore all in silence, and even spoke kindly to those who were so cruel to her. In a short time people came to know that she was really good, and those who had tried to destroy her good name were filled with confusion.

The priest of the place where she lived was full of joy when he saw in his parish one who gave such good example, because he knew the benefits others would receive from it.

One day he went to see her mother, who was now happy because she saw how good her child had become. While he was there Dorothy came in.

"Come, my child," he said to her, as he drew her to his side, "you must tell me what has made you so good, for you know that you were once very different."

"Father," she meekly answered, "I am not good, but I would like very much to be good, and I am trying very hard to be good."

"Tell me, then," said the priest, "what makes you better now than you were before."

"When I was at the convent," she answered, "one of the Sisters asked me if I wanted to be good. I said: 'Yes, Sister, I would like to be very pious.' 'Then,' said she, 'the easiest way to be pious is to take Jesus Christ for your model, and whatever you do, do it to please Him, thinking that He is beside you, asking you to do it in the way He did it Himself.' So when I rise in the morning and say my prayers, I think I see the Child Jesus rising when His Mother called Him, and praying to His Heavenly Father. When I am at my work, I think I see Jesus helping St. Joseph in the workshop, or Mary in the house; and when I am told to do anything, I think I see my dear Jesus told by His Blessed Mother to do this or that, and that I see Him doing it immediately. And when I am told to do a thing I don't like to do, I remember how Jesus willingly obeyed His Father in Heaven when He told Him to die on the cross, although He felt it so much; and then I say to myself, 'Since my dear Jesus suffered so much for me, surely I will suffer a little for the love of Him, and then I find it easy to do it."

"But, my child," said the priest, "when people were speaking against you, and calling you a hypocrite, did you not feel angry with them?"

"Ah, dear Father," she replied, "that was a heavy cross; but the Sisters had told me that I would have many crosses to bear if I wanted to be good, so when I heard the falsehoods they were telling about me, and the names they called me, I remembered how the Jews called Jesus names, and that He said nothing, but only prayed to God for their forgiveness. So I did the same."

"Then you do sometimes find it difficult to be good, do you, my child?" said the priest.

"Ah yes, Father, sometimes I am very much tempted, and sometimes I become so weary that I feel very, very sad, and often think it is no use trying to be good. But then I remember that Jesus Himself was sometimes weary and sad, especially that time when He saw so many people turning their backs upon Him and leaving Him after He had, through love for them, fed them in the desert by a miracle. I think I see Him looking at the Apostles, and that I hear Him asking them if they too are going to leave Him. Then I think I hear Him saying to me: 'And you, my daughter, are you also going to leave Me? Surely you will not sin against Me after I have been so good to you?'

"Then I say: 'No, my God, I will never leave Thee. To whom should I go if I left Thee? I promise Thee to go on loving Thee in weariness as well as in joyfulness till I die; but O my God, help me.' Then I feel a kind of happiness which gives me courage to suffer patiently everything for the love of God."

"My dear child," said the priest, "you have learned your lesson well, and, what is far better, you know how to practice it. Go on as you are doing, and if you persevere, you will certainly have fought the good fight well, and will have gained much merit for Heaven."

What is easier than to take Jesus for our model, and do everything, as Dorothy did, for His sake? As long as we are in this world, we must fight against sin and our own evil inclinations, and if we do that we shall one day see God in Heaven; that is what is meant by the good fight.

Instructions for Youth.

35

OUR ONE GREAT DESIRE SHOULD BE TO GAIN HEAVEN

While the Saints were on earth, their one only thought was of the Kingdom of Heaven, and their one great anxiety was how they might secure it.

"Thy Kingdom come."

THE LEGEND OF THE LITTLE SCHOLARS.

When the blessed Bernard filled the office of sacristan in the Convent of Santarem, there were two little boys who were sent daily to the convent from their father's house nearby to be instructed in their religion, and to receive their education in secular knowledge.

They were placed under the care of Father Bernard; and the good man felt a great joy in training them, because he was sure their gentle goodness and innocence made them very dear to his Divine Master.

The little boys were allowed to go into a small chapel not far from the high altar, and there they would spread out their books on the steps, and learn their lessons happily and quietly, or eat their dinner, which they brought with them from home.

On the altar was an image of Mary, with the Holy Child Jesus in her arms; and the two children, with all the simplicity of their age, would speak to Him as if He were alive like themselves.

"Dear Holy Child," said one of the boys one day, "how is it that You never move as we do, and never eat, but always stay in Your blessed Mother's arms? We will give You a share of our dinner very gladly if You will only come down and eat it with us."

It was God's will to reward the simplicity of His little ones by a wonderful miracle. The carved image of the Divine Child took the appearance of life, and, coming down from Our Lady's arms, sat with the boys before the altar, and took some dinner with them.

This happened more than once, and that little chapel seemed full of the joys of Heaven. The love of Jesus became so great in their hearts that they cared for nothing but Him, and longed so much for the time when they hoped to see Him come down to them and speak with them.

Their parents saw that a great change had come over the children, and that they were never so happy as when they were in the convent.

One day they asked them why they were better pleased to stay in the convent than at home; and the children told them their wonderful story. But their parents would not believe them, and said that it was all a foolish fancy, and that such a thing was impossible.

But when the blessed Bernard heard it, he thought that it might indeed be true. He knew that to God, Who loved little children so much, nothing was impossible, so he also questioned them; and when he had heard their story, he knew that they had spoken the truth, and that it was no foolish fancy.

When they told him in their childish way that they wondered why the Holy Infant did not bring some food too, Bernard said to them: "My children, the next time your heavenly visitor comes to see you, ask Him if He would be good enough to invite you to dine in His Father's house."

The boys were delighted, and when the next day came, they asked the Divine Child the question their master had told them to ask.

Jesus smiled upon them with a look of great affection, and said: "Within three days you shall indeed come with Me to My Father's house, and eat of the food He has made ready for you." The boys at once ran back to tell their master what had been said to them.

Bernard looked lovingly on the children, although there was a feeling of sadness in his heart, for he well knew what the message meant. He knew the innocence and purity of their young hearts, and was sure that in some wonderful way God was going to take them from the world before they had been stained by sin.

Then a great longing came into his own heart to go to Heaven with them. He had fought the good fight manfully, and he felt a great desire to enter his eternal home in Heaven, where he might rest from his labors in the arms of his Heavenly Father. So he bade the children return and ask the Infant Jesus if he also might be allowed to go with them.

The Holy Child answered: "Go back to your master and tell him to prepare; for on Thursday I will receive him along with you into My Father's house."

Bernard's heart was filled with the greatest joy and love when he received this happy message, and he began to prepare himself for death.

The day fixed was Ascension Day. That morning the blessed Bernard said Mass early; his little pupils served him, and received Holy Communion from his hands; and when Mass was ended, he knelt upon the altar-steps, with one of the children on each side of him, and commended his soul to God.

About an hour afterwards some of the brothers passing through the church saw Bernard still kneeling there, vested as for Mass, with the little boys clad in their snow-white surplices at his side; but the three were quite dead, and the soft smile upon their faces showed that they had indeed gone home with the Holy Child, in the very act of prayer. They were buried in the chapel where Our Lord had visited them so often, and a picture was hung above the altar, representing the two children seated upon the step, with the Divine Child Jesus between them.

Lives of the Saints, May 8.

ST. TERESA AND HER BROTHER RODERICK.

When St. Teresa was a girl, not more than seven years old, she used to spend much of her time with her little brother Roderick in reading the lives of the Saints, and in speaking about holy things.

The thought of eternity and of Heaven made a deep impression upon their young minds, and they were never tired of saying over and over again these words: "Forever, forever, forever! What a blessed thing it will be to see and enjoy God forever!"

When they read about the monks and the hermits who left the world, and went to live in desert places, far away from the company of those who might make them forget God, they also wished to be like them.

So they set to work in their father's garden to build little houses or cells for themselves, where, like the hermits, they might think only of God and of Heaven, on which all their thoughts were fixed; but because they were so young and so feeble, they were not able to accomplish what they desired to do.

Sometimes, when they read the history of the holy martyrs, they were so filled with delight that they seemed to be more in Heaven than on earth.

"Oh, how much I would like to be a martyr!" said Teresa to her brother; "how happy they were to get to Heaven after such short sufferings!"

"Yes," said Roderick, "and I would like to be a martyr, too! Come along with me, and we will go into the country where the Moors live, and they will put us to death because we are Christians, and then we shall get to Heaven, and be like the holy martyrs."

"Oh, that will be delightful!" ejaculated Teresa. "This very day we will go, that we may get to Heaven sooner."

So these innocent children set out to go to the country of the Moors. As they went along the road, they prayed with great fervor, and wondered when they would reach the end of their journey.

When their mother, who knew nothing of their intention, missed them from table at dinner-time, she became alarmed, and diligent search was made for them everywhere.

Now, it happened that as they were crossing a bridge over a river near the town, they were met by an uncle, who asked them where they were going.

"We are going to the country of the Moors," they replied, "because we want to be martyrs, and so get to Heaven."

Their uncle took them back with him to their mother, who was very glad when she saw them again. She asked Roderick why he was guilty of such a foolish thing; but he put all the blame on Teresa, his sister, saying that she was the first to speak of it. Upon which Teresa got a great scolding.

No doubt Almighty God was pleased with their great fervor, and although they did not receive the crown of martyrdom, they continued to become more and more fervent; and this fervor was increased by the thought of Heaven, and the glory God would one day give them, if they were good.

Life of St. Teresa.

THE LITTLE BOY CELSUS.

At the beginning of the fourth century a terrible persecution was raging at Antioch. The faithful were put to death without mercy because they would not deny Jesus Christ, nor offer incense to the gods of the pagans.

Amongst those who were brought before Marcian, the governor, was the holy martyr Julian. After having inflicted on him the most terrible torments, he ordered him to be dragged through the streets of the city, amidst the insults of the mob.

Now, while St. Julian was being thus led through the public places, it chanced that he passed by the house where Celsus, the governor's son, was at school. The shouts of the mob that crowded around the holy martyr drew Celsus and his schoolfellows to the window, to see what was the matter.

As he stood at the window, the boy saw a most wonderful vision. "Oh!" he cried out to his companions, "I see a most wonderful thing!"

They asked him what it was.

"I see," he said, "a great multitude of men, clad in white garments; they are speaking to that Christian whom they are leading to death. And I see above his head a crown of glory, which his God is to give him. Oh, how beautiful it is! It seems to be made of the purest gold, and it shines so brightly that it far surpasses even the light of the sun. And there are angels of the most ravishing beauty standing by his side, and encouraging him to win that bright crown."

Then the child, struck by the grace of God, cried out: "Great is the God of the Christians, Who can thus reward those who serve Him! I, too, will be His servant, that I may win for myself a crown of glory like the one I now see."

Then, in a transport of holy joy, he ran after the martyr, and when he reached him, he cried out: "O servant of the true God, I renounce forever my earthly father, who has brought me up in unbelief, and I now take thee for my father, that thou mayest teach me the true Faith, and show me how to worship the true God."

In the meantime news of this strange event reached Marcian, his father. At first he refused to believe it; but when he saw that it was true, he was filled with rage and indignation, and ordered Julian and his own boy Celsus to be immediately brought before him.

"Thou treacherous Julian!" he cried out, "thou hast, then, succeeded in robbing me of my dear and only son, the hope of my race, and the pride of my heart."

At the same moment the boy's mother, who had also been told of what had occurred, came in great haste to the place. Her hair was all in disorder, and her face bathed in a flood of tears; all those who were with her were likewise overwhelmed with grief.

Seeing this, his father said to him: "O cruel boy, are you not moved by your father's sorrow and your mother's tears? Repent of what you have done; I will yet obtain your pardon."

But Celsus answered: "I set no value on my life; I have this day been born to a new life that will never end. The tears that stream from your eyes shall never soften my heart. Take, then, from me the life you gave me, that I may enter at once into the possession of that crown of glory that God has this day shown to me."

The heroic child was condemned to suffer the most cruel tortures, but he bore them all with heroic patience; and in the end, when he was condemned to be beheaded, he joyfully bent his head to receive the stroke of death, which, in a moment, opened for him the gates of eternal life in Heaven.

Surius: Vit. SS., Jan. 9.

THE BOY-MARTYRS OF SPAIN.

In a town of Spain called Alcala there lived, in the time of Diocletian, two little boys, whose names were Justus and Pastor. Their parents, who were Christians, brought them up very carefully in the fear of God. They were also taught all the things that children generally learn, and for this purpose went every day to school.

The Roman governor of Spain at that time was called Dacian. He was a very cruel man, and went about from town to town seeking out the Christians and putting them to death. When he came to Alcala, he issued a proclamation commanding everyone, under pain of death, to offer sacrifice to the heathen gods.

This proclamation made a great stir in the town. Justus was at that time seven, and Pastor was nine years of age. They were both at school, when a person came running in and told the news to the master. Most of the boys were so busy trying to finish their lessons quickly, in order to get out the sooner to play, that they took no notice of what the man said.

But it was not so with Justus and Pastor. As soon as they heard about the governor's proclamation, they were seized with such a wonderful desire to die for Jesus that, throwing down their books, they rushed out of the school, and, running up to the tribunal of the wicked Dacian, cried out: "We are Christian boys, and you must put us to death, because we will not sacrifice to your gods."

Dacian at first would not listen to them. He thought they were foolish little children who were talking nonsense, and told them to hold their tongues, and not interrupt him, for he was very busy.

But they would not be silent, and continued to speak so boldly that at last Dacian, in very great anger, turned round to them and asked them who they were.

"We are Christians," they again said, "and we want to be put to death, that we may go to God in Heaven."

Dacian was at first amazed at what he heard, but, persuading himself that some childish fancy had got into their heads, he thought he would soon cure them of it, so he ordered them to be privately whipped, and then sent home.

So the two little brothers were led away like innocent lambs to be whipped. As they were going along together, they encouraged each other to bear every kind of torment for the love of Jesus.

As Justus was the younger of the two, he thought that perhaps his brother would think that such a little fellow as he was could not have courage to bear the tortures, so he said to him: "I hope, dear Pastor, you are not afraid of dying, or of being whipped, or of that sharp sword with which they may perhaps cut off our heads. As for me, I am not the least afraid of them."

"I am not afraid for myself," answered Pastor, "because, you know, I am a big boy now; but I am afraid of you, dear Justus, for you are such a little fellow."

"Don't trouble yourself about me," replied Justus, "for though I am such a little boy yet, by God's grace, I shall be as strong as the biggest man."

"Are you quite sure?" said Pastor.

"Yes, quite sure," he answered, "for God, Who has called on us to suffer for His holy Name, will be sure to give us strength to bear our martyrdom."

"Dear Justus," cried out Pastor, "I am so happy to hear you speak so bravely. I am sure it is God Himself that speaks through your mouth; so now I am not at all afraid of you, and it will be quite easy for me to die with you, so that we may both together go to live with our dear Lord Jesus, in Heaven."

"God will be sure to carry us through, even although we are such poor weak boys," replied Justus, "and will take us quickly to that happy Paradise which papa and mamma have so often told us about, where we shall be with His angels and Saints, and shall see Himself in all His glory." Pastor answered: "Yes; and just think, too, what a glory it will be for us to shed our blood for that dear Jesus Who shed His blood for us!"

Thus did these little children encourage each other as they went along. The soldiers, who heard what they were saying, were amazed, and they thought there must be something very strange about them, when they were so willing to die. So they went to Dacian, and told him what they had seen and heard, and asked him what they were to do with them.

Dacian thought what a disgrace it would be for himself, a powerful man, if he should be vanquished by two little boys; and he was afraid, also, that their heroic example might encourage other people to suffer martyrdom. So he ordered them to be taken to a place where no one would see them, and to be secretly beheaded.

They were accordingly led into a field, where they were beheaded on a great stone; and to the present day there remains on this stone the mark of the knees of those two innocent children. The Christians of Alcala took up their precious relics, and buried them with great reverence on the spot which they had sanctified by their glorious death; and when the days of persecution had passed away, a magnificent church was built over their tomb, and dedicated to God in their honor.

When we read of the great love of these two little boys for God, and their great desire of going to see Him in Heaven, we should try to love God more than we are doing, and pray to Him to give us a place in His happy home above when the short time of our trial on earth is ended.

Surius: *Hist. Sanct., Aug. 6.*

36

THE KINGDOM OF GOD ON EARTH.

When we read the lives of the Saints, my child, we see that their greatest desire was to see the Kingdom of God extended on earth; and we read that many of them spent their whole lives in laboring for the salvation of souls

THE SLAVE OF THE SLAVES.

Many years ago, when traffic in human beings was common in the East, cruel men went to the coast of Africa, carried off the people who dwelt there, and brought them into America, where they were sold as slaves.

These poor people had much to suffer from their cruel masters. They were overworked, badly clothed, and poorly fed; but, what was worst of all, they received no religious instruction. Their masters, indeed, took care of their bodies, that they might be able to labor for them, but there was no one to look after their souls till God, in His mercy, raised up a holy man, who became their apostle. This was Peter Claver, who was born in Spain in 1581.

He was the son of noble and pious parents. In his youth he joined the Society of Jesus; and while yet a novice, begged that he might be sent to America, to spend his life among the poor negroes.

His request was granted. As soon as he reached that country, he began his noble work. Whenever a slave-ship arrived, Peter went on board to meet the unhappy men. He received them with great kindness, and spoke to them consoling and encouraging words. In this way he soon won their confidence.

When the time came to leave the vessel, Peter helped them out; he carried the sick in his arms, and placed them in a wagon he had prepared for them. The others he accompanied to their new homes, begged their masters to treat them kindly, and left a promise to see them soon again.

Afterwards he instructed them in the truths of our holy religion. Nothing discouraged him—neither the dulness of some, nor the rough, coarse ways of others. Day after day the holy man carried hope and comfort to those in sadness, and for many who had offended their masters he obtained pardon.

When not thus occupied, his time was spent in the hospitals, where he sat at the bedside of the sick, dressed their wounds, and waited on them as a servant. The name he loved best to be called was "The Slave of the Slaves."

On Sundays and holidays he gathered together all his dear slaves who were well into an open square, where he had put up an altar, and placed benches and matting for their comfort. It is no wonder that Peter gained the love of these poor negroes.

If they lived piously, he made them little presents to encourage them; but if they did wrong, he gently reproved them. In this way did he win these ignorant people to God; and it is said that during his life he converted and baptized no fewer than forty thousand.

The holy man spent thirty-six years in this heroic work. At last he fell sick, and for four years lay on his death-bed. During all that time his poor slaves came in crowds to visit him. Day by day he instructed and consoled them, till at last, on September 8, 1654, God called him to his reward in Heaven.

Lives of the Saints, Sept. 9.

OUR LADY'S CHILD.

It was a beautiful evening in the summer-time. The birds were singing their sweetest songs, and the sun shone brightly over the earth. All nature seemed full of joy, as if to remind us of the love of Our Father in Heaven, and to tell us of the happiness He will give in Heaven to those who have faithfully served Him on earth.

Under the shadow of a wide-spreading tree sat a little girl all alone. She was poor, and had no one in this world to care for her. Her occupation was to take care of a few sheep that grazed peacefully near her, for which she got her scanty food and clothing from the farmer to whom they belonged.

But she was happy—happy in the company of her dear Father above, Who seems to have a more especial care for His little ones on earth the more they are neglected and unheeded by men.

By her side was a little heap of flowers which she had gathered in the fields, and with them she was making a floral wreath.

When it was finished she rose up, and directed her steps towards a little chapel by the wayside. In this chapel was an altar, and on the altar a statue of Our Lady. There was no grandeur in this lonely place like what may sometimes be seen in stately cathedrals. Everything was humble, and of little value; even the statue of Our Lady was of the rudest construction.

To this humble spot, then, did the little shepherdess proceed, and, kneeling down before the altar, she poured forth her prayers—those simple prayers so pleasing to the Queen of Heaven.

"My Mother," she said, as she looked up with tears in her eyes towards the image of Our Lady—"my Mother, you have no crown on your head. Oh, if I were able, I would place upon your brow a golden crown, all sparkling with jewels; but I am only a poor, simple girl, and I have nothing to give you but this crown of flowers which I gathered in the fields. My Mother, they are the prettiest I could find. Accept it, then, as a sign of the love I bear to you."

She then rose from her knees, and, going up to the altar, she placed the wreath upon the image of Our Lady. Then, kneeling down again, she thought of the glory which God must have bestowed on His Holy Mother, the Queen of Heaven, and prayed that she might one day be so happy as to see her in her kingdom.

Thus did the lonely child pray day after day; and every evening, whilst the flowers bloomed, she crowned Our Lady's statue with a fresh wreath.

But it is now time to see how Mary recompensed this little act of homage. The poor child grew ill, and the hour of her death was fast approaching.

It happened that two religious were passing through that country. It was during the great heats of the day, and they sat down to rest under a tree by the wayside. One of them fell asleep, and the other remained awake, but both saw the same vision.

They saw coming towards them a group of virgins clad in dazzling white. In the midst of them was one more beautiful and majestic than the others. When they came up to the place where they were reposing, one of the religious asked her who she was and whither she was going.

"I am going," replied the Most Holy Mother of God—for it was she—"I am going along with these holy virgins to visit one who often came to visit me—a little girl who used to tend the sheep in this place. She is now at the point of death."

When she said these words, the vision disappeared. The holy religious said one to the other: "Let us also go and see her."

They rose immediately and went towards a lonely cottage nearby. When they entered, they saw the young girl lying on some straw. A heavenly smile was on her wasted countenance, and her eyes seemed to gaze in rapture on something beautiful which they could not see.

She looked towards the two religious as they entered, and saluted them. Then she said: "My Fathers, pray to God to let you see the beautiful company that is around me."

They knelt down beside her, and as they prayed, they saw again the same beautiful vision that they had seen before. Our Lady was speaking to the dying girl sweet words of comfort, and held in her hand a beautiful crown.

Suddenly the beautiful virgins who accompanied Our Lady began to sing, and at the same moment the soul of the poor lowly child left its frail body. Mary took it in her arms, and, crowning it with a crown of glory more resplendent than the sun, carried it along with her to Paradise.

It is thus that the faithful child of Mary dies. It is not granted to us to see it as these religious saw it; but if we are faithful in her service and in that of her Divine Son, she will come at the hour of death and conduct us safe to our home above.

St. Liguori

WHAT ST. CATHERINE SAW.

St. Catherine of Sienna loved God with her whole heart, and God often showed her that He also loved her very much by many special favors which He granted her.

One day He was pleased to give her a little glimpse of the glory of Heaven which He would one day bestow on her and on all His children, if they would be faithful to Him while they dwelt in this world.

When the vision was over, she went down to the other nuns in the convent; but her face was so bright that they could scarcely look upon it. They knew at once that she must have had a vision, so they asked her to tell them what she had seen.

"Oh," she exclaimed, "I have seen such wonderful things—such wonderful things!" But she could say no more.

When her confessor heard about it, he asked her to tell him more plainly what God had been pleased to show her.

"Father," she answered, "it is quite impossible for me to tell you what I saw: no human tongue could express, and no words could describe, the beauty of the heavenly things God showed me—the reward which He is to give to everyone who serves and loves Him in this world. Oh no! it is beautiful beyond all that can be imagined."

Since Heaven is so beautiful, we should all try to love God now, that we may one day enjoy its happiness.

Life of St. Catherine

37

A HAPPY DEATH THE ENTRANCE INTO LIFE

"Precious in the sight of the Lord is the death of His Saints" (Ps. cxv. 15).

ST. GERTRUDE'S HAPPY DEATH.

St. Gertrude was so anxious to see God and be forever with Him in Heaven, that during her whole lifetime this was her only thought.

When the day of her death, which she so much desired, had come, Our Lord appeared to her with His Divine countenance all radiant with joy.

On His right hand stood His ever-blessed Mother and on His left the beloved disciple St. John. An immense multitude of the heavenly host accompanied their King, and along with them were many of the religious who, when on earth, had lived under the guidance of St. Gertrude, and were now in Heaven.

One of the nuns who was present, and who also saw this vision, ventured to address Our Lord in these words: "O most sweet Jesus, I beseech Thee, by the goodness that prompted Thee to give us so dear a Mother, that, since Thou art about to take her from this world,

Thou wouldst receive her with the same affection as Thou didst receive Thine own blessed Mother when she went forth from the body."

Then Our Lord turned to His Holy Mother, who was at His side, and said to her: "Tell Me, My Mother, what I did most pleasing to you when you were leaving the world, for they ask Me to bestow a similar favor on their Mother here."

"My Son," replied the Holy Virgin sweetly, "my greatest joy was the grace which Thou didst give me in receiving me so lovingly into Thy sacred arms at the moment of my death."

Then Jesus answered: "Yes, My Mother; I granted you that favor because, after My departure from you into Heaven, you always remembered so affectionately My Passion and death."

Then, turning to the religious, He said: "I granted that favor to My chosen one, My Mother, in recompense for her grief and the tears she shed, while thinking of My Passion and death. Gertrude must merit in some way that same favor by bearing with patience the sufferings she shall have to endure to-day."

St. Gertrude, therefore, continued in her agony all that day. But Our Lord did not leave her to suffer alone; she drew from His Sacred Heart the help and the consolation she needed. Celestial spirits also appeared to her coming down from Heaven, and inviting her to Paradise. She heard their heavenly harmony as they sang, in tones of celestial sweetness, "Come, come, come, O Lady; the joys of Heaven await thee. Alleluia! Alleluia!"

Then Jesus turned towards her, and her happy soul, at that instant leaving the body, flew into His blessed arms.

"Behold, now," He said, as He pressed it to His Sacred Heart—" behold, now; you are to be united to Me, and to be My own beloved one forever; and in the close embrace of My Heart will I present you to My Eternal Father."

It was thus St. Gertrude died.

Life of St. Gertrude.

HEROIC FAITH OF A CHILD.

In the year 1833 a violent persecution was raised against the Church by the King of Cochin China, and many of the Christians were cruelly tortured and put to death for the Faith.

These good people showed the greatest joy in the midst of their sufferings, and even the little children nobly confessed the Faith, and offered themselves to the judge to receive the crown of martyrdom.

One day a little boy presented himself before the tribunal of the judge. He threw himself on his knees before him and asked permission to speak.

When he obtained permission, he said: "Mandarin, cut off my head with the sword, that I may go to my own country."

"Where is your country?" asked the judge.

"It is in Heaven," replied the child.

"And where are your parents?" "They are gone home to Heaven, and I want to follow them. Oh, sir, give me a stroke with the sword and send me there too."

The Mandarin was struck with admiration at the faith and courage of the boy, but refused to grant him his request. But this child received from God the glory of the martyrs on account of his great desire of being a martyr.

Annals of Prop. of the Faith.

My child, with Whom shall we be in Heaven? With God, Who is our Father; with Jesus Christ, Who is our Brother; with the Blessed Virgin, who is our Mother; with the angels and Saints, who are our friends.

A King in his last moments said with regret: "Must I, then, leave my kingdom, to go to a country where I know no one?" This was because he had never thought of the happiness of Heaven. We must make friends there for ourselves now, that we may meet them again after death, and then we shall not be like that King, afraid of knowing no one.

Blessed Curé of Ars.

PART VI

"THY WILL BE DONE"

38

WHAT IS MEANT BY DOING THE WILL OF GOD?

The third petition of the Lord's Prayer is, "Thy will be done on earth as it is in Heaven." To do the will of God is to keep His commandments, and to receive with joy from His hands whatever He is pleased to send us during the short time we are in this life.

"THY WILL BE DONE, O LORD."

Every time St. Gertrude said the Lord's Prayer, she said this third petition, "Thy will be done," with the greatest fervor. Sometimes she would say it over and over again, because every time she did so she felt her heart all on fire with the love of God.

One day, as she was saying it in this way, Our Lord Himself appeared to her in a visible manner. In His right hand He seemed to carry health, and in His left hand sickness. He said to her: "Gertrude, my daughter, which of the two do you wish Me to give you—health or sickness?"

Did she choose health? No. Then was it sickness? No. She only said: "O my God, Thy will, not mine, be done." This answer was so pleasing to Our Lord that He gave her, even in this world, many special marks of His love. One day He appeared to a holy nun of the same convent called Mechtilde. He was seated on a beautiful throne, with St. Gertrude at His side. She was gazing with rapture on His sacred countenance, and He also seemed to be looking on her with eyes beaming with love.

Mechtilde then understood that this great favor had been given to her because she was always so submissive to His blessed will.

Life of St. Gertrude.

NO CONSOLATION.

There was once a very holy man, who spent his life in the midst of great spiritual consolations. He was always very happy, and seemed to have none of those temptations which are so common amongst poor sinners in this world.

One day he was reading the holy Scriptures, and saw there that Jesus Christ had said that if we desire to be His disciples, we must take up our cross and follow Him.

"I have no crosses," he said; "I never had any. I seem to be living more like the angels of God in Heaven than like one on trial on earth. O my God," he cried out, "take away from me these favors Thou art daily heaping upon me, if Thou seest that I shall be more pleasing to Thee without them."

God heard his prayer. For the next five years he was continually tormented with temptations, and during all that time he received no consolation from Heaven. In his prayers, too, he felt no fervor, and his life was embittered by continual sorrows.

One day as he was weeping bitterly over his sad condition two angels appeared to him. "God has sent us to console you," they said. "He is pleased with what you have done for Him, and if you so desire it, He will put an end to all your afflictions, and give you back again the peaceful happiness of former days."

But he answered: "No; I do not desire any consolation. It is enough for me that the holy will of God be accomplished in me; I seek nothing else."

The angels then left him. To the end of his long life he had to endure the same afflictions and the same bitter trials. But now they are all ended, and he is with God in Heaven, in possession of that eternal joy which God has promised to all who do His holy will on earth.

P. Huguet: *Christ. Perf.*, p. 733.

THE SUFFERINGS OF ST. VINCENT DE PAUL.

When St. Vincent was growing old, he had most acute pains to suffer. His legs were swollen to such an extent that, whenever he tried to walk, he suffered great pain.

One day when they were dressing his sores, one of the Fathers who was standing near him said: "O my dear Father, what cruel agony you must suffer!"

The Saint answered: "What is that you say? How can you say that anything is cruel which God is pleased to send? Could anything be bad enough for me who am such a great sinner? May God forgive you, dear sir, for saying such a thing! That is not the way we should speak of what our dear Lord Jesus sends us. Is it not but just that we should suffer everything God wants us to suffer? For we do not belong to ourselves, but to Him, and therefore He has a right to treat us as He thinks proper."

Another time the same priest said to him: "My Father, I think your pains seem to be increasing every day."

"Ah, yes; it is quite true. From the crown of my head to the soles of my feet I suffer much—very much. But, alas! what an account I will have to give to God when I die, for having made such little use of these many and great graces!"

THE STATUE IN THE NICHE.

What could be more beautiful than the following advice of St. Francis de Sales to St. Jane de Chantal to encourage her in the practice of this virtue of conformity to the holy will of God?

"Remain in the place where God has put you, and perform in it all the duties He has placed upon you. Be before God like a statue which is placed in a niche, remembering that we belong not to ourselves, but to God alone, and that He is our All.

"If the statue in the niche could speak, and if someone were to ask it, 'Why are you there?' it would answer, 'Because my master has placed me here.'

"'And why do you not move?'

"'Because his desire is that I should not move', "'And what will you gain by remaining there immovable?'

"'It is not for myself that I am here; it is to fulfill the desire of my master who placed me here.'

"'But you cannot see him?'

"'No, indeed; but he sees me, and he finds pleasure in seeing me in the niche in which he himself has placed me.'

"'But would you not desire to have the power of moving, so that you might approach nearer to him?'

"'No; because the will of my master is the only desire of my heart.'"

This was, indeed, what the Saint himself daily practiced. All his desires were centered in this one thought: "To please God: to do the holy will of God." It was the only end he proposed to himself in all his thoughts, words, and actions.

St. Francis de Sales and St. Jane Chantal.

FLOWERS OF THE LORD'S PRAYER—"THY WILL BE DONE."

A hermit who dwelt in the deserts of Egypt one day asked St. Macarius, who dwelt in the Thebaid, and was renowned for his great piety and experience, how he ought to pray.

"My dear brother," answered the Saint, "to pray well you do not require to utter many words; it is sufficient to raise up your hands and eyes to Heaven, and to say: 'O my God, may Thy holy will be done.'"

When St. Martin was lying on his death-bed, his disciples stood around him weeping. They said to him: "O Father, why are you about to leave us, or to whom will you confide us who will so soon be orphans? Hungry wolves will come and attack your flock, and who will stand by us to defend us from their ferocious assaults if you depart from us?'"

The Saint, moved with the deepest compassion, mingled his tears with theirs; and, looking up towards Heaven, with outstretched hands, prayed thus to God: "O Lord, if I am still necessary for Thy people, I do not refuse to labor still longer for their sakes. May Thy holy will be done!'"

When St. Herion, a young man in the flower of his age, was being dragged away by the soldiers to suffer for the sake of Christ, his mother stood beside him weeping.

"Weep not for me, my beloved mother; it is God Who calls me. May His most holy will be done! We will meet again in Paradise."

On one occasion St. Richard, Bishop of Chichester, suffered much from the effects of a fire which had broken out in a house near his dwelling. The people came to offer him their condolence at the loss he had sustained; but he answered them: "My friends, it is by the holy will of God that this has occurred to me. May His holy will be done! Who can tell but He may have sent me this accident to punish me for my too much attachment to the perishable things of this world?"

St. Hedwige, Duchess of Poland, had for her husband and her children an intense affection; yet when her husband died, after a long and painful captivity, it is related that she shed only a few tears; likewise, when her eldest son Henry, in the flower of his age, fell on the battle-field in a combat against the Tartars, she seemed almost unmoved.

When asked why she was so unaffected under such a heavy afflic-tion, she answered: "It was God's holy will that they should die in this manner, and He knows what is most advantageous for us."

When the city of Hamburg was assaulted by the Normans, who were pagans, the holy Bishop of that place, by name Auscarius, and all the inhabitants had to seek safety in flight. They escaped only with their lives, and were obliged to leave behind them all their possessions.

St. Auscarius, seeing their sadness in their great affliction, consoled them by saying to them: "It was God Who in the beginning gave us all these things; now it has pleased Him to take them from us. May His will be done, and may His holy Name be forever blessed!"

When Joseph II., Emperor of Germany, was lying in bed suffering from a painful illness, the sad intelligence was brought to him that his wife had just died. For a few moments he lay in silence, then, piously raising up his eyes to Heaven, he said these words: "O my Lord, it is Thy holy will. May Thy holy will be done in all things!"

Count Leopold of Stolberg, on hearing of the death of his beloved wife, fell into a deep melancholy, and wept, and uttered words of great lamentation. "Alas!" he cried out, "she is gone from me. She is dead; never shall I see her again;" and he would not be consoled, so great was his sorrow.

"My lord," gently whispered one of the attending maids of the late Countess, "who is it that has taken her from you? Is it not God Himself, Who had given her to you? and you know that whatever God does is always for the best, and is well done."

These words touched the heart of the Count, and, sighing, he said aloud: "You are right; it is indeed God Himself Who has sent me this sorrow; it is He Who has taken away my beloved spouse. It is my duty to submit to His adorable will."

ST. JOHN THE ABBOT'S DYING COUNSEL.

When the Abbot John was about to leave this world, his brethren besought him to give them a counsel, which they might cherish as his last legacy.

He said to them: "My children, never do your own will. Consider what is the will of God, and accomplish it. This has always been the aim of my life, for I would not teach to others what I myself did not practice and show forth by my own example."

Vit. Patr., c. v., lib. i.

39

HOW THE SAINTS AND THE JUST OBEYED THE WILL OF GOD

My child, the Saints had no will of their own. As soon as they knew what God desired them to do, they did it at once. They were like little children who are always obedient to their father's orders. It was this great virtue that made them always joyful, even in the midst of great trials and sufferings.

"BE MY FATHER, AND I WILL BE YOUR CHILD."

Not many years ago there was a little girl belonging to Genoa who had the misfortune in her childhood to be captured by pirates and sold as a slave.

She changed masters several times. At last she fell into the hands of one more savage than the rest, who seemed to be devoid of all human feeling, and who, in consequence, treated her with the utmost cruelty.

One day he struck her so fiercely that she fell to the ground, and fainted under the blow. He then went away, leaving her as dead, and thought no more of her than if she had been a brute beast.

In a short time she returned to her senses, and her first thought was to try and escape from the ruffian who had been so cruel to her. This she was able to do in a few days without much difficulty.

By a happy chance, Monsignor Dupuch, Bishop of Algeria, came into the city that same day. The poor child saw him as he passed along the street, and although she did not know who he was, she was struck by the look of kindness that was on his venerable countenance.

"Oh," she said to herself, "if I only could have that man for a master, how happy should I be! I am sure he at least would treat me kindly, and would not beat me."

A sudden thought at that moment came into her mind. She ran towards the place where the Bishop was, and, making her way through the crowd that surrounded him, threw herself at his feet, and cried out in accents that reached the Bishop's heart: "O kind sir, be my father, and I will be your child!"

The Bishop kindly raised the poor girl from the ground, asked her in the gentlest tones who she was, and how she came to be covered with so many bruises.

She told him all in a few words, and again asked him to be a father to her, and not allow her to fall again into the hands of her cruel master.

The Bishop was touched with the girl's story, and more still with the child-like confidence with which she had spoken to him. He promised to protect her, and told her she should have to suffer no more cruelty, but would find peace in the home to which he would take her. He then brought her to a convent, and placed her under the charge of the Sisters, that they might instruct her and take care of her.

At the end of a few months she asked to receive Baptism, and to be made a Christian. The Bishop at first did not grant her request. He thought that a little longer time would be needed to prove that her desire was sincere, and that her instruction was sufficiently advanced.

But this delay made the little girl sad; she desired so much to be a child of God that she could not be comforted when she heard that this favor was to be put off for a time. So the Sisters again asked the

Bishop to grant the child's request, and to allow her to be baptized immediately.

The Bishop himself then went to the convent to speak to the child. "O my Father," she said as soon as she saw him, "let me be baptized, that I may become at once the child of God." The Bishop said to her: "My child, you know that when you are baptized you must be always good, and never sin again, and love God with all your heart. Are you willing to do this?"

The child took up a crucifix, and, pressing it to her breast, said: "I wish for no other master but my dear Lord Jesus Christ Who died for me."

Then, seeing the ring on the Bishop's finger, she pointed to it, and said, with tears in her eyes: "As you carry that ring with you wherever you go, and as you turn it about on your finger just as you like, and as it is always with you, so when I am made a Christian I will always be like a ring on the finger of God's hand."

The Bishop was moved at this beautiful and simple answer. He hesitated no longer, and at once baptized her. "Oh, what a happiness it would be if all children would try to be like this little child!" he said to the kind Sisters who were present, "and to be as rings on the finger of God, by being obedient to His holy will in all things!"

Notes d'Alger.

ST. EDMUND OF CANTERBURY IN HIS LAST MOMENTS.

Those who in the course of their life seek only to accomplish the holy will of God enjoy the greatest peace and happiness at the hour of death.

St. Edmund, Archbishop of Canterbury, during his whole lifetime, endeavored to conform himself in everything to the most holy will of God.

When, in the year 1242, he saw that his last hour was at hand, he desired to receive the last Sacraments of the Church; and when the priest brought into his room the adorable Viaticum—Our Lord

Himself—he, with a supreme effort, raised himself in his bed, and, lovingly stretching out his dying arms, as if to embrace Him Whom he had ever so faithfully served, he said: "Thou art my Lord and my God: I have ever believed in Thee, and preached Thee to the people Thou didst confide to my care. Thou art my witness that I never sought on earth anything but Thee, and that I never had any will, and have now no other will, but Thy most holy will, and at this moment my sole desire is that it should be accomplished in me."

After saying these words of faith and love, he received his Divine Lord and Master into his heart. For a long time he seemed to be filled with a peaceful calm; his countenance was sweet to behold, and his eyes were bathed in tears. Not long afterwards, without for an instant losing that serenity which makes death so sweet to the children of God, he resigned his soul into the hands of his Divine Master on November 16, 1242.

From his Life.

40

GOD KNOWS WHAT IS BEST FOR US

God always knows best what is most useful to us, although we may not see it; and during our short life on earth we shall have many sufferings to endure if we love and serve God. It is when the glory of Heaven opens before our eyes that we will see the unspeakable reward that God will bestow on us for accomplishing faithfully His holy will on earth.

THE FAITH AND OBEDIENCE OF ABRAHAM.

"After these things," says the Scripture, "God tempted Abraham, and said to him: 'Abraham, Abraham.'

And he answered: 'Here am I.'

"And He said to him: 'Take thy only-begotten son Isaac, whom thou lovest, and go into the land of vision: and there thou shalt offer him for a holocaust upon one of the mountains which I will show thee.'

"So Abraham, rising up in the night, saddled his ass: and took with him two young men, and Isaac his son: and when he had cut the wood for the holocaust, he went his way to the place which God had commanded him. And on the third day, raising up his eyes, he saw the place afar off.

"And he said to his young men: 'Stay you here with the ass: I and the boy will go with speed as far as yonder, and after we have worshipped, will return to you.' And he took the wood for the holocaust, and laid it upon Isaac his son; and he himself carried in his hands fire and a sword.

"And as they two went on together, Isaac said to his father: 'My father.'

"And he answered: 'What wilt thou, son?'

"'Behold,' said he, 'fire and wood: where is the victim for the holocaust?'

"And Abraham said: 'God will provide himself a victim for a holocaust, my son.' So they went on together.

"And they came to the place which God had shown him, where he built an altar, and laid the wood in order upon it; and when he had bound Isaac his son, he laid him on the altar upon the pile of wood. And he put forth his hand and took the sword to sacrifice his son.

"And behold an angel of the Lord from Heaven called on him, saying: 'Abraham, Abraham.'

"And he answered: 'Here I am.'

"And he said to him: 'Lay not thy hand upon the boy, neither do thou anything to him: now I know that thou fearest God, and hast not spared thy only-begotten son for My sake.'

"Abraham lifted up his eyes, and saw behind his back a ram amongst the briers sticking fast by the horns, which he took and offered for a holocaust instead of his son."

Genesis xxii. 1 et seq.

AMONG THE ANGELS.

The following beautiful story is from the history of the ancient monks of Egypt:

There was a certain rich lady who had a great devotion to St. Maurice, the heroic commander of the Thebian Legion. This lady had an only child, a boy, and she resolved to spend her whole life in teaching him to be a Saint.

On the day of his baptism she consecrated him to God; and when he grew up to boyhood, she placed him in the monastery of St. Maurice, that he might be safe from all danger, and grow up piously in the fear of God.

For some years the mother's earnest desires were fulfilled even beyond her expectations. The boy was not only pious and good, but he was clever, and held a high place among his fellow-students.

He had, moreover, a sweet musical voice which charmed everyone who heard it, and it was his delight to join with the Fathers of the monastery as they sang the Divine Office.

His mother was in raptures of joy as she sat and listened to him singing the praises of God, and most earnestly did she pray to her Father in Heaven to preserve her dear child in his innocence, that one day he might join the holy angels in Heaven, to sing the praises of God for all eternity there.

This prayer was heard sooner than she desired; for in his youth he was seized with a fever and died. His mother was inconsolable at his loss. Sad and disconsolate, she watched by the dead body of her child; and when it was carried to the grave, and hidden from her sight forever, her grief was painful to behold. Day after day she sat in the church and listened to the religious as they chanted their holy prayers, and every time she heard them, the memory of the boy she had lost would come back to her, and fresh tears would burst forth from her eyes.

One day as she knelt in the church, weeping as usual, she fell asleep. And as she slept, her patron, St. Maurice, appeared to her.

"Why do you still continue to weep?" he said.

She answered: "I weep for my dear boy who is dead, and shall weep for him as long as I live, for he was my only consolation on earth."

"O woman," replied the Saint, "banish all sorrow from your heart, for the boy whom you love is now with us in Paradise. God took him to Himself, lest the world might stain his innocence, and he is now singing the praises of God in Heaven." These words gave the desolate mother great comfort. The Saint continued: "That you may know that my words are true, rise tonight, and go to the church at the hour of Matins, and you will hear the voice of your son singing along with the rest of the religious. Console yourself, therefore, for you have reason to rejoice rather than to weep, seeing that your son is now with God."

The woman awoke, and, not knowing whether it was a real vision or only a dream, she waited impatiently for the time of Matins.

At length it came, and she went in haste to the church. But no sooner had she entered it, than she heard the voice of her child singing beautifully as before. From that moment all her sorrow disappeared, for she knew now that her child was certainly in possession of eternal glory, and she thanked God with her whole heart.

Rodriguez: *Christ. Perf.*

THE SCHOOLMASTER'S CHILDREN.

There was a schoolmaster who had two children—a boy and a girl—who were distinguished among all the other children for their great piety and their childlike innocence. They were their father's joy, and he looked forward to them to be the support of his old age.

But God, Who disposes of all things in the manner He sees most useful to us, had arranged otherwise.

One day both the children became suddenly ill. The father happened to be absent from home at the time, and before he returned they were both dead.

The poor mother was afflicted beyond all that can be imagined. Tears of grief fell from her eyes in torrents as she gazed on the lifeless forms of her two little children, a short time before so happy and so full of mirth.

But she, like so many other saintly mothers, was full of faith. She looked beyond this weary world, and she knew that at that very moment her beloved children were gazing on the all-beautiful face of God in Heaven. She tried to dry her tears, and, taking the bodies, she herself carried them into another room, where with her own hands she prepared them for their burial, and covered them with a white cloth.

In the meantime the father returned home; he had not yet heard of the sad event that had occurred. Not seeing the children coming as usual to meet him, he said to his wife when he reached the house: "Where are the children?"

"They are not very far away," she answered, and then tried to speak of something else.

The husband, seeing that his wife was, as usual, calm and cheerful, thought that, although he did not see them, they must be quite safe, sat down to table and partook of the dinner she had prepared for him.

When he had finished, and had returned thanks, as was his custom, his wife said to him: "I am going to ask you a question. Some time ago I received from a rich gentleman a valuable treasure, which he wanted me to keep for him till he would come to ask me to give it back to him. He has come today to ask it from me. Do you think I should give it to him?" The schoolmaster looked at her in surprise. He thought it strange that he had never heard of this treasure before; but he at once answered: "Most assuredly; return it to him, since it belongs to him. Why do you ask me such a question?"

She replied: "Because I wanted you also to consent to my doing so."

As she said these words she rose, and, leading her husband into the room, raised the white cloth, and his eyes fell upon the lifeless bodies of his two children.

"O my God!" he cried out, pale with anguish; "O my children!" and he sank down in a chair that was near, and buried his face in his hands. His grief at length found relief in a flood of tears. His wife also wept.

Taking the trembling hand of her husband, she said to him: "Did you not tell me a few moments ago that it was my duty at once to return the treasure confided to my care, as soon as the owner came to seek it? God gave us these two little ones to keep for Him, till He would come and ask us to return them to Him. He has come for them to-day. Let us, then, with willing hearts give them back to Him, since they belong to Him, not to us."

The good man threw himself on his knees at the bedside, and with hands and eyes raised up to Heaven, he cried out: "The Lord has given, the Lord has taken away; blessed be the name of the Lord!"

The next day he laid them in their grave. Tears, indeed, fell from his eyes, for he loved his little children; but his heart was calm and resigned to the holy will of God.

From that day to the end of their lives the schoolmaster and his wife lived in the practice of piety, loving God with their whole hearts, and beloved by all their neighbors. Their bodies are now lying beside those of their children in the village churchyard, and their souls are, let us hope, reunited to their little ones above, according to the promise of Our Lord: "He that shall do the will of My Father Who is in Heaven, the same shall enter into the Kingdom of Heaven."

41

OUR PERFECTION CONSISTS IN DOING GOD'S WILL

Your perfection, my child, consists in fulfilling the duties of the state of life in which God has placed you, and in such a way as to please Him.

THE EMPORER WHO WANTE TO BE A MONK.

Henry, Emperor of Germany, was a Prince loved by all his subjects, not only on account of the firm and gentle way in which he governed them, but also because of his piety and valor. He had been victorious in many a battle, and lived in the enjoyment of great wealth.

But all these things had no value in his eyes; he aspired after higher and more lasting riches.

There was, at a little distance from his palace, a monastery over which the Blessed Richard was Abbot. Often did Henry go thither to spend some time in prayer, and to speak with the monks on heavenly things. Often also did he regret his high position in life, which hindered him from renouncing the world altogether, to live in that holy solitude where his heart already was.

One day, as he was entering the monastery accompanied by the Abbot and Haimon the Bishop, he suddenly stood still, as if some great thought had come into his mind. At length he cried out: "This is the place of my repose; here I shall dwell forever."

The Bishop took the Abbot aside, and said to him, "Did you observe the words the Emperor has just now spoken? He has resolved at last to lay aside the crown and scepter and to become a monk. Now, if you yield to his request, and receive him among your brethren, the empire which God has entrusted to his care will suffer a loss that nothing can repair."

The Abbot was lost in thought for a few moments. "I know what I shall do," he said; "I will both satisfy the pious desire of the Emperor, and at the same time preserve the peace of the State."

He then assembled all the monks, and in their presence asked the Emperor what he intended to do.

Henry burst into tears. He thought that now at last his great desire was to be granted him. "Venerable Father and brothers," he cried out, "I have resolved to forsake the vanities of the world, and to spend the rest of my days in this holy house in solitude and prayer, that I may save my soul."

The Abbot said to him: "Then, do you promise me that, according to the rule of this house, and according to the example of Jesus Christ, you will be obedient in all things till the day of your death?"

"With all my heart I promise," answered the Emperor.

"Then," said the Abbot, "I receive you into this monastery, and admit you among the number of my monks, and from this day I myself will take charge of your soul. But you must promise me again to do whatever I command you, in the Name of God."

Henry once more promised.

"It is therefore my will, and I command you in the Name of God to return to your palace, and continue to govern the empire which God has entrusted to you, that by your watchfulness and your zeal you may procure the eternal salvation of your subjects."

Henry, who never expected to receive this command, burst into tears; but, seeing now that it was the holy will of God that he should be placed on a throne, he cheerfully obeyed.

Lives of the Saints, July 15.

HOW HE BECAME PERFECT.

In a certain monastery in Spain there lived, in the fourteenth century, a very humble monk, who by his prayers worked many miracles.

Everyone was astonished at it, because, although he was a very good man, there was nothing very wonderful about him, and the other monks in the monastery seemed to be just as good and fervent as he was.

One day the Superior took him aside and asked him to tell him what he did more than the other monks, that God should choose him to work such wonderful miracles.

"Father," he replied, "I myself am astonished at it, and I do not know the reason of it: I am a great sinner, and have done much to offend God in my lifetime, and yet He is pleased to make choice of me to do these great things."

"But, my child," said the Superior, "do you not perform in secret some great penances, or say some long prayers? for it seems to me that you must do something more than the rest, to be so highly favored by God."

"No, Father," he replied; "I know of nothing; I do not perform any great penances, nor do I say any more prayers than the others do. I just content myself with trying to do everything to fulfill the will of God. When I am sick, I say to God, 'O my God, Thy will be done.' When my superiors tell me to do this or that, I consider it is the voice of God Himself I hear, and I do it immediately, even although I do not like it, and I always say, 'O my God, Thy will be done!'"

"But, my child," said the Abbot, "what did you do the other day, when that enemy of ours came and set fire to the house, which caused us so great a loss?"

"Father," replied the humble monk, "I said the Lord's Prayer, and when I came to these words, 'Thy will be done on earth as it is in Heaven,' I thought it was the holy will of God that this affliction happened to us; and I said again, 'O my God, Thy will be done on earth as it is in Heaven.'"

The Abbot at once saw that the reason why God loved this good monk so much was because of his humble submission to His holy will, and that he was so perfect because he was so obedient.

Let us be the same, obedient and submissive to the holy will of God, and if God does not give us the gift of miracles, He will at least bestow on us as great, or even greater, graces.

Schmidt: Cat. Historique.

THE PRIEST AND THE BEGGAR.

Thaulerius, a religious of the Order of St. Dominic, a very learned man, and very eloquent, had for many years earnestly prayed to God to send him an angel, or some great Saint, who would show him the way to become perfect.

One day, when he was in the church at his prayers, he heard a voice that said to him, "When you go out of the church, you will meet a person who will show you the way to become most perfect."

Full of delight at this, he rose up at once and went out, expecting to find some great Saint or learned man, who would tell him what he so much desired to know.

While he was standing on the steps leading to the church, looking on all sides for the person he had come to seek, he saw sitting there a poor old man, with scarcely any clothes to cover him, and these were only rags; his body was all covered with sores, and most loathsome to look at.

Thaulerius said to him, "Good-day, my poor man."

"Reverend Father," he answered, "I have never seen any bad day."

The monk was somewhat surprised at this unexpected answer, and, thinking that the poor man had not heard him rightly, he added, "May God grant you every good thing!" "God has sent me good things all my lifetime," he replied. Thaulerius, looking at the miserable appearance of the man, said again to him: "May God, then, make you always happy!"

"Thanks, dear Father, for your kind wishes," said the beggar; "but I have always been most happy, and, more than that, God has always given me everything I could desire."

"Well, that is indeed strange," said the monk; "but tell me how that can be; tell me how it can be possible that you who are so poor and so miserable should be able to say that you have always received good things from God; that He has given you everything you wished for, and that you have always been happy."

"Reverend Father," he replied, "it is all quite true; I never in my lifetime had a bad day nor a misfortune. Why are you astonished at this? Does not everything that takes place in this world, whether it be agreeable or disagreeable, come from the hand of God? And is not God my Father? And does He not know what is best for me, His child?

"This thought makes me always content, and I unite myself closely with God, and I try to be one with Him, my dear Father in Heaven; so that God's will is my will, and whatever pleases Him pleases me, because I am certain He always knows best what is good for me.

"If I am hungry, I praise God; if I am cold, I also thank God; if the wind is boisterous and the rain falls upon me, and if sickness afflicts me. I am quite content, because I know that God wishes it to be so. If men mock me, if they persecute me, and if the Devil assails me, I am still content, because I know that God, my Father, sees all, and will reward me; and that neither the Devil nor all the malice of men can ever do me any harm, since God is watching over me.

"And who am I, that I should think of preferring my own will to that of God? He is my Creator, and I am His creature; and didn't He love me much when He died for me upon the cross? How is it possible, then, that He could ever send me anything to harm me? Oh no! These things which you call misfortunes, such as my poverty and misery, are not evils, but a great good, because they will procure Heaven for me.

"On the contrary, the things which the people of the world call good are real evils, because they hinder us from going to God. I am quite indifferent, then, to whatever God sends me, for I know that whatever he sends is for the best, and must be for my good.

"Now, tell me, good Father, was I not right in saying that I never had a bad day, and never can have a bad day, so long as I keep resigned to the holy will of God?"

"But, my good man," said the monk, "if after all this God should condemn you to hell-fire, would you be content then?"

"God condemn me to hell-fire for trying to please Him! Never, Father; He never could do that! But even if God should wish this, I have two arms, and with these two arms I would seize hold of Him, and I would take Him with me, and most certainly I would rather be in Hell with God than in Heaven without Him. But I have no fear of that, because Hell was made, not for those who try to do God's holy will, but for those only who willfully rebel against it."

This poor man was the one God sent to the learned theologian to teach him how to become perfect, and if we do as he did, we shall also be perfect and reach Heaven; for Jesus Christ has, as we have often heard, expressly said: "He that doeth the will of My Father Who is in Heaven, the same shall enter into the Kingdom of Heaven."

Blosius: *Append. c. 1.*

BLESSED CATHERINE OF GENOA: A SAINT IN THE WORLD.

Blessed Catherine of Genoa, though living in the midst of the world and of its attractions, led the life of a religious in a convent.

One day a member of a religious Order said to her: "Why do you not renounce the world altogether, and embrace the religious life? for being retired from the world and its surroundings, you could love God more fervently, and serve Him with greater devotion."

She answered in words of holy indignation: "How can you say these words to me? Are we not best in the place to which God has called us? Until this time no creature or any created thing has hindered me from loving God as much as I wished and as much as I was able."

Our perfection, my child, therefore does not consist in any particular state of life, but in living piously in that state in which God desires us to serve Him.

Mansi: Disc. vi., n. 8.

My child, it seems impossible in the eyes of the world, and even to good Christians it appears at first sight to be very difficult, to be submissive to the holy will of God in many of the occurrences of this life; but in reality it is not so; for God has promised us to give us always sufficient grace to perform what He requires of us; and therefore it becomes not only possible, but easy, considering the recompense promised to those who do the will of God on earth as it is done in Heaven.

ST. JANE FRANCES RENOUNCES THE WORLD AT THE CALL OF GOD.

St. Jane Frances de Chantal, having lost her beloved husband, thought that she heard, and did really hear, the voice of God in her heart saying to her the words He, in the distant ages of the past, had said to Abraham: "Go forth out of thy country, and from thy kindred, and out of thy father's house, and come into the land which I will show thee" (Gen. xii. 1).

Obedient to the voice of God, she formed the resolution of renouncing the world and all its comforts which she had until then enjoyed; and as soon as possible she began to accomplish her design.

But who can describe the consternation of the household when she first made known to them that she was soon to leave them forever? Who can depict the grief that filled her own heart when she considered in detail the sacrifice she was about to make? The poor, who venerated her as their benefactress, expressed their sorrow in loud lamentations. The servants and domestics who served her sighed and wept. Her relatives, who confided in her as their adviser in all difficulties; her family, who loved her as only devoted and dutiful children know how to love, were all in dismay. Her father, now far advanced in years, who had looked on her as his only mainstay in the evening of his days, besought her not to forsake him.

She was, indeed, moved to the very depths of her being as these distressing cries reached her, but she was not shaken in her determination. God had called her: "Go forth from your father's house," He had said to her, and she obeyed.

There was still one trial left to her, and it was the greatest of them all. Her son, who had never ceased weeping since the terrible news had been brought to him, and who had prayed continually to God not to allow his mother to leave him, made one more last effort to overcome her constancy.

"O my most beloved mother, and dearer to me than anything else on earth," said he, as he fell prostrate at her feet on the day of her departure, "surely you cannot refuse the earnest request of one who owes to you his very existence. Since my tears and my supplications have hitherto been fruitless, and since you are determined to leave me, it will only be by passing over my body lying prostrate at your door. I am not able by force to detain you, but I will be the first victim you will immolate." Saying these words, he threw himself on the ground before the door, so that to be able to pass out it would be necessary for her to step over him.

His mother, on coming to the place, stopped for an instant; her courage seemed for a moment to desert her; her eyes were filled with tears, while her affectionate heart was torn within her.

But God supported her by His grace, and grace triumphed over nature. God spoke to her in her heart, and she overcame. Courageously she stepped over him as he lay on her path, and gained the victory—a victory which the world cannot comprehend, at which nature is dismayed, and at which even religion itself is amazed. That victory, gained for God's sake, assured to her in His own good time a reward, a hundredfold in this life and eternal happiness in the next.

May we always say with the same resignation, "May Thy will be done on earth as it is in Heaven!"

From her Life.

42

ALL THINGS ARE ARRANGED FOR OUR GOOD

Those things which people call misfortunes are often marks of God's special love for us. My child, your Heavenly Father always knows what is best for you.

POISON IN A FLOWER.

An English lady went from her own country to India, where she was for some time the guest of a French officer.

One morning she went out alone into the garden to enjoy the morning air. As she was walking among the gay flower-beds, she saw a flower of a most beautiful color; going over to it, she plucked it and began to smell it.

But hardly had she done this, when a negro who was in the garden sprang quickly to her side, and, snatching the flower out of her hand, crushed it to pieces, and threw it into a ditch. He said some words to her which she did not understand, and then ran away.

The lady was very angry at the rudeness of the slave. As soon as she entered the house, she told his master of the insult she had just received. The slave was at once sent for, that he might be punished for his fault.

But in a few words, spoken in the same language in which he had addressed the lady, the slave explained to his master why he had done what at first seemed so rude, and showed him that, unless he had done so, the lady would most certainly have been poisoned.

The flower the lady had plucked was one which, though very beautiful to look at, contained the most deadly poison. The slave, seeing the lady pluck the flower, and not being able to make her understand by words the danger she was in, saw no other way of saving her from death than by snatching the flower from her hand as he had done, and destroying it.

When the lady heard this explanation, instead of being angry at the good man, she thanked him for his kindness, and gave him a handsome reward.

SCHMIDT.

"YOUR MONEY OR YOUR LIFE!"

A rich merchant was returning home from a certain town with a large sum of money in his purse. He was on horseback. The way was long and solitary, and he had scarcely set out on his homeward journey, when the rain, which had for some time been threatening, began to fall in torrents, and he was soon wet through and through.

"They say God is good to us," he said to himself, "and that He ordains everything for our good. But what good can possibly come of this? I am already nearly drowned, and I have yet many weary miles to ride before I can reach shelter. I think God would have acted much more wisely if He had allowed me to reach my home before He sent down such a deluge of water."

As the gentleman was thus speaking, he came to a part of the road which was bordered on both sides by a thick wood. In this place robberies had often before been committed, because the thickness of the wood gave shelter to the thieves.

The gloom of the night, which was deepening every moment, and the dullness of the weather, made the gentleman anxious to reach the other end of the wood, so he began to ride more quickly that he might the sooner reach it.

But he had not gone far, when the horse suddenly stood still and threw its rider. The gentleman had scarcely time to regain his saddle, when he saw standing in the middle of the road a man disguised from head to foot, holding a pistol in his hand.

"Your money or your life!" were the words that reached the ears of the gentleman, and caused him to shudder.

In an instant he put spurs to his horse, thinking thus to gallop past him. But the robber, foreseeing this, raised his pistol and fired. The gentleman shut his eyes as he saw the flash in the darkness, and, thinking that his last hour had come, recommended his soul to God. It was all the work of an instant.

But he was not shot dead; he was not even hurt. He opened his eyes, saw the man still standing before him, and heard him uttering words of blasphemy and cursing. The pistol had missed fire, for the rain which had fallen so heavily had wet the powder while the ruffian had been loading it.

The gentleman saw at a glance what had occurred, and before the robber had time to rush upon him, he galloped onwards, and was soon beyond all danger. He did not once look behind him till he reached his home.

His wife and children saw him enter, pale and trembling, and, thinking that some terrible misfortune had happened to him, asked him in hurried accents to tell them what it was.

"I am quite safe," he said, "and without any injury. But had it not been for the deluge of rain, which I thought so great a misfortune when I set out on my journey, I never would have reached home alive."

He then related to them his adventure in the wood and his narrow escape from death. He ended with these words: "How foolish it was of me to complain of the weather that God sent, and how good it was of Him to have sent down such a heavy rainfall, which was most certainly the cause of my being preserved from death. It is evident that the robber, whoever he may be, knew that I was to pass that way with a large sum of money. If the pistol had gone off, I or the horse on which I rode would have been at least wounded, and I certainly would have been killed, for it would have been foolishness to have expected to have been spared by so desperate a villain.

"Let this be a lesson for you, my dearest children," he continued, speaking to his little ones, who, through joy at his escape, had thrown their arms around him; "God does indeed ordain everything for the best, although we cannot sometimes see the reason of it. Whenever you say that petition of the Lord's Prayer, 'Thy will be done,' think of this: If there had been no rain today, the powder would not have been wet, and you would not now have a father to speak to you again, or to cling to as you are now doing."

Catech. en Examples.

"THANKS BE TO GOD."

A young man was on his way to the ship that was to carry him over from France to England.

From his earliest childhood his parents had taught him to submit in everything to God's holy will, and to see in everything that happened the work of God.

To keep this always before his mind, he had the custom of saying every time anything good or evil happened to him, "This is for my greater good: thanks be to God."

The ship was on the point of leaving her moorings, and the young man began to run that he might reach it in time. But as he kept his eyes fixed on the ship, he did not see a block of wood that lay upon the street. He stumbled over it in his great haste, and fell to the ground. A heavy box which he carried on his shoulder fell upon his leg, and broke it in two.

His first words were, as usual, "This is for my greater good: thanks be to God."

The people who saw the accident, and who ran to lift him up, were astonished to hear him say these words. One of them said to him, "How can this accident, which has hindered you from going on your journey, be for your greater good?"

"I cannot tell you," he replied; "but God knows; and although I may never know why He has hindered me from proceeding on this journey, which I thought so necessary and important, He certainly willed it, and that is enough for me. May His blessed will be done."

Some of the people laughed at him and said he was foolish, but others with better feelings were greatly edified.

In the meantime the ship sailed without him, and he was carried home.

During that night a terrific gale, so common on that coast, sprang up, and the next day many shipwrecks were reported. Amongst the vessels lost was the one in which the young man was to have sailed to England.

"Was I not right," he said, when he heard of the disaster, "in saying that God sent me a broken leg for my greater good? Do you not see that had I been able to reach the ship, I would now be at the bottom of the sea?"

The people saw in this event how wise are the ways of God's providence, and how happy are those who submit in all things to His blessed will. It will be for you also, my child, a lesson; try to think of this every time you say these words of the Lord's Prayer, "Thy will be done on earth as it is in Heaven."

Schmidt: Catch. Hist., i. 123.

43

"AS IT IS IN HEAVEN."

LITTLE BARTHOLOMEW'S PRAYER.

There was a poor boy named Bartholomew, who lived at Ulm at the beginning of the seventeenth century. His pious parents taught him every day how he was to serve God, so that he might possess Him in Heaven forever; and the child endeavored every day to keep from all evil, and to do all for God.

When he was about eleven years old, a terrible plague broke out in that country, which carried off daily a great number of the people. Bartholomew was struck by it. As he lay on his little bed, suffering and preparing to die, he said to God: "O my God, how little is everything that is in this world! I cannot take anything out of it with me but the good works I have done for Thy glory. Ah, they are very few, it is true, but Thou knowest, O my God, that I tried to keep away from the smallest faults, and that I love Thee above all things. Oh, have pity on me, my dear Heavenly Father, and if Thou hast decreed to take me out of this world by this illness, receive me, I beseech Thee, into Thy paradise, where I may be forever happy with Thee, and be pleased to console my parents when I am gone. 'Thy will be done on earth as it is in Heaven.'"

Bartholomew recovered from his sickness; he spent his whole life in the service of God, and died a happy death in the year 1658.

My child, may your only desire in this life be like his, to live with God here, that you may live eternally with Him in Heaven.

PART VII

"GIVE US THIS DAY OUR DAILY BREAD"

44

OUR DEPENDENCE ON GOD FOR EVERYTHING

"Give us this day our daily bread" is the fourth petition of the Lord's Prayer. When we say these words, we pray that God may give us daily all that is necessary for our souls and bodies.

When we say "Give us," we humbly acknowledge that God is the Master of all things, and that if we desire anything, it is Him we must ask for it, because of ourselves we have nothing; all must come from God. Let us therefore ask Him with confidence for our daily bread, when we say this petition of the Lord's Prayer.

THE BLESSED CURÉ OF ARS ON THIS PETITION.

"We are made up of two parts, my children: we have a soul and a body. We ask God to give us the food we need for our poor body, and He answers us by making the earth produce what is needful to support it.

"But we also ask Him to nourish our soul, which is the better part of us. But the earth cannot do this; it is by far too little; it hungers after God, and God alone can satisfy it. Therefore the good God did not consider it too much to come into this world, and take a body like ours, so that that body might become the nourishment of our souls.

'My flesh is meat indeed,' says Jesus Christ, 'and the bread that I will give you is My flesh for the life of the world.'

"The food we need for our souls is in the tabernacle. Oh, how beautiful this is, my children! When the priest takes the Sacred Host in his hands and shows it to you, your soul can truly say, 'This is my food!'

"O my children, we have far too much happiness! It is only when we get to Heaven that we will be able to understand it. What a pity!"

From His Life.

THE BISHOP AND THE HUMBLE GARDENER.

Monseigneur de Flammeville, Bishop of Perpignan, one day met a gardener who was returning home from his work in the evening.

During his short conversation with him he asked him in what manner he served God, and how he said his prayers.

The humble man replied that he was not learned, and could not say long prayers, but that he tried to speak to his Heavenly Father as a little child does to his father in this world whom he loves. "I speak to Him in words like these: 'O my Father in Heaven, how happy I am in having Thee for my Father, and with what joy I am filled when I think that Heaven will one day be my dwelling-place!' Give me Thy grace that I may always show myself to be a child worthy of Thee. Never allow me to do anything that will keep me from seeing Thee in Heaven.

"And since Thou hast commanded me to ask Thee for my daily bread, I beseech Thee to give me three kinds of bread. In the first place give me the bread of Thy Divine Word, that I may learn what I should do to give Thee the greatest pleasure; then be pleased to give me often the Body and Blood of Thy beloved Son Jesus to be the food of my soul; and lastly, bestow on me what Thou seest necessary for my body, that I may be enabled to live for Thy honor and glory."

The Bishop, filled with astonishment and admiration in seeing such sublime knowledge in one so humble, said, with tears in his eyes, "Would to God that the great ones and the learned ones of this world would pray as you do!"

A LITTLE CHILD'S FAITH.

In a certain town in Holland there once lived a very poor widow, who had a large family. One night her children went to her, and said, "O mother, have you no bread for us tonight? We are so very hungry."

The poor woman burst into tears, and could not answer them. She fell on her knees, and, raising up her tearful eyes to Heaven, prayed to her Father there not to allow her little ones to die of hunger.

When she rose from her knees, her eldest child, a boy of about eight years, whispered softly to her, "Dear mother, did you not read to us a short time ago that God once sent a raven to feed one of His prophets when he was hungry like us?"

"Ah, yes, dearest child," she said; "but that was long, long ago; and, besides, he was a very holy man whom God fed in that way."

"But, mother," said the child, "could not God do today what He once did long ago? And are we not His dear children as much as the prophet? I will go and open the door, and perhaps he may send a raven with bread to us also."

So the child, in his simple faith, went to the door and opened it. The light of the little lamp in the hut shone through the open door on the pathway that led towards it.

Now, it came to pass that a gentleman who was on a journey happened to pass near the place, and seeing the light burning in the hut at so late an hour, and the door wide open, he thought that there must be something amiss; so he went in and asked them the reason of it.

The widow answered that her little boy had opened the door, and then told him what he had just said, and how he hoped that the raven might come to them and bring them something to eat.

The gentleman sat down, and, taking the boy to his side, caressed him. "My dear child," he said, "God has not sent you a raven with bread, but He has heard your prayers, and has sent me instead. Come with me, and I will give you that bread which you expected, with such confidence, to receive."

So he led the boy to a village, and procured enough bread for that night. He also gave him a sum of money to purchase sufficient bread for many days to come.

When that little family had satisfied their hunger, they knelt down to thank their Father in Heaven, Who sends help to those who ask Him with confidence for it in their necessities. The good gentleman went on his journey, happy in the thought that God had chosen him for this good work, and the children prayed that night for him in these words: "Be pleased, O Lord, to give to our kind benefactor, for Thy Name's sake, life everlasting."

45

GOD WILLS US TO LABOR FOR OUR DAILY BREAD.

Although we must pray to God for everything we need, since, as St. James says, "every best gift and every perfect gift is from above, coming down from the Father of lights," yet it is the will of God that we should labor and do what we can, on our part, to receive the gifts we ask; for God has given us all certain talents, and it is His holy will that we should make use of them, for our temporal support.

ST. JOSEPH AND THE INFANT JESUS.

The Eternal Son of God, Who was confided to the care of St. Joseph, in order that he might provide for Him what was needed for His temporal support, assisted His foster-father, not by working miracles, but by the labor of his hands. We know that he could have procured food for the holy family in a miraculous manner, if such had been His will, as easily as He was able in after times to feed with a few loaves the thousands who had accompanied Him to the desert; but we do not read that He ever did this. He was pleased, for our example, to labor at the trade of a carpenter to contribute to the support of His humble home.

ST. PAUL LABOURS WITH HIS HANDS FOR HIS SUPPORT.

St. Paul, who had learned the trade of tent-making, not infrequently worked at it during his apostolate. It is thus he writes to the Thessalonians: "For you yourselves know how you ought to imitate us; for we were not disorderly among you, neither did we eat any man's bread for nothing, but in labor and in toil, we worked night and day, lest we should be chargeable to any of you; not as if we had not power, but that we might give ourselves a pattern unto you to imitate us. For also when we were with you, this we declared to you; that if any man will not work, neither let him eat."

And when he was bidding a last farewell to the clergy of Ephesus, he said: "I have not coveted any man's silver, gold, or apparel, as you yourselves know: for such things as were needful for me and them that are with me, these hands have furnished. I have showed you all things, how that so laboring you ought to support the weak, and to remember the word of the Lord Jesus, how He said: 'It is a more blessed thing to give, rather than to receive.'"

Acts of the Apostles xx. 33.

46

THE FOOD OF OUR SOULS IS, FIRSTLY, THE HOLY EUCHARIST

S ince the soul is incomparably more precious than the body, we should, above all other things, ask for that food which is necessary for its maintenance.

The food of the soul is, in the first place, Our Lord Himself in the Holy Eucharist, and we ought to receive Him daily at least in spirit and desire.

"I AM THE LIVING BREAD."

"When therefore the multitude saw that Jesus was not there [in the ships that came in from Tiberias], nor His disciples, they took shipping and came to Capernaum, seeking for Jesus. And when they found Him on the other side of the sea, they said to Him: 'Rabbi, when camest Thou hither?'

"Jesus answered and said: 'Amen, amen, I say to you, you seek Me, not because you have seen miracles, but because you did eat of the loaves, and were filled. Labor not for the meat that perisheth, but for that which endureth unto life everlasting, which the Son of man will give you. For Him hath God the Father sealed.'

"They said therefore unto Him: 'What shall we do, that we may work the works of God?'

"Jesus answered and said to them: 'This is the work of God, that you believe in Him Whom He hath sent.'

"They said therefore to Him: 'What sign therefore dost Thou show, that we may see, and may believe Thee? What dost Thou work? Our fathers did eat manna in the desert, as it is written: He gave them bread from Heaven to eat.'

"Then Jesus said to them: 'Amen, amen, I say to you; Moses gave you not bread from Heaven, but My Father giveth you the true bread from Heaven. For the bread of God is that which cometh down from Heaven, and giveth life to the world.'

"They said therefore unto him: 'Lord, give us always this bread.'

"And Jesus said to them: 'I am the Bread of life: he that cometh to Me shall not hunger; and he that believeth in Me shall never thirst. . . .'

"The Jews therefore murmured at Him, because He had said: 'I am the living Bread which came down from Heaven. . . .'

Jesus therefore answered, and said to them: 'Murmur not among yourselves. No man can come to Me, except the Father Who hath sent Me draw Him: and I will raise him up at the last day. . . . I am the Bread of life. Your fathers did eat manna in the desert, and are dead. This is the bread which cometh down from Heaven, that if any man eat of it, he may not die. I am the living Bread which came down from Heaven. If any man eat of this bread, he shall live forever: and the bread that I will give is My flesh, for the life of the world.'

"The Jews therefore strove among themselves, saying: 'How can this man give us His flesh to eat?'

"And Jesus said to them: 'Amen, amen, I say unto you: except you eat of the flesh of the Son of man, and drink His blood, you shall not have life in you. He that eateth My flesh, and drinketh My blood, hath everlasting life: and I will raise him up at the last day. For My flesh is meat indeed, and My blood is drink indeed. He that eateth My flesh, and drinketh My blood, abideth in Me, and I in him. As the living Father hath sent Me, and I live by the Father: so he that eateth Me, the same also shall live by Me. This is the bread that came down from Heaven. Not as your fathers did eat manna, and are dead. He that eateth this bread shall live forever.'

"After this many of His disciples went back, and walked no more with Him (for hearing these words, they said: 'This is a hard saying, and who can hear it?').

"Then Jesus said to the twelve: 'Will you also go away?'

"And Simon Peter answered Him: 'Lord, to whom shall we go? Thou hast the words of eternal life. And we have believed and have known that Thou art the Christ, the Son of God."

St. John vi.

THE FOOD OF THE STRONG.

There was a rich merchant in Paris who had for a long time neglected his religious duties, and was leading a very worldly life. He had lost his wife a few years after his marriage, and was left with two infant daughters. As soon as they were of age, he sent them to a convent to be educated by the nuns.

In this happy home they received an education which fitted them for the position they were afterwards to occupy in the world. They also learned there, what was of still greater importance, how to practice their religion as became good and pious Christians.

When the elder of the two had reached her sixteenth year, her father took her home, as she was then of age to attend to the affairs of his household.

At home she was as attentive to her religious duties as she had been at the convent; but she had to perform many of them in secret not to displease her father.

One morning her father happened to go out much earlier than usual, and met his daughter coming along the street. He was at first surprised to see her there at so early an hour, and he asked her where she had been.

"I have been to church to hear Holy Mass," she replied.

"And have you been to Communion today?" he asked in an angry tone.

"Yes, my dear father, I have, and I prayed very much for you."

"Do you often go to Communion?" said the father, in still greater anger.

"Yes, dearest father, I go very often," she replied, "and it is there that I get strength and courage to accomplish all my duties at home."

The father turned away his head, and did not speak. When his daughter looked up, she saw tears in his eyes; and when he was able to speak, he said, in a voice half choked with emotion: "Oh, what a happiness it is for me to have a daughter like you! Go to Communion, my child, as often as you wish, since it makes you so good and dutiful, and continue to pray for me." That man did not at once become a fervent Christian, but in a short time the prayers of his daughter and her good example obtained for him that grace. He is still living, and may often be seen kneeling by his daughter's side at the holy altar, nourishing his soul with the bread of eternal life.

Monsigneur de Ségur.

"GIVE HIM TO ME AGAIN."

One day St. Francis de Sales was giving Holy Communion to the faithful in the little church of a country village.

An old man came up to the altar-rails for Communion. The Saint at once remembered that he had seen him approach to Communion that same day, at an earlier Mass. So he said to him, "My good friend, have you not already received Our Divine Lord this morning?"

"Yes, Father," replied the old man.

"Well, then, my child," said the Bishop, "you must not come twice to Communion in one day; so go back to your place again."

"O my Father," cried out the old man, "do give Him to me again; I felt so happy, so very happy in His company."

St. Francis could not help admiring the fervor and simplicity of the good old man, and as he could not grant him his request, he said to him, "Well, my dear old friend, go away this time, but come back again to-morrow morning, and I promise you that I will give you Our Blessed Lord once more."

The man went away consoled; and next morning, as soon as it was light, he was in the church, and had the happiness of again receiving Holy Communion.

This he did every day as long as he was able, and when the hour of his death came he felt no fear, but was full of joy; for he saw that he was now about to see face to face Him Whom he had so often received in Holy Communion.

Life of St. Francis de Sales.

A GREAT SINNER CHANGED INTO A GREAT SAINT.

In the days of St. Philip Neri there was in Rome a student who had for a long time been a slave to certain grievous sins. One day he heard of this great Saint, and of his kindness to those especially who had fallen into great sins. So he went to Confession to him, and told him that he had been in the custom of committing certain very grievous sins, and that, although he had often tried to break off the bad habits, he had never been able to succeed.

St. Philip told him to take courage, and asked him to promise to do what he would tell him.

"Yes, Father," he answered, "I promise. I will do anything you tell me if I shall only be able to become good again."

"Well, my child, I will now give you absolution, because you are very sorry for your sins, and you will go to Holy Communion tomorrow morning. And if it should happen, as I pray God it may not, that you fall into the same great sin again, come back to me at once, and I will tell you what to do."

The next evening St. Philip saw the same young man coming back to Confession. He had fallen again. The Saint helped him as he had done before, bade him try again, and told him, as he had done on the previous day, to go to his Communion next morning.

The poor young man, attacked on one side by the force of his evil habit, and on the other by the desire to return to the service of God, found in the Holy Eucharist such courage to persevere, that for thirteen days in succession he came back to St. Philip with the same sad tale, and was always told to go to Communion.

At last the grace of God triumphed. Jesus, in the Holy Communion he had daily received, gave him so much strength that he was able to banish the temptation and to remain faithful.

He did not live long after his conversion, but during the short time that elapsed before he died, he edified the whole city by his zeal and his virtues.

He liked to tell on all occasions the story of his conversion, in order to encourage poor sinners, and make young people understand that their salvation lay in frequently receiving Jesus Christ in Holy Communion.

47

GOD'S HOLY GRACE IS ALSO THE FOOD OF THE SOUL

The food of the soul is also God's grace, which enables you, my child, to bear patiently the trials of this world, and so gain merit for Heaven.

THE BURDEN OF LIFE.

An old man was walking along the road with a heavy load of fire-wood on his shoulders. He was carrying it to his cottage, where his little grandchildren were anxiously waiting his return. But as he was old and feeble, as well as hungry, his strength gave way, and he fell down on the ground beside his burden.

"Oh," he cried, "is there no one to help me? My children are cold and hungry at home, and I am not able to reach them to give them what they need."

A young man who was passing by heard these words, and, coming up to him, said: "Do not worry yourself about your burden, my friend; I will help you. But first let us rest while we eat something."

Saying this, he spread out before him bread, meat, and wine, and, sitting down beside him, they both ate and drank.

When the meal was finished, they prepared to continue their journeys. The young man bade his aged companion goodbye, and at once went away. The old man stood surprised and disappointed. "I thought that he was going to help me to carry my heavy burden," he said, "and he has gone off and left me alone."

With a heavy heart he stooped to lift it up, when, wonderful to relate, he found he could carry it with ease. The food the young man had given him had refreshed him so much that he had now sufficient strength to carry his burden home alone.

So it is with the grace of God. It does not take away from us the burden of life, but it gives us strength to bear it. Hence in our daily prayers we ask God for the help we need to accomplish the work He has given us to do each day, when we say, "Give us this day our daily bread."

Bishop Gilmour.

48

WE FEED OUR SOULS BY HEARING THE WORD OF GOD

Our souls are also fed by hearing the Word of God, and by reading good books. Alas! my child, how many people willfully neglect to listen to the words of those who speak to them in God's Name, or to read those books which are written for their instruction. They expose their souls to die of hunger by depriving them of that food which makes God's will known to them, which encourages them in their temptations, and supports them in their trials, and also makes them increase in virtue.

My child, be not like them; remember that Jesus Christ said: "Blessed are they who hear the Word of God." Endeavour, therefore, to be among the number of these blessed ones.

ST. PETER OF ALCANTARA AND THE NOBLE LADY.

There dwelt in one of the cities in which St. Peter was preaching his missionary sermons a lady of high rank, who was especially conspicuous for her great fortune and her vanity. She spent most of her wealth in dances, plays, and other vain amusements suggested by the spirit of the world to those who are in love with it.

One day, while conversing with some ladies of her acquaintance about the wonderful conversions effected by the preaching of the Saint, she said to them that she attributed these conversions to his instability and to the weakness of his mind. But they, on the contrary, said that they considered them to be the effect of the power and holiness of the preacher, in whose praise they said so much that the noble lady felt within her a great desire to go and see him, and hear him preach.

She accordingly one day went to the church where the Saint was preaching. As usual she was magnificently attired, and entering the church with great dignity, took up her position near the pulpit. She then, for the first time, raised up her eyes towards him. But at that moment what a change came over her! At this first glance she beheld before her a man whose body was emaciated and worn out with austerities, and she was so much covered with shame and confusion, when she contrasted her condition with his, that she let down her veil to hide her face, for she thought that the eyes of the man of God were fixed upon her, reproaching her with her contemptible conduct and her love of dress.

She listened to his words with the deepest attention, and when he had ended, she rose up and returned silently to her dwelling. From that moment she began a new life, for the words of the Saint had shown her the deplorable condition of her soul. She laid aside her jewellery and her superb dress, and assumed one more modest and more becoming a Christian; then she hastened to the house where St. Peter resided, and in deep humility threw herself upon the ground at his feet without being able to utter a single word.

He received her with the most tender charity, and with words inflamed with the love of God, encouraged her to persevere in the new life she had begun. She made a good confession of the sins of her whole life, and changed her prodigality into abundant alms; in a particular manner she applied herself to prayer and mortification, in the exercise of which virtues she persevered fervently till the hour of her happy death.

Life of St. Peter Alcantara.

THE HERMIT AND HIS BASKETS.

"Father," said a hermit one day to his Superior, "what is the use of my going to hear sermons, because no matter how attentively I listen to the words of the preacher, I can never keep in mind what he is speaking about?"

The Superior, wanting to show him, in a manner which he would not forget, that he always gained some little benefit from every sermon he heard, although he might not perceive it, said to him: "What are these things you are carrying in your hands?"

"Two baskets, Father," he answered.

"Go, then, take one of these baskets, and bring me some water in it from the river down there."

The hermit looked with surprise into his master's face to see if he had understood him rightly, for he knew very well that he could not carry water in a basket; but seeing that he appeared to be in earnest, and thinking that he must have some good reason for giving him so strange an order, obeyed, and went at once with the basket to the river.

He dipped it into the water, and, drawing it out quickly, ran in haste to his master, but long before he reached him the water had all run out.

The Father told him to go again a second and a third time. The obedient man did so, but the result was the same; the basket was always quite empty before he reached the place where his Superior stood.

When this was done the third time, he told the hermit to place the basket at the side of the other one, and asked him if he saw any change in the appearance of the basket, or any difference between it and the other one.

"No, I do not see much," he replied; "the only difference I can see is that the one I put into the water looks much cleaner than it did before, and much brighter than the other."

"Ah," replied the father, "that is just the difference; and so it is with your soul. As the basket could not contain the water on account of the many openings by which it rushed out, yet became cleaner and brighter every time it was dipped into the river, so also your soul, although it seems it cannot retain the Word of God, yet it derives much profit from hearing it: for it inspires you for the moment with a hatred of sin and a love of virtue, which in itself is a great grace. Continue, my child, to hear God's holy Word as often as you can, for you will always learn something about Him which perhaps you did not know before, or hear something about him which you may have forgotten."

Vit. Patrum.

WE FEED OUR SOULS ALSO BY READING GOOD BOOKS

Next to hearing the Word of God, there is nothing so profitable as to read pious books; this is another of the many ways which God in His goodness has appointed for feeding our souls.

ST. JOHN COLUMBINO'S CONVERSION.

St. John Columbino, who became the founder of a religious Order in the fourteenth century, owed his conversion to reading a pious book.

One day when he came home, after having passed a busy day at his employment, and was in consequence tired and weary, he asked his wife if his dinner were ready. She answered that it was not, but that it would be so in a short time.

John was so angry at this that, giving way to his passion, he turned over some of the furniture of the room, shut the doors with great violence, and burst forth into words of terrible imprecation against his poor wife. She tried to calm him, and said to him with great meekness: "Have a little patience, John; I will make all the haste in my power, and dinner will be ready in a few minutes. In the meantime, just sit down and read a few pages of this book." At the same time she handed him the Life of St. Mary of Egypt.

John took the book into his hands, and threw it with violence at the head of his wife, who, by quickly bending down her head, avoided the blow. The meekness, patience, and piety of his worthy spouse touched Columbino, and he began to be ashamed of his cruelty towards her. He took up the book which had fallen on the ground, and at first contented himself with examining the cover. Then he opened it to see what like the interior was, and finally began to read it.

As soon as he had read a few lines he felt a desire to read more. He continued to read in silence, and as he read the thought of his dinner soon passed entirely out of his mind, so great was the interest he felt in the book.

At length his wife drew near to him, and said: "The dinner is now ready, John; come and eat it."

But John, without as much as raising up his eyes from the book, said to her: "My good wife, would you be good enough to wait a little till I have finished what I am reading?"

When he had finished the part he was reading, he laid down the book. All was changed now. He raised his eyes towards his wife, asked her to forgive him for his conduct, and begged her to pray for him; "because," he said, "I am going to become a Saint. This book has opened my eyes, and has made me hear the voice of the Lord, and I am determined to listen to that voice."

John from that moment totally changed his life, and became a Saint. His happy death took place in the year 1367.

Life of St. John Columbino.

My child, St. Augustine says: "When we pray, we speak to God; and when we read good books, God speaks to us."

HOW ST. IGNATIUS BECAME A SAINT.

Ignatius of Loyola was a young man whose only ambition in life was to gain for himself a great name by his bravery and deeds of valor. He had forgotten altogether the one great end of his creation, and lived as if he had nothing to hope for hereafter.

He had not, it is true, lost the gift of faith, but had imbibed so much of the spirit of the world that all his thoughts were fixed upon it, and although he never yielded to any dishonorable act or anything that would stain his moral character, yet he lived at enmity with God, and thought only of the honors, the glory, and the pleasures of the present life.

An occasion soon occurred which gave him the opportunity he continually aspired after, of gaining renown. A war broke out between Charles V., Emperor of Germany, and the King of France. Ignatius hastened to offer his services to aid in the defense of Pampluna against the attack of the French army, which was advancing to besiege it. His offer was accepted, and he was left in Pampluna by the Viceroy, not to command, but to encourage the garrison. He did all that lay in his power to persuade them to defend the city, but in vain.

However, when he saw them open the gates to the enemy, to save his own honor he retired into the citadel with only one soldier who had the courage to follow him. The garrison of this fortress deliberated likewise whether they should surrender, but Ignatius encouraged them to stand their ground. The French attacked the place with great fury, and with their artillery made a wide breach in the wall, and attempted to take it by assault. Ignatius appeared upon the breach at the head of the bravest part of the garrison, and with his sword in his hand endeavored to drive back the enemy; but in the heat of the combat a shot from a cannon broke from the wall a bit of stone, which struck and bruised his left leg, and the ball itself in the rebound broke and shivered his right leg. The garrison, seeing him fall, surrendered at discretion.

The French used their victory with moderation, and treated the prisoners well, especially Ignatius, in consideration of his quality and valor. They carried him at first to the General's quarters, and soon after sent him in a litter carried by two men to the castle of Loyola, which was not far from Pampeluna.

It was long before he could be removed from his couch even after his legs had begun to heal. He was in perfect health, but found the time of inaction tedious to his martial spirit. As he had a special attraction to tales of chivalry, he asked his attendant to bring him some book of romances, or the fabulous histories of knight-errantry. None such books being then found in the castle of Loyola, his servant brought him books containing the lives of Our Divine Savior, of His Blessed Mother, and of the Saints. This kind of reading was not what the wounded man would have chosen, but as no others could be procured he was glad to read them to pass away the time.

He read first one and then the other, and soon began to relish them and to spend whole days in reading them. He chiefly admired in the Saints their love of solitude and of the Cross. He learned there also that among the anchorites there had been many persons of quality and possessing great riches, who, renouncing all these things for God's sake, buried themselves alive in caves and dens, pale with fasting, and covered with haircloth, and he said to himself: "These men were of the same nature and frame as I am; why, then, should not I do what they have done?"

As he read the Life of Our Divine Redeemer, he felt his heart inflamed with the great desire to love Him more and more. Not only did he read it over and over again, but he wrote down in a book the pious thoughts that moved his heart, for now he could think of nothing else. The world had now passed out of his mind, and he thought only of God and of heavenly things. It is related that in this book, whenever he wrote the holy Name of Jesus, he always did so in letters of gold, and that he always wrote in letters of silver the august name of Mary.

It was thus that, by reading pious books, one of the greatest Saints in Heaven, and the Founder of the Society of Jesus, was changed from being a child of the world to become the means of leading so many myriads of souls to God and to Heaven.

Let us, then, feed our souls daily with this same spiritual food, that we also may become more and more fervent in the love of God.

Life of St. Ignatius, July 31.

MY ABC AGAIN.

A gentleman went to make his retreat in a certain monastery in order to prepare himself for a happy death.

It was the custom in this monastery to lend some pious books to those who went to make their retreat, to enable them to do so with greater fruit. Amongst these books there was always a Little Catechism of the Christian Doctrine.

As soon as the gentleman entered the house, he was brought to the Superior, who gave him the books and the necessary instructions about how the exercises of the retreat were to be performed.

When he was looking over the various books put into his hands he came to the Little Catechism. He looked at it, and after turning over a few of the pages, he said: "This is a child's Catechism, Father; what am I going to do with it?"

"Read it from the beginning to the end with the utmost attention," replied the Superior.

"O Father," answered the gentleman, "you surely do not mean to say that you are going to send me back to the ABC again. I knew that little book from beginning to end when I was only ten years old, and I do not require to learn it again."

"But, my child," said the other, "may you not have forgotten it since then?"

"Oh no," he replied; "it is true I may not remember the exact words of the Catechism, because, having been so long engrossed with business in the world, it is quite natural that I should forget them; but that does not matter much if I retain the meaning of what the words express."

"And are you quite sure that you do retain this knowledge? May you not have forgotten even that? Your business connections with the world, which may have impaired your memory in the one, may have also done so in the other. Let me see."

And he began to question him about God and some of the most

essential points of our holy Faith, and the gentleman was obliged to admit that he had not so clear a notion of some of them as he once had, and that he had even erroneous notions about many things.

"You see, my dear sir," continued the Father, "we act wisely in placing this little book in the hands of those who come here, and it would be well if people in the world would bear in mind that the ordinary way which God in His wisdom has ordained to instruct us, His children, in the knowledge of Who He is and what He requires of us, is by means of sermons and instructions. The little book which you hold in your hand is as much for the old man as for the child, for the learned as for the ignorant. And the man who knows it well, little as it is, knows more than the most profound philosopher in the world."

The gentleman saw at once the truth of these words, and during the leisure moments of his after life he might be seen sometimes reading a small book which he constantly carried with him in his pocket; it was the Little Catechism.

Noël: Cat. de Rodes.

50

THE SUFFERINGS AND TRIALS OF THIS LIFE FEED THE SOUL

S ufferings, trials, and afflictions are sent by God to feed the soul; by them we are led to think of Him, and of the end for which He made us.

THE SHEPHERD AND THE LAMB.

There once lived in a village in Germany a gentleman and his wife. They were both Catholics, but they thought more of this life than of that which is to come, and were very careless about their religious duties.

They had only one child. But as they were not good themselves, the boy would have been left to grow up without religion, and in ignorance of his duty, had not God had pity on him, and visited him with a fatal illness. He took him out of this world, and the child went to Heaven before he had lost his baptismal innocence.

If the parents had been pious, they would not have grieved so much over their loss; but instead of submitting to the holy will of God with Christian resignation, they murmured against Him for having taken from them a child whom they so much loved.

One day they went to the priest. "You tell us that God is good," they said, "and that He loves us as a father loves his children. If such is the truth, tell us why He has been so cruel to us? He has taken away from us our only child, and left us to spend the rest of our days in sorrow. How, then, can you say that God is good or that He loves us?"

The priest answered: "My friends, do not murmur in this way against God. He indeed loves you, and as a special mark of His love for you He has taken your little one to Heaven."

The child's parents were about to make an angry answer, but the priest held up his hand as if to keep them silent.

"Hear me to the end," he said. "There was once a shepherd who had a large flock of sheep. He prepared in the sheep-cot some delicious food for them; but when he opened the door and tried to make them go in they would not enter. He made use of every effort to entice them, but in vain. At last he went in amongst them, and took in his arms a little lamb, and carried it in. As soon as the rest of the sheep saw the lamb in the sheep-cot they all went in after it.

"Now this is what Jesus Christ has done to you. He has prepared for you in Heaven a beautiful feast, and has over and over again asked you to make ready to partake of it.

"Till now you have always refused; you have allowed yourselves to be so much taken up with earthly things that you have forgotten the heavenly home your Father above has prepared for you. But now He has taken from you your child, whom you loved so much, and placed him in Heaven, that you may be, as it were, compelled to lead a good life and go in after him."

51

GOD'S CARE OF OUR TEMPORAL NEEDS

Jesus Christ has again and again declared that if we seek in the first place the food of our souls, He will take care that we shall have sufficient for our bodily wants.

HERMANN, THE PIOUS TAILOR.

There lived in another village in Germany a tailor, whose name was Hermann. For twenty years this good man supported his family by working at his trade, and during all that time they never knew what want was. He had also, by his good example and by watchful care, taught his children to serve God in this world, that they might be happy with Him forever in the next.

But in the year 1770 a great famine broke out over the country, and the good Hermann often passed three or four days without any work. Very soon he had to sell even the furniture of the house to buy bread for his little ones. At last even this failed him, and one morning he rose from his bed without knowing where he was to find a morsel of food for his famishing children.

He was surrounded by them crying out to him for bread, and

holding out their little hands to him. "O father, we are so hungry," they cried; "give us something to eat."

These words pierced his very heart. To console them he said: "I have nothing just now to give you, my dear children, but try and have a little patience till midday, and then we shall have enough to eat."

"But where will it come from?" they all cried out.

He pointed with his finger towards Heaven, and then, rising up, he left them, that they might not see his tears.

He went into the next room, and falling down on his knees, prayed to God in these words: "O my God, shall I have the grief to see my little ones die of hunger before my eyes? Canst Thou, Who givest food to the birds of the air, allow these Thy children to perish from hunger? Oh no, for Thou art so good, and Thy mercy is above all Thy works. Oh, then, come and help us, for now is the time." As he was ending this prayer, one of the children came running to tell him that there was someone at the door who wanted to speak to him. It was a lady, who came to ask if he could make some clothing for her three children, who were to assist at a marriage in a few days. To induce him to do the work more quickly she brought him a little present, which she said would likely be acceptable in these hard times.

Saying these words, she took from a basket she was carrying in her hand a loaf of bread, some flesh-meat, a little bag of flour, and other kinds of food.

When the children saw all these good things they became wild with joy; they ran about the house, and began to clap their hands to show how happy they were. As to their father, he was silent. He raised his eyes to Heaven, and from his inmost soul thanked his Heavenly Father for this speedy answer to his prayer.

He then told the lady, who was looking on in wonder at what she saw, of the sad state to which they had been reduced by the famine, and how he had that very hour promised his children food, without knowing whence it was to come.

The lady was moved to tears at his story, and his pious confidence in God. Before going away she told him that as long as the famine lasted, she herself would provide for him and his family.

Who can describe the joy of that happy family and their gratitude to God for His Fatherly assistance? They sat down to table, and after begging the blessing of God, they partook with joy of the food which God had sent them.

Christ. Perfection.

THE BREAD WHICH THE LORD SENT.

About the year 1217 the great St. Dominic went to Rome with some of his disciples. While he dwelt there, people came every day to ask admission into the Order which he had established. The Saint in his sermons had spoken so fervently of the happiness of living for God alone, that many were led to give up all worldly goods for the sake of God and Heaven.

The friars lived in extreme poverty. But so great was the sanctity, and so powerful the prayers, of the holy Dominic, that when the resources of the earth failed them those of Heaven were ready to meet every need.

One day in particular their supply of provisions was quite done, and two of their members, Brother John and Brother Albert, were sent out to seek alms according to the custom of the Order. They wandered through the streets of Rome for many hours, but obtained nothing. At last they turned homewards, feeling full of sorrow, when they thought of the brethren who were expecting them at home, but whose wants they would be unable to relieve.

As they were passing the Church of St. Anastasia, not far from their own house, they met a woman who had often assisted them.

When she saw that their sacks were empty she offered them a loaf of bread, saying she would give what she could rather than see them return home empty-handed.

She had hardly left them, when they came upon a man of most wretched appearance. His clothes hung in tatters upon him, his cheeks were sunken, and his eyes bright with the glitter of hunger. In a feeble voice he asked them for alms.

"We would give you an alms most gladly," said Brother John, "but we have nothing to give; we are as poor as yourself. We have been begging all the morning, and have nothing to carry home but this one small loaf."

"But you are not as hungry as I am," said the stranger, and at the same time he held out his hand, so thin and wasted that it seemed as if the sunlight could pass through it. "Oh, give me a morsel of bread for the love of God," he cried.

The two monks looked at him with pity, and took counsel together as to what they would best do. "For ourselves," they said, "it would be far better to fast than to leave this poor creature to perish with hunger; and, after all, we would not greatly wrong our brethren by giving him this loaf, for of what use can a few ounces of bread be among a hundred men? Let us, therefore, for the love of God, give this famishing man what help we are able."

Having come to this conclusion, Brother Albert handed the loaf to the beggar, and they departed with his blessing.

When they arrived at the monastery St. Dominic met them. "You have brought nothing today, my children," he said to them.

"Nothing, holy Father," they replied; and they then told him all that had occurred to them on the way.

"It is well, my children," the Saint answered with a cheerful countenance; "the poor man you helped was an angel of the Lord, Who knows well how to provide for his own. Let us, then, pray to Him"; and leaving them he went into the chapel.

A few minutes afterwards he returned, and sent for Brother Roger, who was the cook, and told him to summon the religious to dinner as usual.

"Of what use is it for the brethren to go to the refectory when there is nothing to put before them?" said the Brother.

"Do as I tell you," replied the Saint, "and God will provide for our wants."

The tables were all arranged in the usual way. A plate and a cup were set for each Brother, and an empty wine-cask stood at the one end of the hall—for in Italy wine was then, as now, the common drink of even the poor people; but neither food nor drink was to be seen.

At the sound of the bell the monks filed into the hall, and stood in their places around the tables, many of them with blank and disappointed looks; but their Father, with his accustomed calmness, pronounced the blessing.

All took their seats, and Brother Henry began to read aloud from a spiritual book, according to their pious custom. In the meantime St. Dominic was sitting with clasped hands absorbed in prayer.

Then, in full sight of the assembled community, two young men, with grave sweet countenances and graceful bearing, came into the hall. Long mantles of pure white linen fell from their shoulders. With noiseless step they moved on, the one taking the right, the other the left, side of the refectory, and beginning with the lowest in rank, they set before each of the brethren a loaf of bread of remarkable whiteness and beauty, which they took from the folds of their snowy mantles.

When they reached the head of the table where St. Dominic sat, they gave him a loaf also, and, saluting him, they disappeared.

Then the Blessed Dominic, raising his eyes, said: "Eat, my brothers, the bread which the Lord has sent you"; and turning to those who were serving the table, he bade them bring wine.

"Holy Father," they said, "there is no wine."

"Go to the cask," replied the Saint, "and draw for the Brothers the wine which the Lord has sent them."

They obeyed, and went and found it full of excellent wine, with which they filled all the cups.

For two days the provisions thus miraculously obtained supplied their table, so that no one was obliged to go out for alms. The Saint then ordered what remained to be given to the poor, saying: "O my brethren, trust to our good God even in your greatest poverty. He never forgets to help those who thus call upon Him in their needs."

Life of St. Dominic.

HELP IN THE HOUR OF NEED.

It is recorded in the chronicles of St. Francis that a certain religious, remarkable for his great piety, was chosen to accompany a young novice to another house of the same order at a considerable distance.

When they had proceeded on their journey for some time, evening fell suddenly upon them in a place which seemed to be uninhabited. Being much fatigued and at the same time hungry, they were at a loss to know where to find shelter and food. But the older brother endeavored to encourage his companion by telling him that God, who never forsakes those who trust in Him, would come to their assistance.

Then, taking him by the hand, he led him gently forward. Suddenly a young man of amiable appearance met them, and, having reverently saluted them, offered to be their guide, and to procure for them the shelter and food of which they stood so much in need. Then, going before them, he led them to a cottage in a secluded part of the neighboring forest, where, on entering, they found a bright fire burning. The two religious, in their surprise, could not find words to testify their gratitude. The young man said to them: "Warm yourselves at the fire while I go to prepare something for you to eat."

In a short time he returned, bearing on a plate a magnificent fish. It was the season of Advent. The religious sat down to table and partook of the fish, which he had placed before them. During their whole lifetime they had never tasted anything so delicious. When they had finished their repast he took them to a little room, where he spread on the floor two straw mattresses. "Here is a bed for each of you," he said. "They are not very luxurious, but they will be most conformable to the rules of your holy Order."

They slept calmly during the night, and on the following morning the young man came to arouse them. When they had partaken of their morning repast, he led them through the forest towards the highway, and pointed out the road that would lead them to the end of their journey. When bidding them farewell, he told them to thank and bless God for what He had done for them.

When the two religious turned round to thank him for his kindness, he was nowhere to be seen. Then they knew that it was an angel whom God had sent them to assist them on their way; and, prostrating themselves on the ground, they returned Him their grateful thanks for the favor He had conferred upon them.

52

THE HAPPINESS OF THOSE WHO "CAST THEIR CARE" UPON THE LORD

The poor man who day by day asks God with confidence for his daily bread is often much happier than the King on his throne who has so much more than he needs.

THE EMPEROR AND THE MONK.

Not far from the city of Constantinople there lived a holy monk, who had thrown aside all the pleasures of life to seek in solitude and prayer the treasures of the Kingdom of Heaven. His food consisted of bread and water, and on this humble fare he lived as happily as the King upon his throne.

The Emperor Theodosius, having heard of him, and the kind of life he led, had a great desire to visit him.

So one day he put on the dress of a countryman, and went to the mountain where the holy man dwelt.

After they had conversed together for some time, the Emperor told him he was hungry, and asked him if he had any food in his cell.

"Yes," answered the monk, "I have here some bread, and plenty of water pure from the stream, but that is all I can put before you."

The Emperor partook of what the monk had set before him, and while he was eating it, he said to him: "My Father, do you feel happy here, and are you contented with the kind of life you have chosen?"

"Yes," replied the holy man, "I am perfectly content; I would not change places even with the Emperor on his throne. I have nothing, it is true; but then, I do not stand in need of anything. No one troubles me here, and I never want for anything, for God always provides me with everything I need."

"Do you know who I am?" said Theodosius.

"No, sir."

"I am the Emperor Theodosius. I have come to visit you, that by your example and heavenly conversation I might be edified. Oh, what would I not give to be able to live like you, free from all the cares of life, and living on a little bread as you do! I would then be able to prepare myself to appear before God."

Theodosius then recommended himself to the holy man's prayers, and departed. He now saw the truth of those words of Our Blessed Lord, that if we seek first the Kingdom of God and His justice, all things else we need will be added unto us.

Traité sur le "Pater."

THE PIOUS STUDENT

There was one time a young man who was studying in one of the Universities of Germany. He was very poor; but although he had not much of this world's wealth, he was rich in piety.

Now it happened that when he was about the end of his course he became very ill. For a long time he was obliged to lie in bed, and the doctor had to come often to see him. When at last he recovered, he found that all the money he possessed in the world was required to pay the expenses he had incurred during his illness.

He was soon obliged to part even with his books and clothing to purchase food, but in a short time these things also were all sold, and he began to feel more than ever the pangs of hunger.

One Sunday morning at Holy Mass, when he was saying the petition of the Lord's Prayer, "Give us this day our daily bread," he thought of his extreme poverty, and said that prayer over and over again with great fervor.

"Surely God will not refuse to hear me today, for I am so much in need of His assistance, and He has said that those who put their trust in Him shall never want."

With this thought in his mind he returned home, but there was not a morsel of food in the house, neither had he any money with which to buy any.

As he was sitting at home, sad and hungry, he heard a little mouse nibbling what seemed to be a crust of bread in the corner of the room. He went to the place, and found there a piece of bread hard and dry as wood. This was for him a treasure. He took it into his hands, but before eating it he knelt down to ask God's blessing on the piece of bread that he had found.

As he was trying to eat it, someone came to the door with a basket full of good and nourishing food. A rich gentleman who lived in the neighborhood had come to know of the poor student's distress, and sent it to him.

The young man fell on his knees, and thanked his Father in Heaven for having sent him this timely aid. But this was not all; the same gentleman, seeing his piety and confidence in God, provided for his wants as long as he remained at the University. He was thus able to finish his course, and obtained a high position in his native city.

PART VIII

"FORGIVE US OUR TRESPASSES"

53

WHAT WE PRAY FOR IN THIS PETITION

When we say, "Forgive us our trespasses, as we forgive them that trespass against us," we pray that God may forgive us our sins, as we forgive others the injuries they do us.

My child, God has promised to pardon us the sins that we have committed against Him on condition that we forgive those who have offended us.

TOM, THE POOR INDIAN SLAVE.

A poor negro known by the name of Tom was once bought by some slave-owners on the coast of Africa, and carried by them over to the West Indies.

In his new home he had the happiness of embracing the Christian religion. After his conversion he led a holy life. Not only did he bear patiently all the hardships which his humble condition in life imposed upon him, but he became a model of Christian perfection even to his master.

In a short time his good conduct raised him so high in the confidence of his master, that he entrusted to his care some of his most important works.

One day his master wanted to purchase a number of slaves. For this purpose he went to the market, and took his faithful Tom along with him.

As they were looking among the slaves for those who might be most suitable, Tom saw an old man there whom he recognized. Going to his master, he said: "Please, sir, buy this old man."

But his master refused. "Of what use will that old man be to us?" he said. "He can no longer do any work, and I cannot spend my money on such useless objects."

But the slave-owner to whom the old man belonged said that if he would buy twenty other slaves from him, he would give this one also, without asking any price for him.

This was agreed to, and the old man became the property of Tom's master.

When they reached home, Tom took the old man specially under his care. He brought him into his own cabin, and made him sit down at his own table, and fed him with the tenderness of a mother. If he felt the cold, Tom took him to the fire to warm him; or if the heats were too great, he led him to a shady place among the trees; in a word, he acted towards him with as much affection as if he had been his dearest friend on earth.

His master, who had observed this singular conduct of Tom towards the old slave, was anxious to know the reason of it.

"Is that old man your father?" he one day asked him.

Tom answered: "No, master; he is not my father." "Then is he a brother older than yourself?"

"No; he is not my brother."

"Then he must be an uncle or some near relative, for it is impossible that you should take so much interest in one who is an entire stranger to you, and show so much kindness to him."

"No, master; he is not a relative, nor a friend even."

"Who, then, can he be?" inquired his master, more surprised than ever; "and tell me why you show him so much kindness."

"That man is my greatest enemy," he answered. "It was he who stole me long ago from my home and my dear parents, and made me a slave. But I cannot hate him; for the father missionary told me that I must forgive my enemies, and do good to those who have injured me; and that if my enemy is hungry, I must give him to eat, and if he is thirsty, I must give him to drink. That is the reason why I am so kind to that poor old man."

Christian Anecdotes.

GOOD FOR EVIL.

There lived in the town of Ajaccio, in Corsica, a rich merchant, whose name was Bordano.

He had in his service a very trustworthy man called Benedict Torcelli, who had a wife and family, all, like himself, living in the fear of God. Benedict occupied a position of great importance in his master's household, and he repaid the confidence placed in him by attending faithfully to his master's interests.

One day, without any warning, Bordano ordered him at once to quit his service, and never to appear again in his presence. In vain did Benedict ask him to tell what he had done to incur his displeasure. Bordano would not listen, and the poor man had to go forth into the world without a home to shelter him.

For a short time he was able to support himself and his family by the little savings he had amassed, but these soon came to an end, and he was reduced to a state of great poverty.

One day, as he was wandering on the mountains, gathering some branches for firewood, he met Bordano, his late master, who was hunting.

He went up to him, and, falling on his knees, said: "O my master, forgive me if I have done anything to offend you! If I did any wrong, it was not done willingly. Oh, have pity on me and my little children, who are now in great misery, and give me something to appease their hunger."

Bordano looked on the poor man at his feet, and, instead of being moved with compassion, told him to go away, and even threatened to shoot him if he did not at once obey.

Benedict rose up and left him, and continued sadly to gather up the dead branches, as he had been doing before.

All that day Bordano had but little success, and this made him still more angry. About an hour after he left his old servant Benedict, he turned homewards. On the way he saw a beautiful bird flying above his head among the trees. He raised his gun and fired. The bird fell into a great ravine among bramble bushes and brushwood. Bordano, anxious not to lose it, ran forward towards the place, without looking whither he was going. In his haste, he stumbled over some loose stones, and fell over a precipice into the abyss beneath. There he lay stunned by the fall, his legs and arms broken.

Not long afterwards Benedict, not knowing what had occurred, happened to pass the place at the bottom of the ravine where Bordano was lying. He suddenly came upon the motionless form, and in an instant recognized who it was. With that Christian charity which forgets all past injuries, Benedict at once ran to his side to help him. He bound up his broken limbs as well as he could, and, taking him upon his shoulders, carried him with great difficulty to the village, which was at a considerable distance. There he received assistance, and the injured man was soon lying safely in his own home.

The physicians who were called in soon restored him to consciousness. He opened his eyes. "Where am I?" he cried.

"You are safe in your own house," was the reply.

"And who was it that saved me from death in that terrible den into which I had fallen? Who brought me here?"

"It was I—your old servant Benedict Torcelli."

"You!—you whom I had so unjustly treated!—you whom this very day I had so cruelly ordered from my presence, whom I even threatened to kill!"

"Yes," replied Benedict; "it is true you did treat me, a faithful servant, with the greatest injustice, banishing me from your service as if guilty of some great crime. But I am a Christian, and the law of God commands me to do good to those who injure me. Today I have only done my duty."

Bordano looked on the good man with tears in his eyes. It was now his turn to beg forgiveness. This was immediately granted, and Benedict and his little family were once more restored to their former position, where they were happy, and respected by everyone as long as they lived.

THE KING TAKES AN ACCOUNT OF HIS SERVANTS.

Jesus Christ shows us in the following parable how we must forgive our enemies if we desire to be forgiven by Him at the Day of Judgment:

"'The Kingdom of Heaven,' He said, 'is likened to a king who would take an account of his servants.

"'And when he had begun to take the account, one was brought that owed him ten thousand talents. And as he had not wherewith to pay it, his lord commanded that he should be sold, and his wife and children and all that he had, and payment to be made.

"'But that servant, falling down, besought him, saying: "Have patience with me, and I will pay thee all."

"'And the lord of that servant, being moved with pity, let him go, and forgave him the debt.

"'But when that servant had gone out, he found one of his fellow-servants that owed him a hundred pence: and, laying hold of him, he throttled him, saying: "Pay what thou owest." "And his fellow-servant, falling down, besought him, saying: 'Have patience with me, and I will pay thee all.'"

"And he would not; but went and cast him into prison till he paid the debt."

"Now his fellow-servants, seeing what was done, were very much grieved, and they came and told their lord all that was done."

"And his lord called him, and said to him: 'Thou wicked servant, I forgave thee all the debt, because thou besoughtest me: shouldst thou not, then, have compassion also on thy fellow-servant, even as I had compassion on thee?'"

"And his lord, being angry, delivered him to the tortures until he paid all the debt."

"'So also shall my Heavenly Father do to you, if you forgive not everyone his brother from your hearts.'"

St. Matt. xviii. 23 et seq.

54

WE MUST PRAY FOR THOSE WHO HAVE INJURED US.

Y ou must not only forgive your enemies and do good to those who injure you, but you should also pray for them. This will bring to you God's greatest blessings.

OUR LORD'S ANSWER TO ST. ELIZABETH.

St. Elizabeth of Hungary was treated in the most cruel manner, not only by her enemies, but even by her nearest and dearest friends.

One day the Saint was praying to God to give great graces to all those who had in any way injured her, and to give the greatest graces to those who had injured her the most. After she had said this prayer, Our Lord appeared to her, and said: "My daughter, never in all your lifetime did you say a prayer which pleased Me so much as the one you have just now said for your enemies. On account of this prayer, I forgive you, not only all your sins, but even the temporal punishment due to them."

Life of St. Elizabeth.

55

THE EXAMPLE OF JESUS CHRIST MAKES IT EASY TO FORGIVE

Jesus Christ on the cross forgave those who were crucifying Him. If you feel it difficult to pardon those who have injured you, think of this, and then you will find it easy.

ST. JOHN GUALBERT'S CONVERSION.

John Gualbert belonged to a rich and noble family. In his boyhood he was brought up in piety, but when he grew up, the attractions of the world deceived him, and he plunged headlong into the life of pleasure it offered him. He even began to think that dissipation and a life of pleasure were privileges that belonged to the position in life in which he was born.

It happened that his oldest brother, Hugh, had been killed in a quarrel with a gentleman of that country. John formed the resolution of avenging his death by taking away the life of the man who had slain him.

One Good Friday, as he was coming from the country into Florence, he met his brother's murderer in a narrow defile, from which there was no possibility of escaping.

In a moment his sword was in his hand, and, full of anger and the desire of revenge, he rushed forward to plunge it into the breast of his enemy. But the man, without attempting to escape, cast himself at his feet, and, stretching out his arms in the form of a cross, cried out: "I conjure you by the passion and death of Jesus Christ, Who on the cross forgave His murderers, and prayed for them, do not kill me."

John, remembering that that very day was the anniversary of Our Savior's death, at once drew back. He threw away his sword, and, stretching out his hand to his enemy, said to him in a tone of sweetness: "I will not refuse you what you have asked me in the name of Jesus Christ my Savior. Not only do I grant you your life, but I also give you my friendship. Pray to God to pardon me."

The two gentlemen, now no longer enemies but friends, embraced each other in sign of their reconciliation, and separated.

John continued his journey, and when he reached Florence, went into one of the churches of that city. He knelt down before the great crucifix, and began to pray with extraordinary fervor. While he gazed on the figure of Jesus Christ on the cross, he saw the head of Jesus move, and incline towards him as if to thank him for having forgiven his enemy for His sake. At the same time he felt a secret voice in his heart, telling him to renounce the world altogether and give himself entirely to God.

"Yes, O my God, I will obey Thee; for if Thou dost reward with so great a miracle this little action which I have done for the love of Thee, how great will be the reward I may expect hereafter, if I serve Thee faithfully to the end of my life!"

John Gualbert went immediately to the monastery of St. Minatus, and begged to be admitted. He spent the rest of his life in works of piety and religion, became the founder of a religious Order, and is now a great Saint in Heaven.

Life of St. John Gualbert, July 12.

THE CRUCIFIX IN THE HANDS OF ST. PHILIP NERI.

A penitent of St. Philip Neri on one occasion refused to forgive a man who had injured him.

The holy man, seeing that his words made no impression on his hardened heart, took a crucifix into his hands, and placing it before the eyes of the impenitent sinner, said: "Behold, and consider well the example which our dear Lord and Master has given us. Not only did He Himself forgive even those who crucified Him, but, hanging in agony on the cross, He prayed to His Heavenly Father also to forgive them. You also daily recite the Lord's Prayer. In doing so," continued the Saint, "you ask of God, not pardon for what you have done against Him, but your own eternal condemnation. Cast yourself on your knees before this image of your Divine Master dying for your sins, and say to Him: 'O Lord Jesus, it was not enough that Thou shouldst die once in the midst of the most awful torments for my salvation; Thou must die again if Thou dost wish to obtain from me that I should pardon my enemy.'"

The Saint said these words in so touching a voice that the young man became mute with astonishment, and began to tremble from head to foot.

When he recovered his power of speech, he burst into tears, and in the midst of sobs cried out: "O my Father, I forgive—yes, I forgive from my heart him who has offended me, and I will do for him all that you may be pleased to ask me, to show the fullness of my forgiveness."

Anecdotes of St. Philip.

"JESUS CHRIST DIED FOR YOU AND FOR HIM."

A certain man belonging to a noble family, whose name was Antony Martin, vowed to be avenged for the murder of his brother, who had been slain by another nobleman called Don Velasco.

To execute his design he went to Grenada, where his enemy

dwelt. Velasco, being made aware of his intention, endeavored by every means to pacify him and obtain his forgiveness, but without success.

As soon as St. John of God, who was in Grenada at that time, heard of this, he went out to meet Antony, praying God to come to his assistance in the work of reconciliation. He saw him as he was passing through the great square of the city, and, running up to him, threw himself humbly at his feet; then, taking in his hand a crucifix which he had concealed in the sleeve of his upper garment, raised it up before the face of the angry man, saying: "Brother Antony, God will pardon you the sins you have committed against Him, if you will only forgive your enemy. But keep this in mind: if you refuse to pardon him, God will never pardon you. If Velasco has shed the blood of your brother, remember that Jesus Christ died for you and for him, and that His most precious blood cries for mercy more loudly than that of your brother does for vengeance." Antony, on hearing these words, was struck as if a thunderbolt had fallen upon him. The grace of God at the same moment entered into his heart, urging him to forgiveness. In an instant he fell on his knees before the Saint, imploring him to obtain from God that pardon for himself which he now, from his heart, granted to his enemy. St. John, rising up, went along with him to the place where Velasco abode, and Antony, in his presence, embraced his brother's murderer in sign of his forgiveness.

Rep. du Catech., iii. 358.

56

WE MUST FORGIVE IF WE DESIRE TO BE FORGIVEN

God has told us that unless we forgive our enemies, He will not forgive us. The following is a terrible example, which should make those afraid who keep in their hearts any anger against their neighbor.

ST. NICEPHORUS AND SAPRICIUS.

St. Nicephorus lived in the city of Antioch, and led a life of solid Christian virtue. There sprang up between him and another Christian named Sapricius an intimate friendship; they loved each other like brothers, and assisted each other with tender solicitude.

But the enemy, who never sleeps, envious of the glory given to God by so virtuous a friendship, did not rest till he had sown the seeds of discord between them. Then the bonds of friendship were broken, and hatred succeeded love to such a degree that when they saw each other on the street they turned away their heads, that they might not meet each other face to face. This conduct was carried on for a long time by these former models of true friendship.

At last Nicephorus, feeling remorse of conscience, saw the greatness of his fault, and resolved to try by every means in his power to be reconciled to his enemy.

He sent to him certain friends dear to them both to try to obtain his pardon, assuring him of the sincerity of his repentance, and his resolution to give him every satisfaction in his power. But all in vain; Sapricius would not even hear the name of his enemy mentioned.

He tried again and again, but was unsuccessful. At last he went to him in person, and, throwing himself at his feet, besought him for the love of Jesus Christ to pardon him. This heroic act of humility had no better effect than the intervention of his friends; Sapricius was as hardened as ever, and not only closed his ears to all cries of reconciliation, but even became deaf to the voice of God crying out in his heart: "Forgive, and you shall be forgiven."

In the meantime a terrible persecution against the Christians broke out at Antioch. As Sapricius was one of the Christians who was best known in that city, he was one of the first to fall into the hands of the persecutors.

When the prisoner was taken before the Governor, he was asked his name.

"I am called Sapricius," he answered.

"And what is your profession?" asked the Governor.

"I am a Christian," replied the prisoner. "We Christians adore Jesus, the only true God, as the sovereign Lord of Heaven and earth, and we hate your gods, because they are invented by the Devil to hold you captive."

The Governor was very angry at this answer, and ordered Sapricius to be put to the torture.

The confessor of the faith was not shaken by this, but suffered it with great constancy, saying to the judge in the midst of his torments: "You have my body in your power, torment it as you like; but you cannot touch my soul; it is subject only to Jesus Christ, Who alone can cast both soul and body into the eternal fire of Hell."

When the tyrant saw that he could not make Sapricius deny his faith, and that neither promises nor threats had any effect on one who looked upon it as a glory to suffer for Jesus, he passed the following sentence on him: "That Sapricius, a Christian, who is obstinate in his mad religion, and who believes that he will one day rise again, be handed over to the executioner, who will cut off his head in punishment for his contempt for the edict of the Emperors."

Sapricius heard the sentence with calmness and even with great joy, desiring to give his life for the glory of Him Who gave His for the love of us on the hallowed wood of the cross.

He was preparing to go to the place of execution with the hope of soon wearing the martyr's crown, when Nicephorus, having heard what had taken place, ran to him and threw himself at his feet, exclaiming: "O martyr of Jesus Christ, pardon the fault I have committed against thee."

Even at that moment, and although he was going to die for the sake of Him Whose first words upon the cross were a prayer for pardon, the unhappy man refused even to open his lips to him.

Nicephorus rose from his knees as the man passed by, but did not yet despair of gaining his object. He ran to another street through which the procession had to pass, and making his way through the crowd, he again hung himself at his feet, and weeping, said to him: "For the sake of Jesus Christ, do not condemn me to despair; pardon the fault I committed more from frailty than from malice. I beseech thee, by the glorious confession thou hast made of Our Divine Redeemer, grant me pardon."

But the heart of Sapricius was hardened more and more. He walked on without even deigning to look at Nicephorus, who followed him in tears. The soldiers also soon grew tired of him, and, wondering at his strange conduct, cried out to him: "What madness is this? The man is going to die, and yet you are imploring his forgiveness."

Even when they had reached the place of execution, Nicephorus redoubled his entreaties and his tears to obtain pardon; but Sapricius remained obstinate in his hard-heartedness and vengeance.

Soon, however, he experienced the anger of God. The executioner had the sword raised, and was about to strike the last blow, when

Sapricius stopped him, saying: "Why are you going to cut off my head?"

"For your disobedience to the Emperor's orders, and for refusing to offer sacrifice to our gods." "Hold a moment," said the unfortunate man; "bring me fire and incense, and I will sacrifice to your idols, but don't kill me."

Nicephorus, who was present, was filled with dismay on hearing this, and cried out to him: "In God's name, what are you doing? Do you thus deny Jesus Christ? For a short span of life do you condemn yourself to eternal death?"

But these feeling words made no impression on the heart of Sapricius, who was now the slave of Satan.

Then Nicephorus, anxious to make reparation to the glory of Jesus, injured by the apostasy of an unworthy Christian, and bitterly bewailing so terrible a fall, cried out to the executioners: "I am a Christian. I adore as my God Jesus Christ, to Whom this unfortunate man has become an apostate. Here I am, ready to suffer a thousand deaths sooner than renounce my Jesus and adore your gods."

This unexpected exclamation put an end to the joy the idolaters began to feel at the fall of the apostate Christian.

One of the soldiers ran to tell the Governor what had happened. "Sir," said he, "the obstinacy of Sapricius has broken down, and he promises to sacrifice to the gods; but another man has come forward who proclaims himself a Christian, and says he will never deny his God, nor worship our divinities, nor consent to obey the orders of our august Emperor."

When the Governor heard this report, he pronounced sentence against Nicephorus, saying: "If this man refuses to offer incense to the gods, let his head be cut off in the place of Sapricius." Nicephorus was faithful to the end, and, bending down his head, received the fatal blow. The angels came down from Heaven to receive that holy soul, and crown it with the diadem of martyrdom, and carry it to Heaven to the throne of glory of which Sapricius was unworthy, through his hardness of heart and his refusal to pardon injuries.

Thus were the crowns of martyrdom transferred. What a terrible lesson for those who keep in their hearts sentiments of hatred and vengeance against their brethren!

Light of the Lowly, i., p. 27.

THE FALSE FORGIVENESS.

There were once two men who for a long time had lived together in the bonds of an intimate friendship which, one would think, nothing could disturb. But this very intimacy in course of time produced a coldness, which ended in mutual hatred for each other. This soon became known to their neighbors, and although many of them endeavored to bring about a reconciliation, they could not effect it.

One of these men at length became dangerously ill. His friends, seeing him in this condition, and knowing that unless he forgave his neighbor before he died he could not obtain forgiveness from God, tried to induce him to forgive him who had trespassed against him. In this they succeeded. He agreed to do this, and sent for the priest to hear his confession, and to administer to him the Last Sacraments of the Church.

When the priest came, he said to the dying man: "You know well, my child, that the first thing you must do in this your preparation for death is to forgive your enemy from your heart; you must send for him to whom you have so long borne sentiments of hatred. He will be pleased, I am sure, to come. You will speak to him as a Christian and child of one common Father should do one to the other, and then your preparation for the Sacraments will easily be accomplished."

This was done, and while the messenger went to call him, he made his confession. When his enemy came into the room, he received him with every sign of sincere friendship, and they became once more attached to each other as in former times—at least, to all outward appearance.

Then the one who had visited the dying man departed. As he was going out, he said to someone near him: "Oh, what a coward that man is! He wanted this reconciliation only because he was afraid to die as he had lived."

Unfortunately the dying man heard these words, and, being seized with great anger, he cried out: "No, I am not afraid, and to show you that I am not afraid, I tell you that I still hate you, and hate you more than ever. Get you hence, and let me never see you again."

The excitement produced by this awful scene brought on a sudden reaction, and thus he died without repentance, finishing his sinful life by a still more miserable death.

God grant, my child, that your death may not be like unto his.

Histoires Édifiantes, p. 102.

ST. JOHN THE ALMS-GIVER AND A GREAT LORD.

A certain great lord in Alexandria had allowed a deep hatred to rest in his heart against one of his neighbors. The Saint frequently endeavored to make peace between them, but in vain. Seeing the nobleman so determined to continue to live in this sinful hatred, he sent a messenger to him, asking him to come to see him, as he had something very important to make known to him.

The great man came with much pomp, and richly attired. The Saint said to him that he was about to offer up the Holy Sacrifice in the Church, and asked him to be present at it. He consented. After the consecration, when the saintly patriarch had intoned the "Our Father," the assistants, according to the custom of those days, said it aloud along with him. When he reached the petition, "Forgive us our trespasses, as we forgive them that trespass against us," he suddenly paused; so also did all the others, according to a previous arrangement he had made, so that the only voice heard uttering the petition was that of the noble lord himself.

The Saint then turned round towards him from the altar, and said to him: "My lord, have you ever thought seriously on the words you have just now uttered in the presence of God, and of all the people? You have asked God to forgive you, indeed, but in what manner? 'As we forgive them that trespass against us.' You have an enmity towards your brother, and you still refuse to forgive him, and you have asked God to forgive you just as you have forgiven him. What a terrible prayer you have uttered against yourself! Repent, therefore, of your folly, and as you desire to be forgiven by the great Judge of the living and the dead, forgive now from your heart your adversary who has sinned against you."

These few words were enough to touch the heart of the nobleman, whose faith was still alive within him, and in his heart admired the ingenious charity of the holy patriarch.

When Holy Mass was ended he lost not a moment, but hastened at once towards him whom he had hitherto considered one of his greatest enemies, and was reconciled to him. From that day they lived together united in the closest bonds of fraternal charity.

LEONTIUS: *Life of St. John the Almoner.*

THE NOBLE DUKE OF GUISE AND HIS ENEMY.

A certain man who was a heretic had conceived the design of assassinating the Duke of Guise, one of the most zealous defenders of the Catholic religion in his days in the kingdom of France. This design was opportunely discovered, and the Duke was informed of it.

Summoning the intending assassin into his presence, he said to him, with an air of astonishment: "Have I ever done you any wrong, that you should thus desire to kill me?"

"No," replied the other, "you have never done me any harm."

"Why, then, did you resolve to put me to death?" "It was because I wished to defend my religion," replied his enemy.

The Duke made him this beautiful answer: "If your religion enjoins you to assassinate your enemy, mine commands me to forgive; I freely pardon you."

What heroic sentiments! May they enter your heart, my child, and remain ever engraved there!

Catéch. de Rodez, ii. 423.

57

THE GREATER THE INJURY FORGIVEN, THE MORE CERTAIN GOD'S PARDON

The greater the injury is that has been done to you, my child, the greater will be your merit before God in forgiving it.

A CHRISTIAN'S NOBLE REVENGE.

A brave Hungarian Count, by name Peter Szapary, was taken prisoner by the Turks, brought to the city of Ofen, and dragged before Hamsa-Bey.

The cruel Turk rejoiced to see his dreaded enemy at length in his power; he loaded him with insult, condemned him to receive a hundred blows on the soles of his feet, then to be chained hand and foot, and to be cast into prison.

It was a dark and loathsome dungeon. The prisoner's bed was only moldy straw; his food was so wretched that he was soon reduced to the point of death.

But the cruel Pasha did not want him to die. He desired first only to torture his prisoner, and then to receive a heavy ransom for him. He ordered the prisoner to be cared for till he was restored to health, then to be sent to work in the kitchen.

One day Hamsa-Bey asked him in mockery how he felt. Szapary

did not answer him a word, but bore this insult without any signs of anger. At this the Pasha was so enraged that he ordered the brave nobleman to be harnessed to a plough, and to till a neighboring field with another unhappy Christian, exposed to the strokes of the lash and the jeers of the populace.

Finally, after three long years of cruel martyrdom, Szapary was given in exchange for a wealthy Turk, who had been taken prisoner by the Hungarians.

Szapary returned home in a most pitiable condition; he was worn to a skeleton, and scarcely able to stand. It was a long time before he was completely restored to health.

Some years after this, it happened that the city of Ofen was captured by the Christians, and the cruel Hamsa-Bey taken prisoner. The Duke of Lorraine gave him into the hands of Szapary, to do with him whatever he thought proper.

A servant of Szapary went in haste to the Turk to announce to him the fact. Soon after Szapary went to the prison in person to visit his cruel enemy.

"Do you know me?" he asked. "I am Szapary."

"I know it," answered the Turk sullenly; "now is your time for vengeance."

"Very well," answered Szapary; "I shall take it, but it shall be the Christian's revenge. I now restore you to freedom unconditionally and without ransom." The Turk smiled with contempt; he did not believe such noble conduct possible.

"I am a Christian," continued Szapary; "my religion commands me to forgive my enemies, and to return good for evil."

He then ordered the chains of his enemy to be struck off, and his liberty to be restored to him, for the sake of Him Who was nailed to the cross.

The hardened Turk was completely overcome by such generosity. He fell in agony at the feet of Szapary. "Your kindness comes too late," he shrieked. "I have taken poison to escape the tortures which I expected. I now curse myself and my cruelty towards you, and I crave your forgiveness. I wish at least to die a

Christian, since the Christian religion teaches so sublime a virtue."

Skillful physicians were speedily called in, but it was too late. Hamsa-Bey was dying; but before he died he was baptized, and Szapary was his godfather.

Hungary.

THE PRIEST AND THE SOLDIER.

About a hundred years ago, when the terrible Revolution broke out in France, a certain priest called Father Aurain gave a beautiful example of doing good to one who hated him.

One day he was in the church at his prayers. Suddenly someone ran to tell him that the Republican soldiers were coming towards the church to take him prisoner.

The priest immediately recommended himself to the protection of God, and tried to make his escape through the sacristy into the garden behind the church.

There two of the soldiers met him; they tried to seize him, but, leaping over the wall, he ran in great haste towards the river about a mile distant. The two soldiers also ran after him.

When the priest came to the banks of the river he looked round, and saw that his enemies were still pursuing him. Without delay he leapt into the water and swam safely to the other side. One of the soldiers attempted to follow him. The priest, seeing this, again began to run, and was soon out of danger.

But as he stopped to rest a little on the top of a hill, he thought he heard cries for help proceeding from the direction of the river. He looked round, and one glance told him all. The soldier who had plunged into the river in pursuit was unable to swim, and was being carried away by the stream.

In a moment the good priest retraced his steps, plunged once more into the river, and was soon at the side of the drowning man. He seized him by his hair as he was sinking, and drew him to land.

It was some time before the soldier regained consciousness, but when at length he opened his eyes and saw who it was who had saved him he was filled with amazement.

"Who are you?" he cried out, thinking that perhaps his senses were deceiving him.

"I am Father Aurain, the priest of Figeac," was the reply.

"Can it be possible?" exclaimed the soldier. "I had sworn to take away your life, for I hated you." "My child," replied the priest, "I have never done you any harm; why did you hate me?"

"Because I was told that you hated us and tried to do us all the evil in your power."

The priest answered: "My child, you have been deceived. What I have now done to you will prove to you that what I say to you is true. You were on the point of perishing while seeking to take away my life, and I have saved you from death. I thank God, Who has given me this opportunity of doing good for evil."

That soldier afterwards became the priest's greatest friend.

ST. JOHN THE ALMS-GIVER AND THE DEACON.

It happened that on a certain occasion the patriarch St. John the Almoner was offering up the most Holy Sacrifice in his church at Alexandria; and when he came to the Lord's Prayer, he suddenly remembered that on the previous evening he had been told that one of the deacons of his church had conceived a great ill-will towards him on account of some injury he imagined he had done him.

Then came into his mind those words of Our Lord to the multitude in His Sermon on the Mount: "If, therefore, thou offer thy gift at the altar, and there thou remember that thy brother hath anything against thee; leave there thy offering before the altar, and go first to be reconciled to thy brother: and then coming thou shalt offer thy gift" (St. Matt. v. 23). He immediately interrupted the Holy Mass, and, leaving the altar, went in search of him who had the enmity against him; and, although there were many persons present, he threw himself at his feet, and prayed him to forgive him, if he had been the cause of giving him any annoyance.

The deacon was so much moved by the prelate's great humility that in an instant all thoughts of animosity disappeared from his heart. He prostrated himself at the feet of the prelate, and cried out: "What are you doing, venerable Pontiff? It is I, and I alone, who should kneel to implore your forgiveness, and to ask God to pardon me."

The Saint refused to rise from his knees until the deacon had first done so, and then he said: "May God, my son, pardon both of us for what we have done against Him!" Then, having embraced him with paternal affection, he returned to the church, and continued the Holy Sacrifice from the place where he had interrupted it to the end.

With what joy now could that holy prelate say the words of the holy prayer, "Forgive us our trespasses"! and with what confidence could he now himself hope to be forgiven by his Heavenly Father and his Judge!

Leontius: *Life of St. John the Almoner.*

58

FORGIVING OTHERS IS OFTEN THE CAUSE OF TEMPORAL BLESSINGS.

To bear patiently the injuries others cause you to suffer is one of those good works that will be specially rewarded by God in Heaven, and even in this life will bring you much temporal happiness.

THE STATUE THAT DID NOT GET ANGRY.

A young man went one day to the Superior of one of the religious houses in the East, and asked him to take him to be his disciple.

The old man, wishing to know with what spirit the postulant was filled, and anxious at the same time to give him a lesson, said to him, "Do you see that statue there near the door of that cell?"

"Yes, Father," he replied.

"Well, go, my son, and strike it with all your strength with that stick you have in your hand."

The young man did so, and returned to the Superior.

"Did the statue get angry when you struck it, or did it complain of the hard blows you gave it?"

"No, Father."

"Go again, and strike it as you did before."

The young man went a second and a third time, but still there was no complaint; the statue stood there immovable, and showed no sign of anger or ill-will against him who had struck it.

Then the old man said: "My child, if you think you can suffer injury and the harsh treatment of others without complaining or having in your heart any thoughts of anger, and be as patient as that lifeless statue, then you are a fit subject for this monastery. But if you keep in your heart any ill-will against those who may have injured you, or any desire of revenge, you are not suited for our kind of life."

A good Christian ought to be as patient under injuries as the statue under the blows that had been heaped upon it.

SURUS: *Vit. Sanct.*

59

GOD READILY FORGIVES THE PENITENT SINNER

The Holy Scripture says that the mercy of God is above all His works. And when Jesus Christ was on earth, He everywhere showed His compassion for poor sinners, and was ever ready to forgive them when they asked Him.

ST. MARY MAGDALEN.

"And Jesus one day entered into a city called Naim, and there went with Him His disciples and a great multitude. And when He came nigh to the gate of the city, behold a dead man was carried out, the only son of his mother, and she was a widow; and a great multitude of the city was with her. Whom when the Lord had seen, being moved with mercy towards her, He said to her: 'Weep not.'

"And He came near and touched the bier, and they that carried it stood still. And He said: 'Young man, I say to thee, Arise.' And he that was dead sat up and began to speak. And He gave him to his mother. And there came a great fear on them all: and they glorified God, saying: 'A great Prophet is risen amongst us: and God hath visited His people.'"

The raising to life of the widow's son is a figure of God's power to raise the sinner from the death of sin to a life of grace.

After recounting the resurrection of the widow's son to a temporal life, St. Luke relates the conversion of St. Mary Magdalen, whom Jesus Christ raised from death to a spiritual life.

"And one of the Pharisees desired Him to eat with him. And He went into the house of the Pharisee and sat down to eat:

"And behold a woman that was in the city, a sinner, when she knew that He sat at meat in the Pharisee's house, bought an alabaster box of ointment; and standing behind at his feet, she began to wash His feet with tears, and wiped them with the hairs of her head, and kissed His feet, and anointed them with the ointment.

"And the Pharisee, who had invited Him, seeing it, spoke within himself, saying: 'This Man, if He were a prophet, would know surely who and what manner of woman this is that toucheth Him, that she is a sinner.'

"And Jesus answering, said to him: 'Simon, I have something to say to thee.' And he said: 'Master, say it.'

"'A certain creditor had two debtors: the one owed five hundred pence, and the other fifty. And whereas they had not wherewith to pay, he forgave them both. Which therefore of the two loveth him most?'

"Simon answering, said: 'I suppose that he to whom he forgave most.'

"And He said to him: 'Thou hast judged rightly.'

"And turning to the woman, He said unto Simon: 'Dost thou see this woman? I entered into thy house, thou gavest Me no water for My feet; but she with tears hath washed My feet, and with her hairs hath wiped them. Thou gavest Me no kiss; but she, since she came in, hath not ceased to kiss My feet. My head with oil thou didst not anoint; but she with ointment hath anointed my feet. Wherefore I say to thee: Many sins are forgiven her, because she hath loved much. But to whom less is forgiven, he loveth less.'

"And He said to her: 'Thy sins are forgiven thee.'

"And they that sat at meat with Him began to say within themselves: 'Who is this that forgiveth sins also?'

"And He said to the woman: 'Thy faith hath made thee safe; go in peace.'"

When she had thus obtained pardon for her many sins, she followed Our Lord wherever He went, accompanying the holy women who were with Him. She witnessed His many miracles, she heard His discourses to the people, and she endeavored with a pious solicitude to attend to the wants of Our Lord and His disciples.

She was amongst the number of those devoted ones who ascended the hill of Calvary, and stood at the foot of the cross and saw Our Blessed Lord die. She followed Him to the tomb, and was the last to leave it on that sorrowful day. And when the repose of the Sabbath was ended she was again among those who came in the early morning to visit the sepulchre.

How great must have been her anguish not to find the body of Our Lord which she had come to seek! "Woman, why weepest thou?" said the angels to her, as she gazed into the empty tomb.

"She said to them: 'Because they have taken away my Lord: and I know not where they have laid Him.'

"When she had thus said, she turned herself back, and saw Jesus standing; and she knew not that it was Jesus.

"Jesus saith to her: 'Woman, why weepest thou? Whom seekest thou?'"

"She, thinking that it was the gardener, saith to Him: 'Sir, if thou hast taken Him hence, tell me where thou hast laid Him: and I will take Him away.'

"Jesus saith to her: 'Mary.'

"She, turning, saith to Him: 'Rabboni!' (which is to say 'Master').

"Jesus saith to her: 'Do not touch Me, for I am not yet ascended to My Father; but go to My brethren, and say to them: 'I ascend to My Father, and to your Father, to My God and to your God.'

"Mary Magdalen cometh and telleth the disciples: 'I have seen the Lord, and these things He said to me.'"

We have every reason to believe, assuredly, that the first one to whom Our Lord appeared after His resurrection was His Blessed Mother—she whom He loved so well, she who had in His passion suffered so much with Him. But the person whom the Evangelist tells us saw Our Lord before all the rest of His disciples was St. Mary Magdalen—that one who had been so great a sinner, that one who loved Him so much, that one of whom He had said: "Amen, I say to you, wheresoever this Gospel shall be preached in the whole world, that also which she hath done shall be told for a memory of her."

And while the remembrance of the great ones of this world is forgotten, that of the penitent sinner is honored throughout the entire universe. Even in this world God bestowed upon her some of His choicest favors. For during the thirty years she lived on earth after Our Lord's Ascension, during which she practiced for love of her Divine Master unheard-of austerities, seven times in the day was she borne up by angels to the summit of a neighboring mountain, where she heard them singing their heavenly canticles to the notes of the sweetest music, and where she conversed with Jesus, as in the days of old, on the "better part which she had chosen, and which would never be taken away from her."

Life of St. Mary Magdalen
Gospels of St. Luke and St. John.

THE BRIGAND CHIEF.

UNDER THE REIGN of the Emperor Maurice there lived a brigand chief, who, with his cruel followers, spread terror throughout the country and made the highways unsafe for travelers. Now, it came to pass that, by the grace of God, this man was suddenly converted, as if by a miracle, and from being a ferocious wolf became a gentle lamb.

Soon after his conversion he went to the Emperor, and with genuine tears confessed his many crimes, at the same time offering himself to suffer any punishment that might be decreed against him. But Maurice, edified at seeing so much unaffected and heart-felt sorrow in one who had been so wicked, granted him full pardon, and, having admonished him with great earnestness to continue to walk perseveringly in the path he had now chosen, permitted him to depart.

Not many weeks afterwards this same man having become dangerously ill, was taken to the hospital. He himself foresaw that his end was near; and during one stormy night—it was in the autumn season—he thought that he would not live to see the light of the following morning. He therefore sent immediately for the priest, again made his confession with tears of sincere contrition flowing from his eyes, and devoutly received the last consolations of religion.

When the solemn rites were ended, raising up his dying eyes to Heaven, he prayed thus to God: "O my Divine Savior, I am not going to ask you for any new favor; I desire only that you will grant to me what you have already granted to so great a number, and that is that you will show me mercy and forgive me, as you forgave the good thief on the cross when he was dying. Be pleased to receive me as the householder received the laborers who came at the eleventh hour: they certainly had not time to do much work in the vineyard, neither have I much time left me to labor for You. Be pleased, I beseech You, to forgive me the sins I have committed against You, and do not cast me out of Your sight, miserable sinner though I be."

For a long time he continued to pray and weep, from time to time wiping away the tears that fell so abundantly from his eyes with the sheet which covered his bed.

Now, it happened that one of the infirmarians who was in the next room heard these words of the dying man, but being overcome with fatigue, he soon fell asleep. During his sleep, about midnight, he had a vision. He saw, as it were, a pair of scales, with plates of gold, coming down from Heaven, and remaining suspended in the air over the bed on which the dying man lay. Around the bed were men, black and hideous to behold, in great numbers; they were occupied in throwing into the plates of the balance pieces of paper, on which were written all the misdeeds of his lifetime. Then he saw two angels appear, clothed in garments of dazzling white, and take up their position near the other plate. They looked very sorrowful as they saw the first plate weighed down so far with the heavy load of the record of the man's sins, which the evil spirits were throwing into it.

Then one of the angels said to his companion: "Must the soul of this unfortunate man, therefore, perish forever?"

The other angel, with a deep sigh, answered: "Where can we find anything to counterbalance this enormous weight? It is only a few weeks since he repented of his crimes, and how could he, in so short a time, have done sufficient penance to blot out so many sins?"

The wicked spirits imagined now that the soul of the dying thief was certainly their prey, and were beginning to exult in their wicked triumph, when one of the heavenly spirits, seeing that the sheet which covered his bed was wet, and knowing that it was the tears of the repentant sinner that made it so, said to his companion: "Let us put this sheet, watered with the tears of the repentant sinner, in the other basin. Perhaps it may be of sufficient weight to turn the scales in his favor, seeing how merciful Our God is to sinners who ask Him for mercy."

Scarcely had they put into the other plate of the balance the sheet, wet with the tears of sorrow, than it suddenly descended, outweighing the other, which as quickly rose up, as if it contained only some little straw.

"Eternal glory and praise be given to the majesty of God!" cried out the angels. "The soul of this repentant brigand has found mercy with God and is saved, and our prayers have been granted."

Then they led the soul of the deceased with them into Heaven, while the black and hideous spirits descended into Hell, uttering cries of despair.

The infirmarian then awoke, frightened at the vision he had seen. He approached the bed of the robber, and saw that he had just died. He beheld also the sheet he had seen in his dream, wet all over with the tears he had shed; and he learned from those who lay near him that he had never ceased, as long as he could utter a word, to implore the mercy of God, and to show his sincere repentance for the sins of his life.

The infirmarian piously kept that sheet, wet with the tears sorrow had caused to flow, and often showed it to others, who at the sight of their many and grievous sins were tempted to despair when their last hour came. Moreover, he recounted to them his wondrous dream, and, thus consoled and encouraged, they were led to die a happy death in the confidence of obtaining a favorable judgment from Him Who said: "Him that cometh to Me I will in no way cast out."

Rep. du Cat., iii. 353.

PART IX

"LEAD US NOT INTO TEMPTATION"

60

THE MEANING OF THIS PETITION

My child, when you say, "Lead us not into temptation," you do not ask God to keep away temptation from you, but only that He may give you the grace not to yield to temptation.

THE ABBOT AND THE YOUNG MONK.

A young monk one day went to visit a venerable Abbot. As they were speaking of spiritual things, the monk said: "My Father, there was a time when I was much troubled with temptations, but, thanks be to God, I am never troubled with them now."

The Abbot asked him how he had been able to become free from them.

"I prayed to God that He would never permit me to be tempted again, and He has been pleased to hear my prayer."

The Abbot answered: "My son, you have done a very foolish thing. Go back quickly, and pray to God again to send you temptations, but along with them to give you the grace necessary to overcome them. If you have no temptations to fight against, you may easily become careless in the practice of virtue, and so may fall into the sin of sloth."

The young monk did as the Abbot had advised him, and he continued to live a holy life.

Lohner Examples.

St. Paul tells us that we must mortify our members that are upon the earth. This mortification means that we must all the days of our life fight against our passions and evil inclinations, and that it is in Heaven only that we are to look for rest and peace

THE ABBOT THEODORE AND THE NOVICE.

A certain novice one day complained to the Abbot Theodore that he had been for eight years trying to overcome his evil inclinations, and that he had not yet been able to do this, but that they still annoyed him.

"My brother," replied the Abbot, "you complain of this warfare of eight years, and I have spent seventy years in solitude, and during all that time I have not for a single day been free from temptations; and every day during all these years I have had to contend with my evil inclinations, so that I might be able to keep them in subjection. It is only when this life is ended that our struggle against temptation will come to an end."

61

"BLESSED IS THE MAN WHO ENDURETH TEMPTATION."

The Apostle St. James says in his Epistle: "Blessed is the man that endureth temptation, for when he hath been tried, he shall receive the crown of life which God hath prepared for them that love Him" (St. Jas. i. 12).

A VOICE IN THE WILDERNESS.

An old man, who had chosen St. John the Baptist as his patron, tried also to imitate his example. He left his home and his friends, to live in a lonely wilderness in the exercise of prayer and penance.

When he had spent about ten years there, the devil tried to fill his mind with thoughts of despair, and to make him think that he would most certainly be lost forever.

When this terrible temptation was at its height, he took the resolution to leave the wilderness, where he had lived so long, and return home.

"Of what use is it for me to remain here any longer, since I am so surely to be lost forever?"

As he was about to depart, he heard a voice which said to him, "What are you going to do?"

The old man, hearing the voice in that solitary place, became afraid; he looked around him, but could see no one. He answered in these words the question that was put to him:

"I am going to return to my home in the world, since I cannot save my poor soul here."

The same voice answered: "That is a temptation of the most wicked one. Remain here in your cell. During the ten years you have spent in this place you have had to fight against many temptations, and you have overcome them all. For each of them there is in store for you in Heaven a bright crown of glory. For the time to come these temptations to despair will no longer trouble you."

The old man received consolation from these words. He lived for many years after that time, serving God in prayer and penance as before. The end came at last, and he is now in Heaven, enjoying the reward he had merited because he had overcome so many temptations.

RUFFIN: *Vies des Pères*, liv. 3.

SEVEN CROWNS GAINED.

Long, long ago, in the desert of Thebais, there dwelt a hermit who was far advanced in years.

This holy man had a disciple whom he loved with a fatherly affection. It was his custom every evening to give this young man a short instruction, and after they had spent some time together in prayer, the old man would give him his blessing, and then both would retire to rest.

It happened one night that the hermit, having been very tired, fell asleep in the middle of his instruction. The young man waited a long time by his side, hoping that he would soon awake, and then that they would, as usual, say their night prayers together before going to rest for the night.

But still the old man continued to sleep. Midnight came, and the disciple began to grow very weary. A temptation came into his mind to leave his master and retire to rest, but he put away the temptation and remained with him.

Shortly after this the temptation returned, but he again drove it away. Seven times was he tempted in this manner, and seven times did he put the temptation away; for he was determined not to leave the old man alone, and not to go to bed till he had first obtained his blessing.

At length the hermit awoke. Finding the young man still beside him, he said to him: "My son, why did you not retire to rest at the usual time?"

"Because, my father, you did not tell me to go."

"And why did you not awake me?"

"I did not like to disturb you, my father, for I saw that you were very weary."

Tears came to the eyes of the good old man when he saw so much virtue in one so young, and he gave thanks to God for the graces He had already given his young disciple. They then knelt and said their prayers; and the young man, having received his blessing, lay down to sleep.

The hermit also fell asleep. During his sleep he had a vision. He thought he saw a beautiful palace, and in it a magnificent throne, and over the throne there were seven bright crowns of glory shining like the sun.

By his side stood an angel, who seemed to have been sent to show him all these things. He said to the angel: "For whom is that throne, and for whom are those crowns of glory that I see suspended over it?"

The angel answered: "The throne is for your disciple, who is so virtuous and obedient, and these seven crowns he has merited this very night."

When the morning had come, he summoned his disciple, and asked him what good works he had done during the night.

"I have done nothing that I can call to mind." But the hermit insisted upon his telling him all that had passed, even to his very thoughts.

"My father," he answered, "I have done nothing that can be of any merit in the sight of God. It is true that when you were asleep I was seven times tempted to leave you and retire to bed, and seven times I put away the temptation. That is all I have done during the night."

The old man then knew how he had gained the seven crowns, and he saw by this that every victory that is gained over temptations, no matter how small they may be, gains much merit before God.

Lives of the Fathers of the Desert.

A NOBLE ANSWER.

When the wicked Judge Rictiovarus ordered St. Macra to deny Jesus Christ, she answered him: "Never will I be guilty of such a crime, for I am a Christian, and the child of God."

The Judge said: "Sacrifice to the gods, else you shall be put to the most terrible tortures."

The martyr answered: "Know, O most cruel tyrant, that your threats shall never be able to take from my heart the faith and love of my Divine Master! Jesus Christ is my God and my all. He is my treasure, my life, my happiness; and nothing shall ever separate me from Him."

This also should be your answer to Satan, my child, when he tempts you to offend God.

BENIGNE DE FREMIOT'S GENEROUS ANSWER.

Benigne de Fremiot, father of St. Jane Frances, was placed in charge of the fortress of Samur during the war of the Huguenots in France. It happened that during one of the skirmishes that took place the son of Benigne fell into the hands of the enemy. They imagined that now they had a favorable opportunity of obtaining the castle of Samur, which they had for a long time tried to capture, but without success. So they went to the gate of the castle, taking with them the son of the governor; and having asked him to come to the gate, told him that if he did not deliver up the castle to them, they would at once kill his son before his eyes.

These words pierced the father's heart as if an arrow had passed through it; but, remembering his duty to his King, he at once answered without hesitation: "Benigne de Fremiot may indeed lose his son, but he will never be unfaithful to his King."

EULOGIUS AND THE LEPER.

In ancient times, there lived in the East a learned man, who found his greatest delight in the study of human science, and only in the second place thought of the science of the Saints.

One day, when alone, he said to himself: "What will all this knowledge avail me, and the acquisition of all human wisdom, if I am ignorant of the only great science which should occupy the mind of man—the knowledge of God and of those things which lead to God?"

Thereupon he formed the great resolution of consecrating the rest of his life to the service of God, and in the performance of those things which lead to God. He began by distributing among the poor all the worldly goods he possessed, and then earnestly besought God to make known to him the kind of life He desired him to embrace.

God was pleased to hear and grant his prayer. One day, in the public square of the city, he met a leper, who, through the terrible disease that had come upon him, had been deprived of the use of his hands and feet.

Filled with compassion at his terrible condition, he took the resolution before God of taking care of him as long as he might live, and of providing for him everything that was necessary for his support, hoping thus to gain for himself the mercy of God here and the Kingdom of Heaven hereafter.

He therefore took the infirm man to his house, and for the space of fifteen years tended him as if he had been his own child.

At the end of that time the man, who had until then showed great gratitude to his benefactor, suddenly became most ungrateful. Under a great temptation of the evil one, who was enraged at seeing

Eulogius gaining so much merit in the sight of God, the leper constantly complained that he was not sufficiently cared for. "You must have been guilty of a great number of crimes," he one day said to him, "since you have been condemned to do so much penance. I will no longer abide in your wicked company. Take me back to the place where you found me. The generosity of the rich, who will see me in passing, will be sufficient to procure for me the necessaries of life. Besides, I will be able to see and converse with my fellow-men, which I cannot do in this place." These words grieved the heart of the compassionate Eulogius, but far from becoming angry with him, he only redoubled his attention to him, and ceased not to beseech Our Lord to change the heart of the poor man, who was so dear to him. A miserly person could not dread the loss of his treasures as much as he feared being obliged to relinquish the care of his dear leper.

Not knowing what more he could do to appease him, and to keep him from leaving him, he thought that he would take him to the place where the great St. Antony dwelt.

When they reached his cell in the desert, the Saint made the poor man whom Providence had so abundantly provided for, and yet who did not seem to acknowledge it, see how sinful his conduct had been, and showed him that it was all a temptation of the most wicked one.

He concluded by predicting to him and to his benefactor that in forty days they would both die. "You have only a short space of time now left for exercising the great virtue of patience the one for the other, since forty days hence you shall both die, and it would be indeed sad to think that by separating yourselves from each other during that short time you would forfeit so much of the glory that awaits you."

At that moment the leper was delivered from the temptation that had tormented him, and Eulogius returned home consoled. They dwelt together in mutual happiness in the place where they had already spent so many years, blessing and praising God.

On the fortieth day, as St. Antony had predicted, they both fell asleep in the Lord, Eulogius dying first. How great must now be his recompense for having served God so faithfully in the midst of so many trials!

L'Année des Saints, p. 316.

THE VISION OF MOSES THE ANCHORITE.

There lived in the desert of Scete a solitary whose name was Moses. This holy man, having been for a long time tempted in many ways by Satan and the spirits of darkness, resolved to visit St. Isidore the Abbot, a great servant of God, to obtain consolation in his trials, and his counsel how to persevere.

The holy Abbot received him with great kindness, and endeavored to impart to his afflicted soul all the comfort in his power, using for this purpose the consoling words of the Holy Scriptures.

Then he led him to the outside of his cell, and said to him: "My son, look towards the west, and tell me what you behold."

Moses did so, and he answered: "I see a great and ferocious multitude preparing to attack me."

"Now," said Isidore, "turn towards the east. What do you see there?"

Moses replied: "I behold an innumerable host of angels standing in the midst of a brilliant light prepared to come to my assistance to defend me."

"Behold, then," said the Abbot, "an image of the conflict in which you are now engaged. The number of your adversaries is indeed great, but who can count the multitude of those whom God has sent to aid you?" This vision, and the inspired words of the Abbot, infused new courage into the anchorite, and he returned to his cell comforted.

Lives of the Fathers of the Desert.

WE MUST NOT EXPOSE OURSELVES TO TEMPTATION

M y child, you must not put yourself willfully into temptation, but rather fly from it; for the Holy Ghost says: "He that loveth the danger shall perish in it" (Ecclus. iii. 27).

THE GOOD GIRL OF MILAN.

Near the city of Milan, on the road leading to Innspruck, a young woman, about seventeen years of age, was taking care of her mother's flock, which was feeding in the valley. Her name was Mary. She had not much worldly wealth, but she was rich in merits for Heaven, and was in a special manner devout to the most holy Mother of God.

One day, as she was singing a pious hymn in honor of Our Lady, the manager of the great theatre of Milan happened to pass by. When he heard her singing so sweetly, he stopped to listen, for he had seldom heard a voice so powerful and melodious.

"If I could only secure that voice for my theatre," he said to himself, "my fortune would soon be made."

Going up to her, he asked her to tell him her name, and where her parents dwelt.

"My father is dead," she answered, "and I live with my mother in that little cottage which you see by the side of the wood."

"Come with me, and take me to your mother. I want to speak to her."

"But I have no one to take care of my sheep," she said.

"You need not be afraid of them," he answered, "for if any of them should stray before your return, I will pay ten times their value."

"But tell me, sir, why do you wish to see my poor mother?"

"I am going to make her rich, and you also. Your voice is so beautiful that it will make you the first singer in the great theatre of Milan."

"But if I were to go with you to that place I would not be able to save my soul."

"Why not?" he asked.

"Because I learned in my Catechism that those who go to such places not only lose their own souls, but make others lose theirs likewise."

"These are all silly stories," said the manager. "Besides, what does it matter?"

"What is that you say, sir?" she answered, with indignation. "Do you think I am going to put my eternal salvation in danger, even for the wealth of the whole world? Never! So you may go away, for you shall never get me to go with you."

When the manager saw that he could not succeed in persuading the young woman, he left her, and went to try to gain the consent of her mother. The mother was exceedingly glad of the offer, and at once agreed that her daughter should go with him to Milan.

When Mary came home at night with her flock, her mother told her what had taken place, and said that she must make ready to go to Milan next day with the manager, who had been so kind as to consent to take her.

But Mary declared to her mother that she would not go, because that would be to put herself willfully into temptation. All the motives both the manager and her mother could bring forward to induce her to change her mind were of no avail; the young woman would not go.

At last, seeing that they were only wasting words on her, they told her that they would give her till the next morning to think of the proposal.

When Mary was left to herself she was assailed by a terrible temptation. She thought of her mother's poverty, and of the many weary and lonely hours she spent in the fields without gaining more than was barely sufficient to keep them from starvation; and she saw now before her the way to wealth and plenty. Her mother would now be rich, and would be able to spend her old age in ease and comfort.

But, on the other hand, she saw that if she accepted the offer held out to her, she would break the solemn promises of her baptism, and would endanger the salvation of her soul.

In her perplexity she besought the most holy Mother of God and her angel guardian to direct her, and she heard in her own heart the answer to her prayer: "Don't go; you must not turn your back on Jesus to go and serve Satan."

When morning came, she announced to her mother that she had made up her mind not to go.

Her mother burst into tears, scolded her, and even threatened to punish her; but all to no purpose. The manager also told her that if she would not go willingly with him as her mother desired, he would take her away by force.

"O my mother," said the young woman, bursting into tears, "ask me to make any sacrifice you like, but, for God's sake, do not ask me to go where I would be in such danger of losing my poor soul."

But her mother would not yield, and told her to go immediately and make her preparations, and to be ready to leave along with the manager in the space of an hour.

Mary went into her own room, and there, aided by the grace of God, put into execution the resolution she had formed during the previous night. She had often heard it said that the loss of certain teeth entirely changes the voice, and takes from it not only its strength, but its sweetness. So she went to the window, and broke two of her teeth on the angle of a projecting stone.

After this she returned to her mother. Her face gave signs of pleasure rather than of pain, so that her mother thought she had at last made up her mind to go. But no sooner had she begun to speak than the manager detected a strange change in her voice. He looked at her for a moment, and he saw what she had done.

Filled with admiration for such heroic courage, he expressed his sorrow at his conduct, and turning towards her mother, begged her no longer to be angry with a daughter who had shown herself so worthy of her affection and esteem.

SCHUPPE: *Instruct. Relig.*, iii. 532.

THE BOY WHO FELL INTO THE WELL.

A gentleman one day passing through a village saw a little boy called Peter leaning over the edge of a deep well, amusing himself by throwing in little stones, and listening to the noise they made as they fell into the water.

"My child," said the gentleman, "keep back from the edge of the well, lest you overbalance yourself and fall in."

The boy did not seem to heed the warning, but continued playing as before on the brink of the deep well.

The gentleman had not gone far away when he heard a scream. Looking round, he saw that Peter had disappeared, and the people cried out that he had fallen into the well. They all ran towards the place. The gentleman also ran back. Some people brought ladders, and others ropes. One was about to let down a ladder.

"No," said the gentleman; "you may crush him with it. Put down a rope. He may seize it, and we will then pull him out."

They did so. The rope was let down, and Peter took a hold of it. He clung tightly to it, and was by means of it lifted out of the well and saved.

"My child," said the gentleman, "you will keep this rope with great care, for if it had not been for it you would now be dead at the bottom of the well. This will also be a lesson for you not to expose yourself to danger. If you had followed my advice, you would not have fallen into the well." The boy was careful never again to put himself in any danger, but ran away as soon as he saw himself exposed to it.

THE LION IN THE MENAGERIE.

In one of the provincial towns of Scotland a number of wild animals were being exposed in their iron-bound cages to a great multitude of people who had gone into the menagerie to see them. Among these animals was a young lion which seemed in a special manner to attract attention.

The keeper, desiring to enter the cage, opened the door, and before he had time to shut it again, the young lion suddenly sprang out of the cage into the midst of the crowd.

In an instant a rush was made for the door of the tent. Everyone, old and young, ran eagerly away, fearing that they might be devoured, and crying out, "Help! help!"

The lion was soon captured, and again placed in its cage, but the people did not return. They went to their homes, and on the way formed the resolution of never again exposing themselves to a similar danger.

My child, how differently do many people act in a still more important danger—the danger of losing their souls! Instead of flying away from temptation they remain in it, and for the most part yield to sin, and are lost. Learn from this example to fly immediately from temptation, crying out, "O my God, help me!" and you shall certainly persevere.

ALIPIUS AT THE ROMAN SHOWS.

It is sometimes very difficult to overcome the temptations which are thrown in our way; but it is much more difficult, it is almost impossible, to overcome those to which we willfully expose ourselves without cause.

Our Lord has promised to help us when we ask Him, if it is not by our own fault that we are in danger; but if it is by our own fault, He has not promised to help us; on the contrary, He has told us that we shall perish if we go willingly into temptation: "He that loveth the danger shall perish in it."

St. Augustine tells us of a sad misfortune of this kind which befell a friend of his called Alipius.

This young man had gone to Rome to pursue his studies there. In those days there were a great many public shows and theatres in that city, and the young men of Rome used to go to these places, and many of them were thereby ruined both in soul and body.

Now it happened that some of the young men, who were studying in the same school as Alipius, went to these places, and the consequence was that they fell into evil. Alipius was warned before he went to Rome of the dangers he would meet with there, and he very soon saw for himself the evil these shows were doing to his companions. So, from the very beginning, he took the firm resolution never to put his foot in any of these places, lest he might be led away from the path of virtue and fall into sin.

One day there was to be a great display in the amphitheater, and the young men, his comrades, were all in a body going to be present. They asked Alipius to go.

"No," he replied, "I will never go there."

"But you must come with us—just for this once. You will never have such an opportunity again; do come."

"You need not ask me," he replied, "for I have already given you my final answer—I will not go."

One of them said: "If you do not willingly consent to go, we will carry you there by force."

"You can do that if you like," he answered; "but if you do, I will keep my eyes shut all the time; you cannot force me to keep them open."

Unfortunately, after much persuasion and friendly words from those who were seeking to drag him on to ruin, he, as many others have done since then, consented to go with them. "But," he said, "I will keep my eyes shut all the time, for I am quite resolved not to look at anything."

So Alipius went to the amphitheater. There he sat in the midst of his companions with his eyes shut while the acting was going on. It would have been well for him had his ears been shut as well as his eyes, for sin can enter the soul by hearing as well as by seeing.

About the middle of the performance, some of the actors having performed their part with great skill, the people began to cheer and show by the applause they gave how delighted they were. Alipius for a moment forgot his resolution. He opened his eyes, and as soon as he opened them he was so attracted by the scene before him that he made up his mind to keep them open till the play was done. So he yielded to the temptation because he willingly exposed himself to the danger.

Night after night saw Alipius in the amphitheater. He could not now think of anything else. He forgot his work and his prayers, the care of his soul, and everything else, and in the end he was amongst the worst of all his companions.

How long he continued in this way St. Augustine does not tell us, but in the end, no doubt by the prayers of that great Saint, he left off his evil ways and returned to the path of duty; but to all of us he has left a sad example of what a dangerous thing it is to go willfully into temptation.

Confessions of St. Augustine.

SATAN'S COMPLAINT.

St. Antony tells us the following example:

"One day someone knocked very loudly at the gate of the monastery.

"I myself went to see who was there.

"When I opened the gate I was very much frightened, for I saw standing before me a man of great stature. I asked him who he was.

"'I am Satan,' he answered.

"'And what do you want here?' I said to him.

"'I want to know why it is that not only you monks, but also all Christians, are always cursing me. For at the first misfortune that comes to them they always say: 'Cursed be the devil!'"

"I answered: 'They have great reason to curse you, O wicked spirit, for you are always tempting them, and laying snares for them to drag them into sin.'

"Satan answered: 'I am often not so much to blame as you think, for people are often the cause of their own ruin by seeking the occasions of sin, hoping that they will not fall, although they know how frail they are. As for myself, from the time that God became man I have lost my power over them, for they have such strong weapons given them to overcome me. I never could overcome them, if they only used the weapons God has put in their hands. So they need not blame me, nor curse me so much, since it is entirely their own fault that they are lost.'

"I then said: 'My Lord Jesus Christ, I thank Thee because Thou hast overcome the Devil, and givest Thy servants help in the time of need.'

"As soon as Satan heard the name of Jesus uttered he suddenly vanished, and was seen no more."

Life of St. Antony.

My child, the Saints call the eyes "the windows of the soul." It is by the eyes that we see good and bad objects. Blessed are you, then, if, shutting them always to whatever is wrong, you keep them open only to see what is good, and what leads you to God.

"I'LL KEEP MY EYES SHUT."

Little Henry had been very ill. When he was slowly recovering, and was just able to rise from his bed and go about a little, he was left alone for a short time in the room, when his sister came in eating a piece of sweet cake.

Henry's mother had told him that he must not eat anything but what she gave him, and that it would be dangerous for him to eat what the other children did until he was stronger.

His appetite was coming back, and the cake in his sister's hand looked very tempting. He wanted very much to take a bite of it, and his kind sister would gladly have given it to him.

"Jeannie," he said to her, "you must run out of the room at once, and take that sweet cake with you. I'll keep my eyes shut till you get outside the door, so that I may not be tempted to take it."

What a beautiful example from so young a child! If not only children, but also grown-up people, would shut their eyes when they are in temptation, they would easily escape much sin and trouble.

63

TEMPTATION MUST BE RESISTED
AT ONCE

W hen you are tempted to do what is wrong, put away the temptation at once; for if you are careless in putting it away at the beginning, it may in the end kill your soul.

THE NEST OF VIPERS.

A countryman one day was walking through a wood. On the side of the path he suddenly beheld a nest full of vipers. As soon as he saw them he started back with fear, but at length he took courage and went to look at the nest. He found in it seven of them, all quite young.

When he saw that they were so young, he took up the nest and carried it home with him. For several weeks he fed them with bread and milk, and showed them to all those who came to see him.

About three weeks from the time he had brought them home, one of those who came to see the beasts said to him: "My friend, I advise you to kill these vipers at once while they are young, for if you continue to keep them, and feed them as you are now doing, you may depend upon it they will one day attack you with their poisonous fangs and kill you."

"Oh, do not be afraid," he replied; "they are quite young yet, and can do me no harm. I will take very great care that, when they begin to grow dangerous, I will soon get rid of them."

"I would advise you to kill them at once," said the other; "otherwise you may one day find to your cost that they have taken you by surprise."

This advice was not attended to. The visitor went away, and the man still kept the vipers.

Not many days afterwards the same visitor returned. What was his surprise to see his poor friend suffering dreadful torture! The vipers had attacked him, as he had been forewarned. His friend went at once to get assistance, but it was too late. The poison had entered his blood, and the wretched man soon afterwards expired.

Mrs. Herbert.

64

TEMPTATIONS ACCOMPANY US THROUGH LIFE

As long as you are in this world, my child, you will have temptations; but be not afraid, for they cannot do you any harm without your own consent.

DANGERS ON ALL SIDES.

One of the holy solitaries who lived in the deserts of the East was one day led by the Spirit of God into a great city, and was shown how the people were being tempted by the evil spirits.

So great was the number of these wicked ones that the skies seemed to be darkened with them. They were going about with the greatest activity, putting temptations before the minds of everyone they met.

They surrounded the merchants in their shops, tempting them to cheat those who were buying from them. They were standing near those who were idle, and tempting them to speak evil of their neighbors. He saw others walking side by side with young people, suggesting evil thoughts to them; and others he saw filling the minds of women with thoughts of vanity, and inspiring them with a high idea of their own attractions.

But their temptations did not stop here. He saw an immense multitude of these evil spirits enter the church along with those who went in to say their prayers; and as soon as they knelt down, they at once put distracting thoughts before their minds, so as to hinder them from praying well.

He saw, too, that they had often to fly away, because those whom they were tempting had recourse to God for help, but only to return in a short time with even greater force; and whenever they succeeded in making anyone yield to sin, they were filled with a fiendish joy, and the greater the evil that had been done the greater was their joy.

When the holy man saw all this, he cried out: "O my God, keep away temptation from me!" And when he returned to his desert home, he never ceased exhorting the religious whom he met to say over and over again with the utmost fervor that petition of the Lord's Prayer, "Lead us not into temptation"; "for," said he to them, "these wicked spirits are to be found not only in large cities, but wherever there is a human being on the face of the earth."

HAUTERIVE: *Catch. de Persu.*

THE FISHERMAN AND THE LITTLE FISH.

A fisherman stood at the river-side with a fishing-rod in his hand trying to catch the fishes that were swimming in the water.

At the end of his fishing-line was a hook, which was hid from the eyes of the fishes by the bait with which the fisherman had covered it. A little fish, attracted by the pleasing appearance of the food, came near to it, and, thinking that it would be as pleasant to the taste as it was to the eye, opened its mouth and swallowed it.

But in a moment it found out the mistake it had made, for the sharp point of the hook entered its side, and it began to writhe in pain. Then the fisherman, seeing by the motion of the fish that it had swallowed the bait, quickly drew out the line, and the fish lay in agony on the bank of the river. The fisherman, proud of his capture, took the fish into his hands and killed it.

It is in this way that Satan tries to capture your soul, my child. He puts before you something which is pleasant to the senses, but carefully conceals from you the remorse which lies beneath. If you yield to the temptation and commit the sin, you are then in the power of Satan, who only waits the moment of your death to drag you into hell. Oh, how careful you should be, then, to resist temptation as soon as you perceive it!

HOW SATAN TEMPTS THE JUST AT DEATH.

St. Odilo, of Cluny, had spent more than fifty years in serving God when he began to feel his end drawing near. Instead of diminishing his penances, he increased them, because he saw that in a short time he would no longer be able to gain merit for Heaven. Satan, who had so often been overcome by his holy prayers, united all his forces for a last assault as the holy man lay in his agony. He appeared to him in a hideous form to frighten him and tempt him to despair; but, as the Saint had been accustomed to resist him all his lifetime, he was able now also to drive him away.

With a holy confidence, and in words of disdain, he said to him: "Begone, thou detestable and wicked beast, the sworn enemy of the honor of God! What has brought you here? What have you against me? Tell me! In the name of the living God, your judge and mine, I order you to depart!" In saying these words, he made the sign of the cross, and Satan, in confusion, suddenly vanished from his sight.

65

BAD COMPANY A GREAT CAUSE OF YIELDING TO TEMPTATION

My child, the reason why so many people fall into sin is because they put themselves willfully into the occasion of sin by going with bad companions

THE GARDENER AND HIS SON.

There was once a gardener who had a son, whom he brought up in the fear of God. He was a gentle boy, and the joy of his parents' hearts, because he was so modest, obedient, and pious.

But when he went to school, he met some companions who had been brought up very differently. Their conduct, and the words they uttered, showed that they had already grown old in evil. These companions soon made his acquaintance, and he himself began to find pleasure in their company.

But his father, who knew well how to fulfill his duty, was watching with a careful eye the kind of children his son had chosen for his playmates, and he soon perceived that they were bad.

"Come with me, my child," he one day said to him. "I want to show you something."

Saying these words, they both entered the garden together, and the father, taking a basket, placed in it seven apples. Six of these were the most beautiful he could find, but the seventh was rotten and full of worms.

"These are for you, my boy. You can do with them what you like."

The boy took the basket with great delight, but when he saw the rotten apple he asked his father if he might throw it away.

"Why would you throw it away?" asked the father.

"Because it will spoil all the others."

"On the contrary," said the father, "do you not think that the six good ones will cure the rottenness of the bad one, and make it sound again? You shall see. Let us leave them all together in the basket for eight days."

The son did not seem to believe that this would be the case; but the father took the basket with the fruit, and placed it in safety under lock and key.

Three days afterwards they went to look at it. Already three of the apples were spoiled. "Did I not tell you," said the boy, "that if you left that rotten apple among them they would soon all be spoiled?"

The father made no answer, but locked the door again. Five days afterwards they returned to the place; but as soon as they had opened the door they felt a most disagreeable smell, and when they looked they found that all the apples were rotten. At the sight of the spoiled fruit the child began to cry.

"Do not weep, my child," said his father; "I will give you other apples. In doing what I have done I only wanted to give you a lesson. Didn't I see you a few days ago in the company of boys who were not good? These boys were, before God, rotten like that apple in the basket. By going with them you also would soon become like themselves, for they would corrupt your innocent and beautiful soul by making you offend God. One bad boy is sufficient to spoil many good ones, as this one bad apple spoiled the six others that were near it. I can easily give you other apples as beautiful as the ones that have been destroyed, but when your soul has once lost its innocence, what can ever restore its lost beauty?"

The boy understood the lesson, and for the future was always careful to keep away from temptation.

SCHOPPE: *Instruct. Religieuses.*

THE LITTLE BOY OF PORTUGAL.

A little boy, only eight years old, was sitting one evening by the side of his father and mother in their comfortable home at Monte Mayor, a little village in Portugal. This was in the year 1503. The name of the child was John.

Someone came to the door and asked hospitality for the night. John's parents received him kindly, and in return for their generosity he recounted to them the beauties of the cities of his own country, Spain, and the magnificence of the palaces and churches of the Spanish capital.

John listened with the utmost eagerness to the account he gave, and during the whole of that night he could not sleep, but spent the hours in picturing to his mind the grandeur of what he had heard described by the stranger. Oh, what would he not give to be able to see them! An idea came into his mind. "I will go along with the stranger tomorrow," he said. So, unknown to his parents, he left his happy home and followed him, keeping him always in sight, but never going up to him, lest he might be sent back again.

But after many days spent in this way, he soon found out that he had allowed himself to be deceived. He had nothing to eat, except some crusts of bread he received in charity by the way, and at night he had often to sleep under the hedges or the trees. He now thought how different all this was from the comforts of home, and the abundance of good food his parents always gave him. He was ashamed to return and to confess he had done wrong, so he continued to follow in the steps of his guide, each one of which was carrying him farther and farther away from his parents and his home.

At length he reached Castile. He could go no farther. He sank down faint and weary upon a stone, his heart nearly broken with grief. "Oh, that I had never listened to the words of that man!" he said; "I would at this moment be comfortable in my parents' home, where I had so much of everything I could desire. What a fool I was to allow myself to be deceived! And now I must die here, for I cannot walk another step." And the child buried his head in his hands and began to sob aloud.

While he was thus weeping, he was aroused by the rough voice of a shepherd, who was tending his flock in the neighborhood; he asked him what he was doing there.

The boy told him his sad story, and the kind man took him to his house, and gave him shelter till such time as he would be able to restore him to his parents.

But he never saw them again, for his mother died of grief, and his father left the place where he had lost the only things he had ever loved on earth—his wife and his child.

This lesson was, for the boy, the foundation of a life of holiness; he became afterwards a great Saint in God's Church. His name is St. John of God, and the Church celebrates his festival on the eighth day of March.

So, my child, when Satan tempts you to disobey God, say to the tempter: "No, I will never turn my back upon my kind Father in Heaven, Who is so good to me, and my dear Mother Mary, who has watched over me since my childhood. I know that if I yield to your temptation, my future life, instead of being full of pleasure, as you tell me, will be one of misery, grief, and remorse. So begone, Satan!"

66

IN TEMPTATION WE MUST WATCH AND PRAY

M y child, there is nothing the Devil hates so much as prayer when we are in temptation, because he knows that if we pray, he can never obtain a victory over us, for prayer is the safeguard of a Christian in all his dangers. Therefore he always tries to keep us from praying when we are in temptation.

"WATCH AND PRAY."

A young man, who was anxious to please God and save his soul, asked his mother one day to tell him how he could most easily overcome temptations. "For," said he, "I am very much tempted to do wrong." His mother went to her room for a box, and, unlocking it, brought out a ring. "Take this ring, my child, and wear it always on your finger."

The young man looked, and saw engraved on the ring these words: "Watch and Pray."

"Now, my child," she said to him, "every morning and night, and as often as you are tempted to offend God, look at that ring, and recall to mind the words you see engraved on it, and you will then easily banish the temptation. It is the advice that Jesus Himself gave to His disciples."

The young man put the ring on his finger, and took care to follow his mother's advice. He never afterwards found any difficulty in banishing temptations.

Catch. en Examples.

WHY HE FAILED.

St. Macarius of Egypt was one day walking along a road at some distance from his monastery, thinking on heavenly things. Suddenly the evil spirit appeared before him. He was clothed in a linen garment, which seemed to be full of holes, and in each of the holes there was a little vial.

The Saint asked him where he was going, and what was the meaning of all the little vials he carried along with him.

"I am going to the monastery," he said, "to tempt the monks who are there; and these little vials represent the different ways by which I will tempt them. I will tempt them first with one temptation, and if I do not succeed with it, I will try another; and if this one also fails, I will try some of the others; and I am sure that before I have tried all kinds of temptations against them some of them will yield."

Saying this, he vanished from his sight; but St. Macarius remained in the same place, thinking on the many dangers we are in every day from the temptations of the Devil.

Towards evening Satan appeared again to him, as if he had been coming back from the monastery, but he looked very angry and disappointed.

The Saint said to him: "I command you in the name of God to tell me how you succeeded in your temptations against the monks."

Satan answered: "All your monks are invincible; I tried temptation after temptation, but all in vain. As soon as I put a temptation before them, they at once began to pray, and, of course, I failed; for as soon as they began their prayer, God came to their assistance. There were some of them who seemed to be tired and weary; at first I thought I would easily succeed with them: but they also were on the watch, and as soon as they saw it was a temptation, they too began to pray, and I had to fly away from them."

"And did you not succeed in making some of them yield?" asked the Saint.

Satan answered: "Yes, there was one whom I got to yield a little."

"Which of them was it?"

"Theopemptus is his name," the evil spirit answered, and then disappeared.

When the Saint returned to the monastery in the evening, he went at once to the cell of Theopemptus.

"Well, my brother," said the Saint, "how are you?"

"Thanks to your holy prayers, Father, I am very well."

After some little conversation, St. Macarius said to him: "I am going to ask you a question; you must answer me, and tell me the truth. When you were saying your prayers today, had you not some very distracting thoughts in your mind?"

Theopemptus, not wishing to acknowledge his fault, added another one to it by deceiving him. "No, Father," he answered, "I had none."

"Well, that is indeed strange," replied the Saint, "for I am very often tempted with all kinds of thoughts at my prayers, although I have been many years longer in the desert than you have been."

The monk, seeing his great humility, at length said: "O my Father, forgive me; today I was very much tempted by distracting thoughts at my prayers. First one kind of thought came to trouble me, and then another and another. I tried to put them away for a long time, till at last, I must confess, I yielded a little, and allowed them for a short time to remain in my mind."

"O my brother," answered Saint Macarius, "you must promise me to resist every temptation for the time to come; and if these temptations are hard to put away, at once raise up your mind to Heaven, and ask God to give you strength, and you will always be victorious."

Some time after this Satan again appeared to the Saint, as he did before, and the Saint asked him: "What success had you this time in the monastery?" "None at all," he said angrily; "every one of them is still watching and praying, and so long as they are doing that, I have not the least chance of success in making them yield. But what makes me more angry this time is that the one whom I succeeded in making yield a little to temptation last time is now more firm and watchful than all the others."

From this example we learn two things: (1) That the Devil is constantly trying to make us yield to temptation. (2) That the way to overcome his temptations is, as Jesus Christ has told us, to watch and to pray.

Lives of the Fathers of the Desert.

SISTER GRACE OF VALENCIA.

Sister Grace of Valencia was one hundred and twelve years old when she died. During her long life Satan ceased not to tempt her; but, knowing she had no strength of herself to overcome him, she always turned towards Jesus for help, and was always victorious.

"Begone, you evil spirit," she would sometimes say—"begone, I am not afraid of you; all your efforts will never separate Sister Grace from her God. I will always live united to Jesus Christ, my beloved Spouse, and your formidable Judge. In spite of all your temptations, I am stronger than you are and all the spirits of Hell put together; so I defy you. Go back, then, to Hell, out of which you came, and leave me alone."

At other times she would say: "What do you want with me? Why do you still torment a poor old woman like me? You indeed show how weak you are when you come in this way to attack a woman who is weighed down with years. I order you, in the name of Jesus Christ, to go away and leave me."

Again, she would sometimes put the evil spirit to flight by saying the holy names of Jesus and Mary. But, although the Devil was always beaten, he always returned to tempt her, for he hoped that one day he might succeed in making her offend God, and this would be for him a great triumph, and a sufficient recompense for all his pains; but in this he failed. Grace always triumphed over him, because she always trusted in God and not in herself.

Let your prayer in temptation always be: "Our help is in the name of the Lord." "My Jesus, help me." And, by frequent and fervent communion, keep Jesus in your soul, and Satan will never be able to touch you.

67

PRAYER TO OUR LADY POWERFUL IN TEMPTATION

O ne of the surest means of overcoming temptations is to have recourse to the most holy Mother of God, who is called the "Help of Christians."

"COME WITH ME TO HEAVEN."

St. Alphonsus relates that there was a certain young man whom the Devil tempted with thoughts of despair. He brought before his mind all the sins he had ever done, and showed him how enormous they were, and filled his mind with the thought that they were too great for pardon.

Now it happened that this man from his childhood had a tender devotion to Our Blessed Lady, and particularly to her seven Dolors. In the midst of his temptations he always had recourse to her, and by her help he succeeded in banishing the thoughts of despair from his mind.

When the hour of his death drew near, Satan redoubled his attacks, that he might at that final moment gain his soul. Thoughts of sadness filled the dying man's mind, because he began to think that after all his sins would keep him out of the Kingdom of Heaven.

But the most holy Mother of God, seeing her beloved child a prey to these terrible thoughts, appeared to him, and said: "My child, why are you afraid, and what makes you so sad—you who so often used to meditate on my sorrows, and feel so much compassion for me in my sufferings? Come, take courage; my Son Jesus has sent me to console you. Come, then, come joyfully with me into Paradise."

When she had said these words the young man breathed his last, and delivered up his soul to God, filled with joy and consolation.

St. Alphonsus: *Virtues of Mary.*

THE HEROIC MOTHER.

Marie Leczinska, spouse of Louis XV. of France, had a son whom she also trained up in the fear of God from his infancy.

When he grew up to be a young man, he had to leave his mother's home and live for a time among strangers.

During his absence word was brought to his mother that he had to spend part of his time among those who would take a pleasure in corrupting his young heart. As soon as she was informed of this, she threw herself on her knees at the foot of a crucifix, and recommended her beloved child to the protection of his Heavenly Father.

"O my God," she prayed, "take my darling boy to Thyself, rather than permit him to offend Thee by sin, or to lose the treasure of his innocence." God heard the prayer of that good mother, and delivered him from the evil that threatened him.

When he returned home, the first question his mother asked him was if he had much to endure from the companions he had to mingle with.

"Yes, my mother," he replied, "great indeed were the dangers they put around me to ruin me; but, thanks be to God, and to your prayers, I have still kept my soul pure and stainless."

Not long after this time the young Prince became suddenly very ill, and died in sentiments of great piety.

On the evening of the day of his death his mother sent for her other children, and, with tears in her eyes, said to them: "Your brother is dead; it is I, your mother, who asked God to take him to Himself. Some time ago I heard that he was in danger of committing sin. I went on my knees, and prayed fervently to God to take him out of this world rather than permit him to lose his innocence. God has heard me, and I thank Him for His goodness to me. Still I weep for him, for I loved him as dearly as any mother could love her child."

The Abbé Fliche

THE LITTLE BOY AND THE SERPENT.

A certain man was one day in his garden in company with his little son. While he was occupied in tilling the ground, the boy amused himself by running hither and thither along the walks, and in gathering flowers.

Suddenly he uttered a piercing cry, which brought his alarmed father to the place where he was standing. He, on arriving, saw a serpent behind one of the trees; it was this that had frightened the boy and caused him to scream. The man soon succeeded in destroying the obnoxious reptile.

"My son," he said, "you see how very ugly is the serpent I have killed, and I am not surprised that you were afraid of it when you saw it; yet it was a harmless one, and was filled with fear when it saw you. One stroke of my stick was sufficient to lay it dead at your feet. But there is another kind of serpent the bite of which is mortal, and which is continually pursuing you, and lies in wait for you night and day to do you harm. That dangerous serpent is sin. It can only be overcome by God's grace. Do not forget, then, my child, to have recourse to God when you see yourself in danger of being attacked by it. You pray earnestly to Him to "Deliver you from evil," which may threaten your temporal life. This is a prayer very pleasing to Him; but how much more fervently should you say these same words when Satan by his temptations urges you to commit sin?"

Schmidt: Instruct. Religieuse.

A HOLY HERMIT'S TEMPTATIONS.

St. Gregory of Tours, in his book entitled "Lives of the Saints," relates that a certain holy hermit, whose name was Caluppa, had been for a long time tormented by remorse of conscience for the sins of his former life. Satan also tempted him with thoughts of despair, frequently appearing to him in the most affrighting forms, that he might harass him in his solitude.

The holy man made use of many different means to free himself from these terrible mental tortures, but all in vain.

One day as he was devoutly reciting the Lord's Prayer, and had come to the last petition, he suddenly stopped, and said it again and again with all the devotion in his power: "Deliver us from evil." The more frequently he said these words, the greater was the calm he felt in his heart, and the evil spirits who had been tormenting him fled away, crying out: "That prayer is for us a terrible torture."

68

HOW GREAT SHOULD BE OUR CONFIDENCE IN SAYING THIS PETITION

W hen you ask to be "delivered from evil," you should do so with a firm confidence that your Heavenly Father will hear your prayer, and come to your assistance, because He is so powerful and so good.

THE FATHER'S PROMISE.

Annie Young lived in the country. The school which she went to was more than a mile from her home, and as the roads were bad, it was too far for her to walk in the winter season. So her father always sent her to school in the morning in a sleigh or carriage, and brought her home at night in the same way.

One afternoon he stopped at the schoolhouse, and told Annie that he was going along the road several miles, and might not return till after school was over. "But wait for me till I come," he said; "I will be here before dark." When school was over, the children wrapped themselves in their cloaks, overcoats, and shawls, and set out for home.

"Are you not going?" asked one of the last that left the school-room, as she saw Annie take her seat by the stove.

"Father told me to wait for him," said Annie.

"But are you not afraid to stay here alone?"

"What is there to be afraid of? It is pleasant and warm here."

"I should be afraid to stay here alone," said the girl; "it will be dark very soon."

"Father said he would be here before dark," was Annie's reply.

"What will you do if he doesn't come?"

"There is no doesn't about it," replied Annie. "Father will come for me; he said he would."

Annie was left alone. Time seemed to move very slowly; the sun went down, and the room began to be gloomy. She went to the door, and looked out for her father. He was not in sight, although from the door of the schoolroom one could see nearly a mile down the road.

When she was standing at the door, a man came along with a yoke of oxen and a sleigh. He was a neighbor of theirs.

"What are you doing here?" he asked of Annie.

"Waiting for father," was her answer.

"It will soon be dark," he said; "you had better get into my sleigh, and go as far as my house. It would not be very pleasant for you to stay here all night." "Father will be sure to come for me," said Annie; "he told me to wait for him till he came."

It was nearly dark, but not quite, when Mr. Young drove up to the door. He had driven fast to get there. He had been kept longer than he expected, and had left his business unfinished in order to keep his promise, and get back to his child before dark.

"Were you not afraid I would not come, Annie?" he asked, as he wrapped her up in a warm rug.

"No, father," was the child's answer; "you said you would come, and I knew you would."

How beautiful this is! If we could have the same trust in our Heavenly Father, in the dangers of this life, as Annie Young had in her earthly father, how happy we would be! And yet Annie's father had not the one-hundredth part of the love your Father in Heaven has for you.

Bishop Gilmour.

THE WORDS KING DAVID SAID.

"Mother," said a little girl one day, "what did David mean when he said: 'Preserve me, O God, for in Thee do I put my trust'?"

Her mother answered: "Do you remember the little girl we saw walking with her father in the woods yesterday?"

"Oh yes, mother. Wasn't she beautiful?"

"Yes, she was a gentle, loving little thing, and her father was very kind to her. Do you remember what she said when she came to the narrow bridge over the stream?"

"I don't like to think of that bridge," answered the child, "for it is very dangerous—just two loose planks laid across, and no railing. If she had stepped to one side or to the other, she would have fallen into the water."

"Do you remember what she said?" repeated the mother.

"Yes, mamma; she stopped a minute as if afraid to go over, and then looked up into her father's face, and, asking him to take hold of her hand, she said: 'You will take hold of me, dear father; I don't feel afraid when you have hold of my hand.' And her father looked so lovingly upon her, and took tight hold of her, as if she were very precious to him."

"Well, my child," said the mother, "I think David felt just like that little girl when he wrote these words you have just asked me about. You know this life is full of dangers; we meet them at every step. But God, our Heavenly Father, is always near us to protect us. When David said these words, it was just as if he had said: 'Please take care of me, my kind Heavenly Father; I do not feel afraid when Thou art with me and taking hold of my hand.'

"You also, my child," continued the mother, "should speak to your Father in Heaven when you are in any danger, either to soul or body, and ask Him, with the same confidence, to protect you, and He will most certainly do it."

The Chimes.

"MY FATHER IS THE CAPTAIN."

Not very long ago a priest, full of zeal for the salvation of souls, was sent by his superiors to the West Indies to preach the Gospel, and labor for the conversion of the pagans who dwelt there.

The ship on which he embarked was very large, and there was on board a great number of people, old and young, who were going to these distant countries to seek their fortunes, or to make for themselves new homes.

As they left the harbor everything seemed to promise them a prosperous voyage. The sea was calm, the weather pleasant and warm. For a few days the good ship was carried along by favorable winds, and the passengers were enjoying themselves without fear. Some of them were even counting the number of days that must pass by before they would arrive at their new homes in the Far West, and making plans in their own minds what they would do when they reached the end of their journey.

But often when we think ourselves free from all danger, danger is very near us. So it was with them. For when they had been about a week at sea the weather suddenly changed. Dark clouds hid the sun, and there came a dead calm, the sure sign of a coming storm.

Very soon the ship began to be tossed from side to side; great waves broke over it, and the wind began to howl with a terrible noise which frightened everyone. Even the captain and the seamen, who had seen many storms, were afraid, and were heard to say to each other: "This will be a terrific gale! We must prepare for the worst!"

When the passengers heard them saying these words their fears became greater than ever, and a deep silence took the place of the mirth of the past few days.

In the meantime the storm increased, and it was soon seen that the words of the sailors were but too true. The great ship, which had ridden so proudly on the bosom of the calm sea, was now in the midst of an awful tempest. All on board gave themselves up for lost, and loud cries of despair were heard amidst the noise of the storm. Strong men, as well as the women and children, fell into dismay, and even the sailors gave themselves up for lost.

In the midst of this confusion there was one on board that ship who was quiet and happy. This was a little boy of six or seven years of age. While the storm was raging, and the ship rolling from side to side, and the people wailing and weeping, he sat by himself playing quietly as usual, as if they were all in perfect safety.

It happened that the priest was near the child, preparing himself calmly to appear before God, for, like the rest, he thought the end was near. His eyes fell upon the boy, and for a few moments he watched him.

"My dear child," he said, "you do not seem to have any fear. Do you not know that there is an awful storm raging, and that we are all in danger of being drowned? How can you amuse yourself as you are doing, and sing so joyfully, when everyone else is weeping and crying in despair?"

But the child answered: "Why should I be afraid? Don't you know that my father is the captain of this ship? He knows how to guide it in a storm as well as in calm weather. He loves me, and he knows that I am in the ship; do you think, then, that he would let me be drowned? Oh no! So there is no fear, and that is why I am not afraid." The storm continued for many days and nights, but at last it came to an end. The passengers, who had escaped from a death which a short time before seemed so certain, with one voice praised the captain, to whose skill and watchfulness, under God, they owed their safety.

Then the priest took opportunity of telling them how calm the captain's son had been, even when the storm was at its height, and also the reason why he had not been afraid.

"It is true," he said, "the poor child expected too much from the power of his father, because, skillful though he has proved himself to be, it might, after all, have been beyond his power to have saved the vessel. Yet we have a beautiful lesson given to us in the boy's conduct.

For if this helpless child, in the midst of so great a danger, had so much confidence in his dear father, whose power is so limited, that he feared nothing, when everyone else was in despair, how much greater ought to be the confidence we should place in our Heavenly Father, whose power is infinite, and who watches over every one of us, His children, with fatherly love! Whenever we are in danger, then, let us ask Him with a childlike confidence to take care of us, and, although the danger may be very great, we shall have nothing to fear: He will be with us."

Rep. du Catéchiste.

JESUS WALKING UPON THE WATERS.

We read the following story in St. Matthew's Gospel (chap. xiv.):

"And forthwith Jesus obliged His disciples to go up into the boat, and go before Him over the water till He dismissed the multitudes.

"And having dismissed the multitude, He went up into a mountain alone to pray. And when it was evening He was alone. But the boat in the midst of the sea was tossed by the waves, for the wind was contrary.

"And in the fourth watch of the night He came to them walking upon the sea. And they, seeing Him walking upon the sea, were troubled, saying: 'It is an apparition'; and they cried out for fear. And immediately Jesus spoke to them, saying: 'Be of good heart; it is I: fear ye not!'

"And Peter, making answer, said: 'Lord, if it be Thou, bid me come to Thee upon the waters.' And He said: 'Come.' And Peter, going down into the boat, walked upon the water to come to Jesus. But seeing the wind strong, he was afraid, and when he began to sink he cried out, saying: 'Lord, save me.' And immediately Jesus, stretching forth His hand, took hold of him, and said to him: 'O thou of little faith, why didst thou doubt?'

"And when they were come up into the boat the wind ceased. And they that were in the boat came and adored Him, saying: 'Indeed Thou art the Son of God.'"

My child, it is the same Jesus Who is now coming to you on the stormy waters of this life. Be not afraid, then, for He is your Father. Go forth to meet Him with faith and confidence and love as St. Peter did, and He will not allow you to sink under the waves of temptation, but will Himself uphold you.

69

WE SHOULD PRAY TO BE DELIVERED FROM THE SNARES OF SATAN

M y child, our great enemy Satan is ever on the watch to destroy us, and is everywhere laying snares to draw us into sin. We should therefore earnestly pray to God, when saying this petition, that He will deliver us from these snares, and never permit us to lose His holy grace.

ST. PERPETUA'S VISION.

St. Perpetua gives us the following account of a vision she had during the time she was in prison for the Faith before her martyrdom:

"I thought I saw a long ladder made of gold, which reached from earth to Heaven, but so narrow that only one could mount it at a time. The two sides of the ladder were covered with sharp swords and javelins, and scythes and daggers, and all kinds of sharp instruments, so that it required the greatest care when mounting the ladder not to be hurt by them, for if the one who was ascending did so with negligence, and did not keep his eyes fixed upwards, straight towards the top, he would most certainly have been severely cut and wounded.

"At the bottom of the ladder there was a terrible dragon, who sat there ready to spring upon anyone who came there to go up. (Many came, but, frightened by the sight of the monster, turned back.) My brother Saturnus thought he would attempt it. He went to the foot of the ladder, and succeeded in passing by the beast; then, keeping his eyes fixed on the top, he was able to ascend without being hurt.

"When he had reached the top of the ladder, he turned round towards me, and said: 'Perpetua, I am waiting for you; but take care of the beast at the foot of the ladder, lest he hurt you.' I answered: 'I am not afraid. In the name of Our Lord Jesus Christ, let him do me no harm.'

"Then the dragon, when he heard that holy name, seemed to become terribly afraid, and turned away his head. Then I put my foot on his head, just as it had been the first step of the ladder, and I mounted without much difficulty to the very top.

"When I reached the top I found myself in a very beautiful garden, in the midst of which I saw a man of most beautiful countenance, very tall, dressed in the garments of a shepherd, with hair white as snow. Around him there was a countless multitude of persons dressed in spotless white. As soon as he saw me, he called me by my name, and said: 'Perpetua, my daughter, welcome.' Then he gave me food to eat which was most delicious, and while I was eating it I joined my hands in rapture, and all the multitude who were dressed in white answered, 'Amen.' Then I awoke, and saw that it was but a dream; but I related it to my brother, and from that time we took the resolution to take off our thoughts from all earthly things and to fix them on Heaven."

This vision which St. Perpetua had is a faithful picture of our sojourn in this world on our way to Heaven. Like the ladder, the way to Heaven is narrow, and on all sides temptations, which put us in great danger of hurting our souls. At our very first step on the way to Heaven Satan meets us to try and keep us from going there, and to kill our souls by inducing us to commit mortal sin. Some people put on the good resolution of walking on the path which leads to Heaven, but, seeing the difficulties on the way, they are frightened, and turn back. There is just one way of being able to pass by and overcome the terrible dragon that is Satan. We must do as in the vision of St.

Perpetua; we must keep our eyes fixed upon the top of the ladder, upon Heaven, and then we will be secure. Jesus, Who is there, will meet us, and take us into His beautiful field of Heaven, where we will see His holy angels and His Saints, clad in beautiful white garments, and He will call us by our names, and will say, "Welcome into My Kingdom"; and He will give us delicious food, and fill us to over-flowing with happiness forever.

Lives of the Saints.

70

PRAY TO BE DELIVERED FROM A SUDDEN AND UNPROVIDED DEATH

As the greatest happiness in the world to come is to enjoy God in Heaven, so the greatest evil is to be separated from Him forever. It should, then, be your constant prayer, my child, that you may be delivered above all things else from the evil of a sudden and unprovided death.

THE DOUBLE VISION OF ST. FRANCIS.

St. Francis of Assisi went one day into the mountains of Alverno, to spend some time in solitude, and to meditate on the eternal truths of the next life. As he was making this meditation, the rocks and the trees around him disappeared from his sight, and he saw the heavens above him suddenly open. There he saw God seated on His great throne, surrounded by an innumerable multitude of holy angels and Saints.

"O my God," cried out St. Francis, "I see Heaven! Oh, how magnificent is the beauty of Thy house, O Lord! Indeed, it is but a small sacrifice to give up all the goods of this world, and to bear with patience all the ills of life, since this enables us to secure for ourselves such a glorious dwelling-place."

While he was saying these words to himself this beautiful vision suddenly disappeared, and was followed by another one of quite a different kind. Beneath his feet he thought he saw an immense abyss. It seemed to be a bottomless ocean of flames, in which were plunged countless multitudes of the wicked, who were vomiting forth cries of despair, and curses and blasphemy.

This sight filled the Saint with fear, and he cried out: "Oh, what an awful place! this must surely be Hell itself! O my God, be so good as to remove from my eyes the vision of this frightful place. Oh, if people did but see this awful abyss, and the torments those have to suffer who are in it, they would never commit sin, that they might never be condemned to it."

This second vision also disappeared, and Francis, having returned to himself again, saw nothing round him but the rocks and the woods of Mount Alverno.

"I am, then, placed," he said to himself, "between Heaven and Hell. This is what God wanted to show me by this vision. One or other of these must most certainly be my dwelling-place forever. O my God, grant me grace, while there is yet time, to secure Heaven, and deliver me from the greatest of all evils—the loss of Thee in Hell."

Life of St. Francis.

Let your prayer, my child, be the same: "From everlasting death, deliver me, O Lord."

ST. BERNARD IN DANGER.

When St. Bernard was nineteen years old he was tempted by many and great temptations, which placed him in danger of losing his soul. He was gifted with great natural beauty, which drew towards him the eyes of all who met him. On the other hand, he was rich, and the world smiled on him, and promised him many pleasures.

"You are young, and have yet a long time to live," whispered the evil spirit. "Why, then, will you throw away these years of your youth? Enjoy yourself for the present, and when you are old, it will be time enough to think of becoming a Saint. And even if you do now sometimes yield to temptation, you can easily repent afterwards, for God is good and merciful, and knows how frail you are, and will forgive you, since His Son Jesus died for you on the cross."

Many of his companions, also, who had already begun to walk on the broad way that leads to destruction, tried, both by word and example, to make him do as they did.

But Bernard, in the midst of these terrible temptations, would raise his eyes to Heaven, and would imagine he saw his beloved mother looking down upon him. "She seemed to me to be weeping," he used afterwards to say, "and sorrowfully to put me in mind that it was not for the vanities of the world she had brought me up with so much care, but that she had hoped to see me aspire after something greater than the pleasures of this life—the joys of Heaven which would never end."

One day, while on a visit to his brothers, as he rode along, and his mind filled with melancholy thoughts, he came to a little church by the wayside; it was dedicated to the most holy Mother of God. He stopped at the door, and, dismounting from his horse, entered the church. Going up to the altar of Our Lady, he prostrated himself on the ground before it, and, with many tears, prayed to her to obtain for him deliverance from these dangerous temptations.

As he prayed a great calm fell upon his soul. God at that moment filled his heart with His holy love, and he, on the spot, took the generous resolution of renouncing forever the vain pleasures the world offered him, and of consecrating himself forever to God. "My God," he cried out, as the tears flowed from his eyes, "Thou alone shalt be my portion forever."

No sooner had he taken this resolution than he endeavored to make others follow his example. He went to his brothers, and spoke to them with such earnestness and zeal that they also determined to do as he did.

A SAINT WHO WAS ALWAYS TREMBLING.

St. Isidore was always a holy man. He had begun to serve God from his childhood, and had served Him faithfully during the whole of his life, yet he was never seen to smile, and was always trembling.

One of his disciples once said to him: "Father Isidore, why are you always so sad, and what makes you tremble so much? You always seem to be full of fear, as if some terrible evil was about to fall upon you."

"My child," he answered, "I am afraid that I may not persevere to the end, and that I may lose my soul."

"But you have always tried to serve God," said his disciple; "why, then, should you be so much afraid, since God has promised Heaven to those who serve Him faithfully?"

The Saint answered: "When a poor man is expecting to receive a rich legacy or a great fortune, and is afraid that something may arise to deprive him of it, how can he have an easy mind? It is only when the money is given to him that he can be free from anxiety. So it is with me. I have not yet received the crown of glory, and as long as I am in this world I am in danger of losing it. Have I not cause, therefore, to tremble?"

"My child, you are at this moment, I hope, in the grace of God, and if you were to die now in that happy state you would most certainly go to Heaven. But the time of your trial is not yet over, and you may yet fall into sin. Many who were once as holy and good as you now are have fallen into sin, and, dying in their sins, are now in Hell. Oh, pray that you may be delivered from the danger of losing God by sin.

HOW WE SHOULD PRAY IN OUR SUFFERINGS AND TRIALS

The sufferings and trials of this life, which are so often called evils, are some of God's most choice gifts, because they are the source of much merit for eternity. We may, indeed, pray to God to take them from us "if it be His holy will," but we should rather pray that He would send us more abundant grace to bear them patiently.

HAPPIER ON EARTH THAN IN HEAVEN.

The venerable Alain de la Roche, who lived four hundred years ago, tells us of a holy nun who died after a long illness of ten years. During all that time her sufferings had been terrible to behold, but she had never been heard to complain, so great was her resignation to God's holy will.

After her death she appeared to one of the Sisters of her Order. She was surrounded by a dazzling light, and seemed to be filled with unspeakable joy.

"Oh, dear Sister," she said, "how happy you are to be still on earth! Oh, that you could only understand how happy it is to be in your place!"

"O holy soul," replied the other, "how can you call me happy, seeing that I am still in this vale of tears, and in so much danger of losing my soul? Ah, it is you who are truly happy—you who are in the presence of God in Heaven, and free from all the evils of this life."

"You say you are unhappy because you are still suffering the sorrows and afflictions of this life," replied the Saint. "It is for that very reason that I call you happy. As long as you are in the world, you possess a treasure we in Heaven cannot obtain."

"And what can that treasure be?"

"The power of gaining merits for Heaven. Now that I am in Heaven, I know and see the reward God grants for the least good work done for His sake, or the least suffering endured for love of Him. Willingly would I endure over again all the pains and sufferings which you saw me endure during the ten years of my mortal life, that I might obtain the glory you can now gain by saying even one 'Our Father.'"

SCHOUPPE: *Instruct. Religieuses, iii. 656.*

It is not, therefore, from this kind of evils that we ought to ask to be delivered, for in the light of eternity these are pearls of infinite price.

THE ANGELS ON THE HOUSE-TOP.

One day St. Antoninus, Archbishop of Florence, was passing through the streets of that city. As he was going past a certain cottage, which had every mark of the greatest poverty, he saw a number of angels on the roof. They seemed to be watching over the people who dwelt within it.

Filled with astonishment at this beautiful vision, he entered the cottage to see who the people were who dwelt there, and he found a widow with her three daughters. They were extremely poor, and were occupied, as he entered, in trying to gain for themselves, by their united labor, enough of food to keep them from dying of hunger.

The compassionate heart of the Bishop was moved at their sad condition. He saw also their great piety, and their entire resignation to the holy will of God. He knew also that God must be in an especial manner pleased with them, since He had sent his angels to watch over them.

"My dear children," he said to them, "I see that you are in great need of assistance, and I beg of you to accept of what I now offer you."

Saying these words, he opened his purse, and gave them enough to supply all their present wants. He promised also to give them as much as would keep them in comfort all the rest of their lives, since they were so deserving of it.

The family thanked their generous benefactor with tears in their eyes for having come to their assistance in their great need; and the Bishop went home glad in heart at having been the means of delivering so deserving a family from the evil of poverty.

Not long afterwards it happened that the Bishop was passing near the same house. He looked up to the place where he had formerly seen the angels. But these had disappeared, and in their place he saw a number of evil spirits.

This surprised him beyond measure. He asked someone who lived near if any change had taken place in the house since his last visit.

He answered him that a very great change had taken place there; that the inmates had become proud and haughty, and had made use of the Bishop's alms to procure the luxuries of life; and that instead of being models of piety and resignation, as they had formerly been, they had now become a source of scandal to those who knew them.

The good Bishop went into the house, and gently reproved them for their conduct. He told them of the vision he had seen, and exhorted them to be content with the humble position in which God had placed them, and not to aspire after a condition in which God never intended to place them.

The Bishop himself saw in this a visible proof of the value of poverty, and that instead of being an evil to be avoided, it was, in the designs of God, one of His greatest blessings, since it brought peace and happiness in this life, and would be the cause of so much merit in Heaven.

Catch. en Exemples.

72

HOW GOD SOMETIMES DELIVERS US FROM TEMPORAL EVILS

God has a special care of each one of us. Nothing can happen without His pleasure or permission, and He often makes use of the most ordinary means to save us from the greatest dangers. This should inspire you, my child, with a loving confidence in Him, when you say "Deliver us from evil."

HOW GOD SAVED A LITTLE BOY FORM DEATH.

Francis, a little boy who lived in a large city, went one fine day into the country to amuse himself in the woods. He spent the day in gathering raspberries and other wild fruits which grew by the wayside.

Towards evening the sky began to be covered with thick clouds; and a terrible silence, the forerunner of a storm, made the boy wish that he was nearer home.

Suddenly flashes of lightning, followed by loud peals of thunder, made the boy tremble with fear. The rain, too, began to fall in torrents, and the boy, seeing a hollow oak-tree by the side of the road, ran to it for shelter.

Scarcely had he gone over to it, and was standing under the

shelter it afforded, than he heard a voice calling out: "Francis, Francis! come, come! be quick!"

He was astonished to hear someone calling him by name, and went out of his hiding-place to see who it could be. The moment he had stepped forth from the side of the tree it was struck by lightning and split in two.

When he saw what had taken place he said to himself: "Ah! that voice came from Heaven; Thou, O my loving Father in Heaven, hast saved me." And he fell down on his knees to thank God for His goodness.

Just at that moment he heard the same voice again calling as before: "Francis, Francis!"

He looked in the direction whence the sound came, and saw, not far from him, a countrywoman. She had come out to look for her son, whose name was also Francis, and it was her voice he had heard the first time.

Francis went over to her, and told her that he had taken shelter under the oak-tree, and that when he heard her calling on her son he had thought it was a voice from Heaven calling on him to go away from the tree; for no sooner had he done so than it was struck by the lightning.

"Thank God, my child, that He has delivered you from this danger, for it was indeed He who saved you. He appointed that I should call you by your name, without knowing anything about you, in order that you might be freed from the danger of death to which you were exposed under the tree."

Catech. en Examples.

73

"FROM EVERLASTING DEATH, O LORD, DELIVER US."

The greatest of all calamities is that of being separated from God in eternity. It is mortal sin alone that can bring on us this awful evil. Oh, how earnestly should we pray, then, to be delivered from this evil, the greatest of all evils.

THE PIOUS SOLDIER ON THE BATTLE-FIELD.

There was, some time ago, a young soldier belonging to the French army whose name was Beauséjour. Faithful to the lessons he had received from his virtuous parents, he continued to be always faithful to his prayers, even amidst the scoffs and railleries of his companions in the regiment. He had promised, before leaving his father and mother, never to omit reciting seven "Our Fathers" and seven "Hail Marys" on his knees every day of his life, to secure the protection of God and His most holy Mother throughout the day, both for soul and body.

Sometimes, indeed, he did forget this holy practice amidst the constant employment of his calling, but if he even there remembered the omission, he would arise from his bed at night, and, kneeling down, recite them.

War broke out, and Beauséjour found himself in the first line on the battlefield. When the order was given to halt and prepare to attack the enemy, he suddenly called to mind that he had not that day said the "Our Fathers" and "Hail Marys" he had promised. Immediately falling on his knees, he made the sign of the cross, and said them. His comrades, seeing this, heaped upon him even more than usual their sarcastic expressions. "Beauséjour is afraid; see, he is saying his prayers. Beauséjour is a coward—a devout fool!" The soldier heard the words, but he heeded them not; he knelt there till he had ended his prayer. Then he rose up calm and even cheerful, ready to enter action.

He had not long to wait, for soon the awful roaring of the cannon and the sharp and quick reports of the guns as they sent forth their messengers of death showed that the battle had begun. Ball followed ball in rapid succession, killing or wounding numberless soldiers in both armies. Those who were fighting side by side with the pious Beauséjour, and who had but a few minutes before heaped reproaches on him because of his devotion to God, were one after another killed or disabled, and lay on the ground covered with blood and wounds. Only one of the first line remained standing: it was Beauséjour, who, when the battle ended, was found without even the slightest wound.

When he returned to the camp his first act was to thank God, his Heavenly Father, for his deliverance; and when in after-years his children and grandchildren were gathered round him, he would over and over again relate to them this incident, and exhort them to be always faithful to their daily prayers, and to say especially with devotion the "Our Father" and the "Hail Mary," as being the most powerful weapon they could make use of in every danger to soul and body.

Schouppe: Instruct. Religieuses, ii. 195.

ST. ABRAHAM AND HIS NIECE.

When St. Abraham went to dwell in the solitude of the desert that he might live for God alone, he left behind him in the world a married brother, who had an only daughter, whom he brought up in simplicity and innocence; her name was Mary.

When she was as yet very young, he died, leaving her alone in the world, for her mother was already dead. She was taken to her uncle in the desert, as being the only relative she had. He received her with kindness, and placed her in a cell which he built close to the one in which he himself dwelt.

Through the window of his own cell he would often converse with her, and gave her lessons in worldly learning, but, above all, in the science of the Saints, and taught her how to live for God alone. The young girl grew daily more fervent, and increased in virtue, so that she was the joy of her aged uncle, who ceased not to pray that she might ever remain the beloved child of God, and never offend Him by any sin.

But Satan, who was angry at seeing so much perfection in one so young, subjected her to terrible temptations. He kindled in her soul a love of worldly things, and the desire of living as those did who passed their lives in the pleasures of life. Fearing to let her uncle know of these new feelings which filled her heart, and thinking herself altogether unworthy of living in the company of so holy a man, she secretly left her cell, and went to the city of Aesus, situated about two days' journey from her desert home. There she put on the gay dress of those who dwelt there, and gave herself up to a fashionable and sinful career.

The Saint was admonished in a dream that some evil had arisen. He saw approaching his cell from the inmost recesses of the desert an enormous dragon, who, seizing on a white dove which reposed there, fled away with it in all haste to the desert whence he had come.

When he awoke he began to consider what this vision might signify. At first he thought, with sorrow and anxiety, that some new misfortune had fallen on the Church of God, or that some new persecution had arisen to disturb the faithful, and he besought God fervently to make known to him what it meant.

On the third day the dragon returned, and placed at his feet the dove he had previously taken away; then he understood, from an interior voice in his heart, that some soul had been deceived by Satan, and had fallen into sin. A terrible presentiment suddenly seized upon him. Going to the window, he cried out: "Mary, why are you now so silent in your prayers, and why do you not as usual sing your hymns to God? And why do you not come to me to learn more of God and His holy law?"

But there was no answer; the silence of the grave reigned in her cell. Then the Saint knew that what he feared had come to pass, and a deep sorrow filled his affectionate heart. Falling on his knees and weeping bitterly, he besought God with the greatest earnestness to bring back again to the fold the lamb that had wandered far away from him by sin, the dove the dragon had carried off.

In the meantime someone came in haste, and told him that his niece had gone away, and where he would find her. Immediately he rose up, and, laying aside the dress he wore, put on one he had long ago laid aside, similar to those worn by men in the world, and went forth to look for his dear lost child.

On arriving at the inn to which she had gone on her arrival in the city, he inquired of the master of the house what kind of life she was leading, and informed him that he would desire to converse with her apart. The innkeeper invited his guest to follow him into the dining-room, where she then was, and where he would find an opportunity of speaking to her. When he entered he saw her there, splendidly attired, but she did not know him under the disguise he had assumed. When the other guests had retired, he carefully shut the door of the room, and, taking off the mantle which covered his head and face, stood before the eyes of the astonished girl as she was accustomed to see him in their desert home.

Then, heaving a deep sigh, he said in accents of sorrow: "Mary, don't you know me, your uncle? Tell me, my child, what caused you to run away from God? What has become of your former love for virtue and purity? Why did you run away from me? Oh, if you had only told me the conflicts you had to sustain, I would have aided you to conquer the enemy, or, if you had fallen, to raise you up again by doing penance for you. I beseech you, my child, by my grey hairs, and by the cruel agony your departure from me caused me, and by my sorrow at seeing you forsake your Heavenly Father, to return at once to God, and He will pardon you. Give me this joy, give me this consolation, and let not my grey hairs descend in sorrow to the grave."

Mary stood in silence before him, as if riveted to the spot, her eyes fixed upon the ground, and her mind filled with fear; but still she hesitated.

"My dearest child," interposed her uncle, "why do you not answer me? Do you not know that it was for your sake alone that I have left my cell in the wilderness to come hither in search of you? And do you not also know that there is no wound so great which God, our Heavenly Physician, is unable to cure? Renounce, then, your evil ways; I myself will be responsible for you to Our Lord Jesus. Only come with me; let us go back together to our happy solitude."

Then the poor sinful child said in a timid and scarcely audible voice: "O venerable servant of God, if shame forbids me even to raise my sinful eyes towards you, how can I draw near to God, covered over as I am with the ulcers of sin?" "Your iniquities, my child, I will take upon myself to expiate; only let us return to our former happy home."

The young penitent, with a heart broken down by sorrow, threw herself at the feet of her uncle, shedding bitter tears.

When she was making her preparations to follow him, she did not know where she would hide the rich garments which she then wore. By the advice of the holy Abraham, she threw them from her, and put on those of a simple country maiden. Then they both secretly left the Inn. The old man, saddling his horse, placed her upon it, and returned to the mountains and to their cells, of which they carefully closed the entrances.

There the poor fallen child entered on a life of rigorous penance; prayers, fastings, tears of sorrow—nothing was overlooked that could obtain the pardon of God. And God Himself, to show that He accepted her humble works of penance, was pleased to work many miracles by her prayers. Her saintly uncle returned thanks to God for being pleased to listen to his prayer and bestowing on her His forgiveness. At an extreme old age he passed out of this world to enter into the assembly of the Saints, and five years afterwards the poor penitent also passed away, her countenance clothed with calmness, the expression of a firm hope, the symbol of innocence regained by penance through the blood of the Lamb.

Vies des Saints illust., iii. 267.

HOW A GREAT BARON BECAME A TRAPPIST.

The Baron de Geramb had brought down upon his head the anger of the French nation because of his disloyal intrigues with the House of Austria. He was, in punishment of this, taken to Vincennes, where he was confined a prisoner in a dungeon, until the allied troops, having succeeded in obtaining possession of the chateau, delivered him from his imprisonment.

During his captivity he had opportunity to reflect on the mutability of all the things of earth which its votaries so highly esteem, and he resolved, if ever he were liberated, to bid an eternal adieu to the world, and to consecrate himself irrevocably to God in the severe Order of the Trappists.

"I became a Trappist," he writes in his great work entitled "A Pilgrimage to Jerusalem," "because my long captivity in the dungeons of Vincennes and the iron-barred windows that kept me in my prison taught me, more forcibly than the most eloquent sermon or the best-written book could do, that we have but one true Friend in this world, our beloved Savior, Who never will forsake us. They taught me that all the prosperity, the joys, and the honors of this earth—in a word, everything that passes away with time—vanish from us like smoke.

"I have become a Trappist that I may do penance for the many sins I have committed during the agitation of the years of my life which have gone past. God forbid that anyone should look on me in any other light than that of a penitent sinner! Let all who know me, or will hear of me, consider me, therefore, as a man who, having recognized that all earthly things are vanity and affliction of spirit, and that he is a great sinner in the eyes of God, has entered the Order of the Trappists to labor, to pray, to weep, and to die on a bed of straw lying on ashes."

THE MAN WOUNDED BY A TIGER.

The celebrated poet Sadi one day found in the wilds of the Eastern forests a poor man who was mortally wounded by the bite of a tiger. Seeing that no material aid could now avail him, he endeavored to give him all the consolation that kind words could impart.

Instead of answering him, the dying man, collecting his remaining strength, raised his eyes and hands to Heaven, and said: "O God of all goodness, I thank Thee with my whole heart for having cast me down upon the ground through the merciless bites of a savage beast. How different would it have been had I been laid down here to die, my soul being stung by remorse of conscience!"

HAUTRIEVE, xii. 633.

THE GREAT EARTHQUAKE AT CONSTANTINOPLE.

On January 24, 447, a Sunday, at about nine o'clock in the forenoon, the inhabitants of Constantinople were surprised to hear a strange, unaccountable noise, followed shortly by another, which resembled the sound of many chariots rushing past. Thinking that this foreboded some terrible visitation on the city, they fled from it to the country with the utmost haste. They carried with them in beds the old and feeble, and the little children in their cradles. In less than an hour afterwards everything in the city presented the appearance of complete desolation; churches, palaces, houses, and the very streets were abandoned.

In a very short time took place what they had all dreaded from the beginning. The first shock of the earthquake came with appalling suddenness, and the magnificent edifices of the city fell to the ground with a terrific crash. This was followed by others without interruption. The very ground under their feet seemed to be in motion, like the waves of the sea in a storm, and a silence—the silence of death—overawed the multitude. The old and the new ramparts of Constantinople, its fifty-two towers, its numerous churches and palaces, the majority of its monuments and its statues, lay in desolation, where but yesterday they stood in magnificence and grandeur.

This earthquake continued for several days. The Emperor, the Senate, the Court, all the people, with the clergy at their head, lay prostrate on the ground in prayer, or raised up their hands to Heaven in fervent supplication and in contrition of heart, beseeching God to show them mercy. The whole country around the ruined city seemed changed into a vast temple, with the heavens above for a canopy; each heart seemed to be an altar from which arose the incense of prayer, imploring the mercy of God in the awful calamity that had befallen them.

It was by this seemingly great evil that God performed one of the greatest works of His mercy. For the people of Constantinople had begun to forget Him in the midst of their temporal prosperity, and had neglected to pray to Him. But now they were forcibly reminded of their neglect, and, like the Ninevites of old, returned to God in the day of their visitation. Even those who had hitherto despised prayer and spoke with bitter and sarcastic words to those who had remained faithful in practicing it, now forgot their railleries, and joined fervently with them in calling on God for mercy.

History records that God, touched with their fervor and repentance, spared the inhabitants, for not one of that immense multitude perished.

History of the Church.

PART X

"HAIL MARY" (FIRST PART)

74

"HAIL MARY"—"O MARY, HOW SWEET IS THY NAME!"

I have now to speak to you of Mary, the most holy Mother of God, and our own heavenly Mother. I know, my child, how much you love her, and how great is your joy when you hear of anything said in her praise. May this little book, then, give some additional glory to her whom we all love so well, and fill your own heart with a still greater love of her.

"Hail Mary, full of grace." The name of Mary is a name of sweetness, and fills with a holy joy all those who say it devoutly.

THE SAINTS AND MARY'S HOLY NAME.

St. Francis of Paul had so often on his lips the holy names of Jesus and Mary that the religious belonging to his Order were at one time called "The Religious of Jesus and Mary."

The pious Father Peter Lefèvre, first companion of St. Ignatius, never neglected to say the holy name of Mary at the beginning of each of the Canonical Hours of the Holy Office, to offer up his prayer through her to her Divine Son Jesus.

It is recorded in the life of the venerable servant of God, Philippa, Duchess of Lorraine, who died in the year 1547, in the one hundred and sixth year of her age, that during the last nine days of her life she pronounced more than three thousand times this salutary invocation: "Jesus, Mary!"

Margaret, Princess of Hungary, had these holy names constantly on her lips, and she used to add to the name of Mary this ejaculatory prayer: "Mother of God and my hope."

There is, perhaps, no more beautiful episode recorded in the history of Japan than that of a certain woman who, whilst she was yet a pagan, was so full of zeal for the worship of the idols of her country, that she used to pronounce the name of the chief of these divinities one hundred and forty thousand times a day. Touched by the grace of God, she became a Christian, and was baptized at the age of seventy-four. To make reparation as far as lay in her power for the superstitious worship of the false divinities of her country, she took the resolution of pronouncing the same number of times each day the names of Jesus and Mary as long as she lived. But as Satan had been accustomed in former times to awake her early in the morning, that she might have sufficient time to pay her daily tribute to the idols she then worshipped, her angel guardian now took his place, and awakened her early, so that she might be able to pronounce, according to her desire, the sacred names of Jesus and Mary.

THE NAME OF MARY BANISHES ALL SORROW.

When St. Bernard was a little boy, we are told of him that he had a great love for the most holy mother of God. All that was needed to banish away all sorrow from him and to fill him with joy was to pronounce in his presence the most holy name of Mary, and to correct him of any fault it was enough to say to him: "Don't do that again, because Our Blessed Lady will not be pleased with you."

"AVE MARIA" ON THE LILY-LEAVES.

The Blessed Francis Patrizi had a great devotion for Our Lady, and found his greatest delight in saluting her with her favorite prayer, "Ave Maria."

As a reward for this little act of homage Mary appeared to him, and foretold to him the hour of his death.

Forty years afterwards there was seen to spring up on his grave a beautiful white lily, on the leaves of which were written in letters of gold the words "Ave Maria."

La Chaîne d'Or, i. 195.

MARY'S GENEROSITY

"It is a most certain truth," writes a devout client of Mary, "that the holy salutation 'Hail Mary' never ascends to the throne of Mary in Heaven without obtaining for the one who utters it some new favor or blessing either for the soul or for the body, for our loving Mother is so generous that she could not suffer us to salute her in this loving manner without showing us her gratitude for this mark of our love.

ST. ALPHONSUS' LOVE FOR MARY'S NAME.

That great servant of Our Lady, St. Alphonsus, had for the name of Mary an unbounded love.

He bowed his head reverently whenever he heard it pronounced, and devoutly kissed the pages of a book on which he saw it written. He always wrote it at the head of his letters and the beginning of all his writings.

"O my incomparable Queen!" he would cry out in rapture. "O my sweetest Mother, I love thee, and because I love thee I also love thy name. O name of the Mother of my God, thou art most lovely to me!"

"HAIL, BERNARD!"

About the middle of the twelfth century there stood in the great forests that separate Flanders from Brabant a famous abbey belonging to the Benedictine Order, called the Abbey of Afflighem.

When St. Bernard was passing through France and Germany, preaching the Second Crusade against the infidels, he stayed at this abbey for a few days to rest.

At one end of the cloister there was a beautiful image of the Blessed Virgin, holding in her arms her Divine Son. Before it the monks used to kneel with great devotion to offer up their prayers to Our Lady, their Queen and their Mother, and countless were the graces they received at her hands for this simple act of homage.

St. Bernard never passed by the holy image without saluting the Queen of Heaven with those two first words of the angelical salutation: "Hail, Mary!"

One day, as he was kneeling at the foot of the little altar on which the statue reposed, and was with loving eyes looking on the image of her he loved so well, he said to her as usual: "Hail, Mary!"

At the same instant the image seemed to assume the appearance of being alive, and he heard, as if proceeding from the lips, the words: "Hail, Bernard!"

When he heard this salutation from the Queen of Heaven, the greatest joy and happiness filled his soul. He never forgot these words as long as he lived; they were a consolation to him in all his sorrows, and sustained him in all his trials.

In his Life.

THE ANGELS AND OUR LADY'S NAME.

The Blessed Virgin herself revealed to St. Bridget that the Guardian Angels approach nearer to those confided to their care whenever they hear them utter her ever-blessed name, and that Satan and his wicked angels flee to a distance from those who, in their temptations, utter it with confidence and love.

ST. STEPHEN OF HUNGARY AND THE NAME OF MARY.

St. Stephen, King of Hungary, had so great a veneration for Our Lady's holy name that he would not even pronounce it. He always called her "The Great Lady." All his subjects also called her by that name, and if it happened that the holy name of Mary was uttered in their presence, they all fell on their knees, and bowed their heads, to testify their veneration for that august name.

THE HOLY NAME OF MARY IN SUFFERINGS.

Blessed Bonaventure was suffering from a most painful swelling in the knee. His condition became at last so serious that the surgeons declared an operation was necessary to preserve his life.

During the operation, which caused him intense pain, the only word they heard him utter was the holy name of Mary. And when, at a certain point, the sufferings had become so awful, that even those who saw what was being done to him could not avoid shuddering with horror, he was calm and even joyful. "Mary, Mary, Mary!" he repeated again and again.

When the operation was over he fell into a sweet repose, as if he had only gone to rest after his ordinary daily labor.

Petitis Bolland., Oct. 26.

IN THE NAME OF MARY.

Alphonsus Rodriguez at the age of four years fixed his eyes lovingly on an image of Mary, and with childlike simplicity said to her: "O my Mother, if thou didst only know how much I love thee! No, thou couldst never love me as much as I love thee."

He had scarcely uttered these words when the Blessed Virgin

appeared to him, and said: "What do you say, my child? The love which I have for you is so great that nothing could ever equal it."

Afterwards, when he became a religious, he could not do enough to testify to Mary the great love that he had for her. He was accustomed to ask everything from God in the name of Mary, and he always recommended this practice to those who were living with him. "If you desire to obtain anything from God," he used to say to them, "ask it with confidence in the name of the Blessed Virgin and you will be certain to obtain it."

NEARLY LOST.

The Blessed Thomas à Kempis was nearly lost because he did not persevere in his first fervor; and very likely he would not now be in Heaven if Our Blessed Lady had not, in a most special way, showed him the danger he was in.

When he was quite a little boy he began to lead a very strict life, and was in a particular manner devout to the Blessed Virgin.

Every day he said a certain number of prayers in her honor, and as he grew up he added more to them; and so great was his devotion that tears of piety would often flow down his cheeks.

This went on for many years. Thomas was happy, not only because his conscience did not reproach him with any sin, but also because he saw that he was daily gaining more and more merit for Heaven.

But he had not yet reached Heaven. Our Lord tells us in the Gospel that when once we begin to be pious we must not look back, otherwise we are not fit for the Kingdom of God. Thomas began to look back, and by doing so nearly lost his soul.

He began at first to feel wearied at his prayers. One day he left out a few of them; next day he left out more. Then he began to leave them out for a few days at a time, then for a whole week, and at length he gave them up altogether. Thomas now was certainly hurrying on towards destruction as fast as he could go.

But Our Blessed Lady, whom he had honored and loved so much, did not allow her child to perish. One night he had a vision. He thought that he was at school, along with the rest of his class-fellows, listening to the words of his master as he was explaining their lessons. Suddenly the Blessed Virgin came into the room at the end farthest away from him, surrounded with rays of glory and with the beauty of Heaven. They were all full of joy when they saw her, especially as her countenance was so beautiful, and her words so kind. She spoke to each of the scholars as she passed along, embraced them all tenderly, and praised them because they were so fervent and so good, and served her Divine Son Jesus so well.

Thomas was anxious for the moment when it would be his turn to receive her sweet embrace. He wondered what she would have to say to him. He said to himself in his own mind: "I know I am not worthy to receive any favor from Our Lady; but after all, I have done much in her honor, and I hope that she, who is so kind to all the rest, will also say something sweet to me."

Mary, by degrees, came nearer to where he stood; it would now soon be his turn. At last it came. Mary stood before him, looked at him, but said nothing, and passed on to the one who stood next to him.

"O my Mother!" he said to her, in tones of bitter disappointment, "have you nothing to say to me?"

Then the Blessed Virgin, turning towards him with a look of great displeasure in her gentle eyes, said to him: "You need not expect caresses from me, for you have forsaken me altogether, and have begun to listen to the suggestions of Satan, who is my enemy. If you had only persevered in those devotions which you used to offer so fervently to me, I would have embraced you as I did your companions, and would have spoken lovingly to you as I did to them. Where are now those beautiful prayers you used to address to me, and the holy Rosary you used to say? You have given them all up; and still you think that I am going to treat you as my child! No, no; go away from me, for you are no longer worthy of my affection."

When she had said this she disappeared, leaving him overwhelmed with anguish. Thomas awoke, and although he saw that it was only a vision and not a reality, he did not fail to profit by it. He examined his conscience and saw his great fault. Once more he began, and this time he did persevere to the end, and is now in Heaven, with Our Lady, praising and blessing God.

Let us examine our conscience also; perhaps we may discover that we are not now so fervent as we once were, because we may have, like Thomas à Kempis, fallen away from our former fervor. If so, let us at once begin again as he did, persevere as he did, and like him we shall certainly one day be in Heaven praising and blessing God.

Lives of the Servants of God.

THE "AVE MARIA" OF ST. FRANCIS DE SALES.

"Hail, sweetest Marie, Mother of God! Thou art my Mother, and I humbly supplicate thee to accept me for thy son and servant, because I desire to have no other Mother than thee. I therefore beg of thee, my good, my beautiful, my most sweet Mother, that thou wilt be pleased to console me in all my troubles and tribulations, both of soul and body.

"Remember and always bear in mind, most sweet Virgin, that thou art my Mother, and that I am thy child, and that thou art all-powerful, and that I am a poor man, vile and feeble. I beseech thee, my most sweet Mother, to guide me and defend me in all my ways and in all my actions.

"Do not say, O gracious Virgin, that thou canst not do this, for thy most-beloved Son has given thee all power in Heaven and on earth. Do not say that it is not thy duty, for thou art the Mother of all mankind, and of me in particular. If it was beyond thy power, I would then excuse thee, saying: 'It is true she is my Mother, and she cherishes me as a son; but then she is poor, and has not the power nor the means of helping me.' And if thou wert not my Mother, then I would try to console myself by saying: 'She is able enough and rich enough to assist me, but, not being my Mother, she does not love me.' Since, therefore, O most sweet Virgin, thou art my Mother, and art most powerful, how can I excuse thee if thou wilt not console me and aid me and succor me?

"Behold, then, my Mother, and see that thou art obliged to grant me what I ask of thee, and to listen to all my petitions. Oh, then, be exalted above the heavens and the earth, most glorious Virgin, my most excellent Mother Mary. And for the honor and glory of thy Son, accept me for thy child, notwithstanding my miseries and my sins. Deliver my soul and my body from all evil, and bestow on me all the virtues which adorned thee, especially the virtue of humility. Bestow on me all the gifts, goods, and graces which will make me agreeable to the most Holy Trinity, the Father, the Son, and the Holy Ghost. Amen."

75

"HAIL MARY"—THE ANGELICAL SALUTATION

A PROMISE OF OUR LADY TO ST. GERTRUDE.

Our Lady once appeared to St. Gertrude, and promised her that when the hour of her death came, she would bestow on her as many graces as would equal the number of times she had, during her life, saluted her with the Angelical Salutation, "Ave Maria."

AN "AVE MARIA" OBTAINS PARDON OF OUR FAULTS.

The Blessed Virgin told St. Bridget to say an "Ave Maria" devoutly to obtain from God forgiveness for some faults of impatience into which she had fallen.

THE LAY-BROTHER WHO KNEW ONLY THE "HAIL MARY."

In one of the convents of the Order of Citeaux there once lived a lay-brother who knew no other prayer but the "Hail Mary"; but this prayer he often said, and always with the greatest devotion.

After his death there sprung up over the place where he was

buried a tree, on the leaves of which were written the first words of the Angelical Salutation, "Hail, Mary, full of Grace' Our Lord is with Thee."

La Chaîne d'Or, i. 195.

THE VENERABLE ARMILLA.

The Venerable Armilla, who from her childhood had lived in poverty, was able to support all the hardships of her condition by her devotion to Our Lady. The Rosary was continually in her hands, and the sweet prayer, the "Hail Mary," was always on her lips; and thus, by living always in the company of her heavenly Mother, she became a model of piety.

One day someone asked her why she thought so much of Our Lady, and said so many times the "Hail Mary" in her honor.

She replied: "If I can only gain the favor of the Mother, I am sure of gaining also that of the Son."

A LITTLE CHILD'S LOVE FOR MARY.

When the Blessed Jane Mary Bonomi was quite a child, she had already a great love for Our Lady. She would often speak to her little companions about her, and teach them how to love her and pray to her.

One day, while wandering through her parents' house, she found in a deserted corner under a stair a picture of the most holy Mother of God. The child made this place her sanctuary, and would spend hours there alone honoring her heavenly Mother by reciting with infantile fervor the "Hail Mary."

Lives of the Saints, March 1.

THE LOVE OF ST. ALPHONSUS FOR THE "HAIL MARY."

St. Alphonsus always loved the Blessed Virgin; he always called her his "Sweet Mother." When he was a little child, he used to say to her: "My own sweet Mother, I don't wish anyone to love you more than I do."

The Rosary was his favorite prayer. From morning to night the beads were always in his hands. One day when they went to bring him to dinner, they found him, as usual, reciting the Rosary. They told him that it was time to come to dinner, and that he might omit the rest of his prayer.

"What is that you say?" he exclaimed. "One 'Hail Mary' is worth more than all the dinners in the world!"

Another time, when it was the hour for retiring for the night, he remembered that he had not that day finished his Rosary. The brother who waited upon him said that he might omit it for once without any scruple.

St. Alphonsus answered: "Never, my brother! Do you not know that perhaps my salvation depends on this devotion?" And he finished his prayer before he retired to rest.

MARY DELIVERS A SINNER FROM THE SLAVERY OF SATAN.

There once lived a poor man who had forgotten the lessons of his pious mother, and had become a great sinner—so great, indeed, that he had sold himself soul and body to Satan.

One thing only he had never forgotten: it was the dying request of his mother that he would every day say one "Hail Mary" in honor of the great Mother of God, and he scrupulously fulfilled this last request.

Mary was pleased to accept this little tribute of honor—the only bright spot in a long life of sin—and obtained for him the grace of repentance before he died.

For when he was very ill and on his death-bed, he had a vision, in which Our Blessed Lady appeared to him. She said nothing, but only looked at him with her compassionate eyes so full of gentle reproach that he could not withstand their influence.

As soon as he awoke, he sent at once for a priest and made his confession, at the same time giving marks of the sincerity of his repentance by the tears he shed.

"Father," he said to his confessor, "if God spares me and permits me to rise again from this bed of sickness, I will become a religious." But God was pleased to accept the will for the deed, and lest he might not persevere, He took him to Himself in Paradise, to be an ever-lasting example of the power of Mary, and the high esteem she has for the smallest act of homage done to her.

La Chaîne d'Or, i. 194.

OUR LADY'S BEAUTIFUL MANTLE.

The shadows of evening were falling on the mountains, and the silver-toned bell had just sent forth its hallowed sound over the valleys, calling on all who heard it to salute the august Queen of Heaven by the evening "Hail Mary" before retiring to rest.

In a little hermitage, built on the slope of one of the mountains, dwelt a holy hermit. He had finished his evening prayer, and had just risen from his knees to retire to rest for the night.

As he lay down on his humble bed of straw, his last thought was of Jesus, and of Mary His Mother, to whose care he commended his soul.

Suddenly his cell was filled with a great light. Our Lady appeared to him, and it was her presence that lighted up his lowly abode. She wore a mantle of magnificent texture, all covered with golden stars, on each one of which he read the words, "Hail Mary."

The holy man was filled with rapture as he gazed on her who is the joy of angels. Then Mary opened her lips and spoke to him. "My child," she said, "you admire the rich stars that bespangle my mantle. It is your work, my child; you placed them there."

"O my Lady," he exclaimed, "how could I, a poor sinner, have ever adorned thy mantle with these most brilliant ornaments?"

The Blessed Virgin answered: "Every time you said the 'Angelus' your angel guardian placed a star upon my mantle, and inscribed on it the 'Hail Mary' with which you praised me. You see, the work is not yet finished; there are as yet a few more stars to be placed upon it. But when this is done, then I will come for you and take you to Paradise, where I will give you an eternal reward for the honor you have given to me by saying so fervently and so frequently that holy prayer."

Mary disappeared, but the holy man fell upon his knees, and raising his hands to Heaven, thanked his heavenly benefactress for this manifestation of her love for him.

Catch. en Exemples, iii. 432.

THE VISIT TO OUR LADY'S CHURCH.

Not many years ago, a young man, who was very clever, resided in a country village in one of the provinces of France. In order to advance him further in his studies, it was resolved to send him to Paris, where he would be under the best masters.

This was for him a subject of great joy, for he desired so much to see the great capital of his country and the many wonders it contained.

Before leaving home he went to bid goodbye to his friends, and told them that he would be very happy if he could be of any use to them during his stay in Paris.

Amongst those to whom he thus offered his services was a pious lady who had known him from his childhood. She thanked him for his kindness, and said: "There is something I would desire you to do for me when you go to the capital, but I do not like to ask you, because you might find some difficulty in doing it."

He assured her that she was mistaken, and that he would be glad and most willing to do anything that lay in his power to oblige one who had been so great a friend of his from his very infancy.

"Well," she said, "what I want you to do for me is to go to the Church of Our Lady of Victories in that city, and there, before the Altar of the Immaculate Heart of Mary, to say one 'Hail Mary' for me."

Now, it happened that the young man was one of those who had given up his religious duties, and had forgotten all the pious prayers his mother had once taught him.

When he heard the lady's request, he was at first about to smile at what he thought to be great folly, but, seeing her eyes fixed on his and awaiting his answer, he replied as calmly as he could that he would gladly do what she requested.

On his arrival in Paris he at once began to fulfill his engagements. But he always put off to some other time his visit to Our Lady's church.

The time for his return home came, and he had not yet made that visit. He was tempted to return home without going at all; but as he knew that the lady would ask him if he had fulfilled his promise, and as he scorned to tell a falsehood, he at last took courage, and went to the church.

He chose a time when he thought there would be no one there, and glided in without being seen. He knelt down, but awkwardly, like one who had not been accustomed to such an action, and began the promised "Hail Mary."

Many years had passed by since he last said it, and now he had to search in his memory for the words of that holy prayer. In consequence of this, the words came slowly from his lips.

As he said them the remembrance of bygone years—the years of his innocence—came before his mind. He felt, too, that he was there in the presence of God, and he began to tremble. Tears also fell from his eyes, and a sigh at times escaped him.

One of the priests of the church was kneeling at a little distance, and seeing him in this condition, went towards him. Taking him gently by the hand, he said: "My dear friend, I am sure that you are one of Our Lady's wandering children whom she sends back to us from time to time."

"Alas! reverend Father, it is but too true; I have indeed wandered far, far away from her."

The good priest took the now repentant sinner under his charge, and in a short time, purified from all the sins of his past life, he knelt down amongst the many devoted children of Mary to receive her Divine Son in the Sacrament of his love.

He returned home to his friends, but his first visit was to the lady who had asked him to say the "Hail Mary" in the Church of Our Lady of Victories.

Catch. en Exemples.

CONFIDENCE IN OUR LADY RECOMPENSED.

One day a poor woman, who was the mother of several children, went to the superintendent of the Holy Family Society, and spoke to him in these words: "Sir, I am not able to pay my rent, and in three days my landlord will put me out of my house, and I will have no roof to shelter me and my poor little ones, and I have come to you to ask your help." "My good woman," said he, "what do you want me to do for you?"

"I come to ask you if you would give me as much as will pay my rent."

"How much do you owe your landlord?"

"Five pounds," she answered.

"Five pounds!" he exclaimed. "Where do you think I could get so much money for you, and in the space of three days, too?"

"Then, if you cannot do this for me, I and my children will have to go out into the cold world without food or home. Could you not try to do something for me?" she cried out in tones of agony which went to the good man's heart.

He seemed to have had at that moment an inspiration, for he said to her abruptly: "I will tell you what to do. Tomorrow, at the sound of the 'Angelus' bell, at whatever spot you may be, kneel down along with your children and say three times the 'Hail Mary' and the prayer 'Memorare.' I will do the same, and we shall see what will be the result of our prayer."

On the following day the gentleman, mindful of his word, was on his way to the church about the hour of the midday "Angelus," when he happened to meet an old friend, who asked him whither he was going.

"I am going to the church to ask the Blessed Virgin to give me five pounds," he answered.

The other said: "For whom do you want the five pounds?"

"I want it for a poor woman and her family; and if I do not get it, she and her children will be without house or food. But it is now midday, and I must hasten to the church!'

"Yes," said the other, "go into the church and thank the Blessed Virgin; then come back to me, and I will give you the money you want for the poor woman."

All this took place at the entrance to the Church of St. Sulpice in Paris, between the first and the last stroke of the "Angelus" bell.

Devotion to Mary, i. 273.

MARY PROTECTS HER CHILD IN DANGER.

On May 2, in the year 1808, an insurrection broke out in Spain against the French, who had invaded that country. It was chiefly at Madrid that the massacres took place. The Spaniards, full of hatred against those who had come to rob them of their homes, slaughtered without mercy every Frenchman they met, and for several hours the streets of that city ran with blood.

In the French army there was a doctor called Claubry, who was most devout to Our Lady, and was a member of the Confraternity of the Holy Rosary. That morning he had received Holy Communion in a church dedicated to Our Lady in Madrid, and was returning to his quarters, when he was attacked by a band of angry Spaniards, who knew by his dress that he belonged to the French army. When he saw that he was in danger of death, he raised up his hands to Heaven, and invoked the holy names of Jesus and Mary.

The men raised their swords to murder him, calling him at the same time a blasphemer and an infidel.

Suddenly, like a flash of lightning, a thought came into his mind. "No," he said, "I am not an infidel nor a blasphemer. If you want a proof of it, look at this." Saying these words, he showed them his Rosary, which he was at that moment carrying in his hands.

When the Spaniards saw the beads, they immediately ceased their cries and lowered their arms. "This man cannot be wicked like the others," they said, "since he says the Rosary." It happened at the same moment that the sacristan of the church in which he had received Communion came to the spot, as if sent by Our Lady herself to defend her child, and seeing them surrounding the man, he cried out: "Do not touch that man; he loves the Blessed Virgin: today I saw him receive Communion in our church in her honor."

On hearing this, the anger of the men was changed into veneration for him; they kissed his Rosary, and showed him every mark of friendship; then, taking him by the hand, they led him to a house where he would be safe from all danger.

When the insurrection was at an end, he returned to his country, and related to everyone the protection Our Lady had bestowed on him on account of his devotion and his love for her. He said the Rosary every day of his life in her honor with the greatest devotion, and kept with pious reverence the beads that had in such a wonderful manner preserved his life.

Huguet: Trésor des Inf. de Mar., 240.

THE PIOUS GENTLEMAN'S MISTAKE.

Towards the end of the fifteenth century, when Gregory Lopez, the hermit, was edifying the world by his holy life, there lived a layman of great piety who was very devout to Our Blessed Lady. He had reached such a degree of sanctity by the fervent recitation of the Holy Rosary, that for some years he was almost always in a state of continual ecstasy.

When he saw that he was so far advanced in mental prayer, he went to the holy hermit Gregory, to ask him if he thought it would be more profitable for him to leave off the Rosary, and give all his time to the prayer of meditation.

Gregory, who was himself a devout servant of Mary, knowing very well how great a help the Rosary is to those who desire to attain perfection, and what progress it enables them to make in the spiritual life, immediately answered "No," without giving him any reason for making this answer. So the good man went away, and, in obedience to the advice he had received, continued as faithfully as before, for another year, his pious custom of saying the Rosary.

At the end of that time, seeing that the favors he was daily receiving from God were constantly increasing, and that now he was far advanced in the way of perfection, he determined, without consulting Gregory this time, to cease the devotion of the Rosary, and to apply himself entirely to meditation.

He did so, but in a very short time a great change came over him. Scarcely had two or three days passed by, when he found himself encompassed by troubles, and felt his soul parched up with spiritual dryness, so that he could not pray at all. This is the danger to which those expose themselves who think that they can sail prosperously on the stormy sea of the spiritual life without Mary, the Star of the Sea, to guide them.

In his affliction, he once more went to Gregory, and told him of the heavy cross with which God had visited him: that all the devotion he used to feel at his prayers was gone, and that God had withdrawn from him all the spiritual consolation He had been accustomed to grant him. At the same time, he did not mention to the holy man that he had for some time past neglected to say the Rosary, although he thought in his own heart that that was the most probable cause of the change that had come over him.

Gregory heard him with patience to the end, and then, looking up into his face, said, with a smile: "My good friend, you have surely been neglecting to say your Rosary."

The other answered that he had for some time been applying himself to mental prayer instead of the Rosary, because he thought that it would be more profitable for him.

Gregory answered: "If you had taken my advice and continued to use your beads, you would not now be in this sad condition. Follow my advice this time. Begin again to say the Rosary, and I foretell you that you shall no longer feel that spiritual dryness of which you now complain."

The good man went home and did as Gregory advised him, and soon regained his former peace and fervor. He then redoubled his devotion to the Blessed Virgin, and often used to wonder how Gregory, without hearing a word from him upon the matter, had laid his finger at once upon the cause of his trouble.

Life of Gregory Lopez, p. 108.

A DEVOUT WORKMAN.

There was a good old man who died at Namur not many years ago. This man had so great a devotion for the Rosary that he had his beads almost always in his hand. He was a picture-framer by trade, and was accustomed to recite his Rosary while engaged with his work, and even held his beads in his hands whenever the work he was engaged in would allow him. When he was asked how long a piece of work would take, he would reply, "It will be a matter of three chaplets," or whatever the number might be, meaning that it would take him the time necessary to say that number of chaplets. So, also, if he was asked the distance from one place to another, he would answer that it would take the time necessary to say so many chaplets.

On his death-bed he would not lay aside his Rosary beads for a single moment. "I want to die," he said, "with my arms in my hands." And he died whilst reciting his Rosary.

Propagateur du Rosaire.

76

"HAIL MARY"—"FULL OF GRACE."

The children of Mary love to call upon her by that holy prayer the Church so often places upon their lips in her honor: "O Mary, conceived without sin, pray for us who have recourse to thee." Mary was full of grace from the first instant of her existence, a privilege which belongs to her alone; and innumerable are the graces she has bestowed upon her clients, who piously invoke her under this her privileged title.

RESTORED TO GRACE

There was a young man who for twenty-one years was a model of piety and edification to all the people, and the joy of his mother's heart. From his childhood he wore the scapular of the Immaculate Conception, and said every morning in his prayers: "O Mary, conceived without sin, pray for those who have recourse to thee."

Two of his companions, whose lives were a scandal to all who knew them, led him by degrees from his early piety. Not long afterwards he left his mother's house, that he might no longer be restrained by her maternal counsels and reproaches, and for three years he plunged into every kind of evil, which brought on a fatal malady. At this time he was residing in a poor dwelling near Geneva. His pious mother, when informed of what had befallen him, and where she would find him, hastened to the place and tended him as only mothers can do.

She took the earliest occasion of gently asking him to return to his Heavenly Father, whom he had abandoned, and to prepare for the judgment which must so soon come upon him. But he coldly answered: "Mother, do not speak to me of that; I have done too much evil to obtain pardon." The priest came twice to visit him, but he would not listen to him: all seemed lost.

His mother spoke to him of his former love for Our Lady, and how often he had said with so much devotion the invocation: "O Mary, conceived without sin, pray for us who have recourse to thee." "Say it again along with me, my child," she said to him. He consented, and repeated the words formerly so familiar to him.

At the same moment his mother beheld his eyes full of tears, and she knew that his heart was moved to repentance; and in the silence of her own breast she thanked Our Lady for the victory. He asked her to send for the priest whom he had so lately dismissed, made his confession, and received the last Sacraments, after which he calmly expired, while his lips repeated for the last time: "O Mary, conceived without sin, pray for us who have recourse to thee."

Guirlande à Marie, p. 46.

77

"HAIL MARY"—"THE LORD IS WITH THEE."

OUR LADY AND ST. ELIZABETH OF HUNGARY.

One night, whilst St. Elizabeth was reciting the Angelical Salutation, she to whom this beauteous prayer is addressed appeared, and among other things said: "I will teach thee all the prayers that I used to say whilst I was in the Temple. Beyond all else I used to beg of God that I might love Him and hate my enemy. There is no virtue without this absolute love of God, by which alone the plenitude of grace descends into the soul; but after entering there it flows away again, unless the soul hates its enemies—that is to say, sin and vice. He, then, who would preserve this grace should endeavor to make this love and this hatred operate in his heart.

"I wish that thou wouldst learn to do as I did. I arose every night, and, prostrate before the altar, I begged of God to teach me to observe all His Commandments, and to grant me those graces most pleasing to Him. I supplicated Him to permit me to see the time wherein should live the holy Virgin who was to bring forth His Son, that I might consecrate my whole being to serve and venerate her."

Elizabeth interrupted her to say: "O most sweet Lady, were you not already full of grace and virtue?"

But the holy Virgin replied: "Be assured that I thought myself as guilty and miserable as thou thinkest thyself; that was why I prayed to God to grant me that grace. The Lord," added the blessed Queen, "did with me what the skillful musician does with his harp, disposing all its cords so as to produce the most harmonious sound. It was thus the Lord was pleased to adapt to His good pleasure my soul, my heart, my mind, and all my senses.

"Thus governed by His wisdom, I was often borne by the angels to God's presence, and then I experienced so much joy, and sweetness, and consolation that this world was entirely banished from my memory. So familiar was I with God and His angels that it seemed as if I lived always with His holy court. Then, when it pleased the Almighty Father, I was again brought by the angels to the place where I had been praying.

"When I found myself again upon earth, and remembered where I had been, the thought so inflamed my soul with such a love of God that I embraced the earth, the stones, the trees, and all created things through affection for their Creator.

"I wished to be the servant of all the holy women who dwelt in the Temple; I wished to be subject to all creatures through love for the Supreme Father. Thou shouldst do this also, but thou asketh thyself always: 'Why are such favors granted to me, who am so unworthy to receive them?' and then thou fallest into a kind of despair and distrust of the goodness of God. Be careful not to speak thus any more, for it displeases God, Who, like a good master, can confer His benefits on whom He pleases, and Who, like a wise father, knows what is best suited to each child. In fine," said her heavenly mistress in conclusion, "I have come to thee as a special favor. This night I am thine. Ask what thou pleasest: I will answer all."

Montalembert: Life of St. Elizabeth.

78
─────────

"HAIL MARY"—"BLESSED ART THOU AMONGST WOMEN."

HOW JESUS REWARDS THOSE WHO HONOUR HIS MOTHER.

I t happened not many years ago that a certain missionary Father was preaching a retreat to ladies in the city of Nancy, in France. In one of his sermons he said to them that they should never despair of the salvation of any soul, although, looking at events in a human manner, there seemed to be no hope; and that actions which in the eyes of men are of little or no importance are rewarded by God, and in an especial manner, at the hour of death.

When he returned to the sacristy, a woman clad in mourning garb followed him.

"My Father," she said, "you have in your sermon today recommended confidence and hope: what has happened to me shows that your words are full of truth.

"I had a husband who was good and affectionate, and who was irreproachable before the world in his private and public life. Unfortunately, he neglected to practice his religious duties. My prayers, and the few words of counsel I presumed to offer him, were alike without effect.

"In the month of May which preceded his death, according to my custom, I erected an altar to Our Lady in the house, which I ornamented with flowers and candles. Every Sunday my husband used to walk into the country, and spent most of the day there instead of going to assist at Holy Mass. Yet he always, on his return home, brought with him a beautiful bouquet of flowers, which he gathered with his own hands, and I made use of them to adorn my little altar. Did he see what I did with them, or did he not? I cannot tell. Or did he do this to please me, or perhaps through a secret sentiment of piety towards Our Lady? That I will never know. But one thing I do know is that he never returned home on Sunday without fresh flowers, the best he could find.

"In the first days of the following month of June he was taken from me by a sudden death, without having time to receive the rites of the Church. This grieved me more than I can describe: my health broke down, and my friends advised me to go to the south for a change of air.

"As I passed through Lyons, I was seized with the desire of paying a visit to Ars, to see the holy curé, M. Vianney, who was then living. When I had prayed for some time in the cathedral church of that city, I wrote to him soliciting an interview, and recommending to his prayers my deceased husband. I gave him no details of his life or death.

"When I arrived at Ars, I went immediately to the church. I had scarcely entered the room where he was accustomed to receive visitors like myself, when he said to me: 'Madame, you are in great sorrow; but have you already forgotten the bouquets of sweet flowers which you placed on Our Lady's altar every Sunday?'

"It would be impossible for me to describe my astonishment at these words of the saintly priest, which so vividly brought back to my recollection a circumstance I had nearly forgotten, and of which I had never mentioned to anyone, and which he could not have known but by revelation.

"He added: 'God has had mercy on the soul of one who honored his beloved Mother, even by the little offering of flowers he made to adorn her altar. At the moment of his death, sudden as it was, he received the grace of repentance; his soul is now in Purgatory; but our prayers and our good works will soon relieve him from his sufferings, and he will then be with God for ever.'"

Confiance en la Miséricorde de Dieu, p. 157.

BLESSED ANDREW OF CITEAUX REWARDED BY OUR LADY.

Blessed Andrew, a religious of the Order of Citeaux, had a great love for Mary. Every day he recited her Office with so great attention that at each verse, and even at each word, he kept his thoughts fixed on Our Lady, and continued in this manner till he had finished it.

Mary, on her side, rewarded her servant with a favor which filled his soul with heavenly joy. For the space of seventeen years had he edified by the sanctity of his life all the religious of the monastery, when the thought came into his mind that he would seclude himself still further from the world by shutting himself up in his narrow cell, and thus be able to spend still more time in prayer.

On one occasion it happened that another religious, who used to provide him with what was necessary for his support, asked him to say something to him for his edification.

Andrew answered: "I will not refuse your request, my brother. Know, then, that I have had a visit from the most Blessed Virgin, who told me that in seven days I shall die; and she added: 'Since you have always served me with so much fidelity, I myself have come to reward you in person.' Saying these words, she smiled sweetly on me."

From that moment this pious servant of Mary began to taste the joys of Paradise. Our Lady had, in the vision she had vouchsafed to him, made known to him that she looked more to the manner in which her children offered up their prayers to her than to the prayers themselves.

Devotion to Mary, i. 217.

THE OFFERING THAT PLEASES MARY BEST.

There lived, a long time ago, a pious young man whose name was Joseph, and who loved the most holy Mother of God with an infantile simplicity. His greatest delight was to adorn her images and to decorate her altars with the most fragrant flowers he could find.

"My dear good Mother is very hard to please," he was often heard to say in his simplicity. "Behold, I bring her the most lovely flowers that bloom, and she says to me: 'I do not want them;' and I bring her the most beautiful cherries I can find, and she says to me that she does not want them either; and when I ask her what I can bring that will please her, she says to me: 'My child, it is your heart that I want.'"

When he spoke thus about Mary, or when he was kneeling before her image, or singing hymns in her honor, his countenance shone with celestial splendor, like that of St. Paul when he was taken up to the third heaven; his face, usually pale, would then shine brightly, and assume the fresh tints of perfect health.

He also desired that all creation would join with him in giving glory to Mary, and would ask the very animals to come with him to honor her. One day he was passing near a flock of sheep grazing in a field, and he cried out to them: "Come with me, and praise the great Mother of my Creator, for He is also yours." Wonderful to relate, the sheep ran after him, without giving heed to the voice of their shepherd calling them back, and stood around him while he sang her Litany. Then he blessed them, and they returned immediately to their pasturage.

Les SS. Legendes.

MARY DELIVERS A YOUNG MAN FROM PRISON.

A pious woman had an only son who had been made prisoner in a war against the Turks, and was cast into a filthy dungeon. As his mother had not, in her poverty, any means of redeeming him from his captivity, she had recourse to the most holy Mother of God to come to her assistance, knowing the unlimited power she possessed of helping all those who are in need. To insure the obtaining of her request, she added to her prayers many other good works.

One day the most holy Mother of God appeared to her and said: "What do you desire of me in those prayers you are so constantly saying to me?" Our Lady asked this that the woman might invoke her still more confidently.

"Alas! my Lady," she replied; "all that I ask of you is that you will be pleased to deliver my son from his cruel captivity, and to restore him to me, his disconsolate mother."

"Be consoled, my daughter," answered Our Lady; "I will soon bring back your son to you."

In a very short time this promise was accomplished, and the happy mother was able to embrace again her long-lost child.

He reached home on the Feast of St. Bartholomew, August 24, 1323. Towards evening he arrived at his mother's house, and knocked at the door. One can easily understand how overjoyed she was at seeing him again. Her first words were to inquire of him how he had been able to effect his escape.

He answered her: "Our most holy Lady herself came into my prison in the middle of the night, surrounded with a most brilliant light, and taking from me the heavy chains that bound me, told me to return to you, at the same time pointing out to me all the ways by which I would accomplish the journey."

During the course of their happy entertainment, both the mother and the son became persuaded that he had been released from his prison during the night, and at the very hour Our Lady had promised to deliver him.

E Calendario Mariano.

79

"HAIL MARY"—"BLESSED IS THE FRUIT OF THY WOMB, JESUS."

THE BEGINNING OF ST. JOHN'S GOSPEL.

"In the beginning was the Word, and the Word was with God, and the Word was God: the same was in the beginning with God. All things were made by Him, and without Him was made nothing that was made: in Him was life, and the life was the light of men: and the light shineth in darkness, and the darkness did not comprehend it.

"There was a man sent from God whose name was John. This man came for a witness, to give testimony of the light, that all men might believe through him. He was not the light, but came to give testimony of the light. He was the true light which enlighteneth every man that cometh into this world.

"He was in the world, and the world was made by Him, and the world knew Him not. He came unto His own, and His own received Him not. But as many as received Him, to them He gave power to become the sons of God: to those that believed in His name, who are born not of blood, nor of the will of the flesh, nor of the will of man, but of God. And the Word was made flesh, and dwelt among us; and we saw His glory, as it were the glory of the Only-begotten of the Father, full of grace and truth."

"HIS NAME WAS CALLED JESUS."

The holy Name of Jesus came down from heaven. "And after eight days were accomplished that the Child should be circumcised; His name was called Jesus, which was called by the Angel before He was conceived in the womb" (St. Luke ii. 21).

ST. PANTALEON WORKS MIRACLES IN THE NAME OF JESUS.

After the conversion of St. Pantaleon to the Christian faith, and while in conversation with his brother, who was still a pagan, on the almighty power of Jesus Christ, some men brought into their presence one who was blind.

His brother said to him: "Since you are held everywhere in great esteem on account of your great knowledge of the medicinal art, let us now see if you will be able to give sight to this blind man."

The Saint without hesitation, and knowing the power of the holy Name of Jesus, approached with confidence towards the blind man. With his hands he touched his eyes, and with his lips he pronounced the holy Name of Jesus, and the man received his sight.

On seeing this miracle his brother no longer doubted, but immediately embraced the Christian religion.

From the Saint's Life.

ST. HILARION AND THE DISCONSOLATE MOTHER.

Elpidius, who afterwards became Commander-in-Chief of the imperial army, was on a journey to Syria, in Egypt, accompanied by his wife and their three sons.

On their homeward journey, as they were passing through Gaza, the three children became dangerously ill. Every means that human art could apply was without effect, and the disconsolate mother went from bed to bed where her children lay, not knowing whose eyes would be the first to be closed in death.

In the midst of her desolation, she learned that a pious hermit lived in a desert place at some little distance from her abode. She at once determined to visit him, and, making what preparations she could in her haste, set out, accompanied by a number of attendants.

When she reached his cell, she immediately threw herself at his feet, and said: "O man of God, I pray thee, in the most holy Name of Jesus, our good Master, and by His cross on which He died for us, and by His blood which He shed for us, to come at once and save the lives of my three little ones." But Hilarion refused to accompany her, alleging as his excuse that he never left his cell, and that he had never visited any city or village, far or near.

On hearing this, the mother broke forth into loud cries of supplication, again beseeching him in the Name of God to come and heal her sons. Those who were with her mingled their sighs and tears with hers, and entreated him to grant her request.

Hilarion found it now impossible to refuse, and, rising up, he went to Gaza, and entered the house of Elpidius. There he found the three children lying at the point of death.

Raising up his hands and eyes to Heaven, he for a little time prayed in silence; then with a loud voice he pronounced over them the holy Name of Jesus, at the same time making upon them with his hand the sign of the cross, and instantly from their bodies there issued forth a copious perspiration.

In less than an hour all dangerous symptoms had passed away. Those who witnessed this miracle were overcome with joy, and joined the happy mother in a prayer of thanksgiving to God, who had, by the power of the holy Name of Jesus, raised up her three beloved children from the brink of the grave.

This miracle took place in the year 328.

ST. APOLLINARIUS, MARTYR.

When St. Apollinarius, the disciple of St. Peter the Apostle, and Bishop of Ravenna, was taken before the pagan governor Taurus, the people with loud cries demanded that he should be put to death.

But God watched over His faithful servant. The governor having called together into the great square of the city the chief men among the inhabitants, he gave orders that Apollinaris should be brought before him, and that a child, blind from its birth, should also be led in.

The governor said to the Saint: "If by the invocation of your Jesus crucified you give sight to this blind boy, we will all acknowledge that Christ is the only true God; but if you will not do so, you shall be cast into the fire, and be burned to death."

St. Apollinaris placed the child before him, and raising up his eyes to Heaven, said: "In the Name of Jesus Christ, let thine eyes be opened." And immediately the child saw.

Those who stood around waiting with eagerness to see the result were filled with astonishment on beholding this miracle, and many of them cried out with a loud voice: "Of a truth the man who has done this wonderful thing must come from God;" and believing in the Lord Jesus Christ, they were baptized.

Lives of the Saints, July 23.

PART XI

"HAIL MARY" (LAST PART)

80

"HOLY MARY, MOTHER OF GOD"— SHE IS ALSO OUR MOTHER

There never could be imagined a greater honor than that one which God gave to Mary in making her His Mother—"Mother of God." To Mary alone was granted that unspeakable privilege. But she is also Our Mother; Jesus gave her to us while dying on the cross. And Mary loves us with the tender love of a mother.

Therefore, while we glory in saluting her with the title of "Mother of God" at the beginning of the last part of the "Hail Mary," we pray that she will always bestow on us a mother's care. "Holy Mary, Mother of God," we say to her, "pray for us sinners now and at the hour of our death. Amen."

A VISION OF ST. MECHTILDES.

St. Mechtildes saw one day, in a vision, a touching manifestation of the love of the Mother of God for her faithful servants. These, under the form of a multitude of little children, surrounded the Queen of Heaven, kneeling at her feet, and offering up to her their prayers.

Mary seemed to look down on them with great love: she listened affectionately to their petitions, and covered them with her mantle, as a sign of the great care she took of them. Sometimes she would raise them in her arms, as if they were her own dear children, and place them near the Sacred Heart of her Divine Son Jesus.

THE GREATNESS OF THE LOVE OF MARY.

Father Nievemburg says that the love of all mothers for their little ones put together would only be a shadow of that which Mary has for each one of us. "She loves us more," he adds, "than all the angels and Saints together love us."

BLESSED ANDREW OF CHIO.

When Blessed Andrew of Chio was suffering the most cruel tortures because he would not deny the faith of Jesus Christ, and when his body writhed with pain under the blows he received, one only word was heard to escape from his lips: "Mary, my Mother, help me." Three different times were his tortures renewed, but each time he burst forth into the same prayer, and by it he obtained the courage to persevere to the end.

"MY MOTHER MARY."

St. Francis Xavier had always a great love for the blessed Mother of God. He used to call her his Mother—"my own sweet Mother Mary."

When he was at the point of death, and when he trembled as he thought of the judgment he was soon to undergo, he turned his eyes heavenwards towards Mary, and said to her: "O Mary, I have always loved you as my Mother; show me now at this terrible moment that thou art my Mother."

He died the death of the Saints. These words, "Show thyself to be my Mother," were amongst the last he was heard to utter.

From his Life.

ST. HYACINTH, DEAR TO OUR LADY.

St. Hyacinth was one of the great apostles of Northern Europe. He loved Our Lady exceedingly, and was a member of the Order of St. Dominic, of which she was the special patroness. The Blessed Virgin took him under her maternal protection, and often came to visit him.

In the year 1221, on the eve of the Feast of the Assumption, St. Hyacinth was meditating before Our Lady's altar on her glorious entry into Heaven, and on her triumphant reception there by the heavenly court. Suddenly a bright light shone over the altar, and the glorious Queen of Heaven appeared to him, surrounded by a multitude of angels.

She said to him: "O Hyacinth, be glad and rejoice, for thy prayers are very pleasing to my Son and to me: you shall obtain from Him whatever you ask of Him through my intercession."

Saying these words, Our Lady disappeared; and such melody of voices and instruments of music was heard as no human tongue could describe. It was to him a foretaste of the joys of Paradise.

"O MARY! O MY MOTHER!"

St. Benedict Joseph Labre left home and parents to live as a poor beggar near the sanctuaries of Jesus and Mary. His ragged and miserable state procured for him insults and blows, and he was even turned out of the Church itself as a hypocrite and an impostor. But the presence of Jesus in the tabernacle warmed his heart, and the thought of Mary turned his sorrows to joy. He wore her Rosary round his neck. Her shrine at Loreto was his favorite pilgrimage; her picture at Santa Maria dei Monti his chosen spot for prayer. There he would spend hours rapt in devotion, unconsciously edifying all around him; while the words, "O Mary! O my Mother!" would burst from his lips. There he knelt for the last time in prayer, and thence his soul made its last pilgrimage to Mary and to God.

ST. JOHN BERCHMANS' DYING COUNSEL.

When St. John Berchmans was lying on his deathbed, and was on the point of appearing before God, the superior of the house where he dwelt came to his room, accompanied by all the other religious of the house. Kneeling by the side of the dying Saint, he said to him: "My dear brother, you are on the point of appearing before God; before leaving us, I beg of you to tell us what special devotion we ought to practice in honor of Our Blessed Lady, that we may obtain her protection every day of our lives, and in particular at the hour of our death."

The dying Saint answered in these words: "Any devotion you choose, provided that it be constant."

BLESSED ALPHONSUS RODRIGUEZ OF THE SOCIETY OF JESUS.

Blessed Alphonsus Rodriguez, a lay-brother of the Society of Jesus, was remarkable for his perseverance in prayer to Mary.

The moment he rose from his sleep he knelt humbly before an image of Mary, and recited most devoutly her litany, to place himself under her special protection during the day. All his leisure moments he devoted to the recital of the Rosary, and at each hour of the day he implored Mary's help by a particular invocation.

When he sat down to table, he besought her to think of the poor souls in Purgatory, as he felt great compassion for them, and towards their consolation he offered all the little mortifications which he imposed on himself during his meals. Whenever he thought of their sufferings, his eyes were moistened with tears, and he often neglected the food before him; and it was frequently necessary for the rector to desire him to eat like the rest.

When he was obliged to leave the house, even should it be in obedience to the orders of his Superiors, he besought Our Lord rather to put an end to his life at once than to suffer him to offend Him even in the least particular; and in order to obtain the support of the Blessed Virgin, he was in the habit of saying often to her this prayer: "O Mary, show me that thou art my Mother."

Ave Maria.

THE LOVE OF THE CHILD ST. BERNARD FOR OUR LADY.

Bernard loved the most holy Mother of God from his earliest childhood. Whenever he saw her holy image, or heard anyone pronounce her name, his little countenance became radiant with joy.

"Oh, speak to me of Mary, my Mother in Heaven," he used to say to those who were with him. "Tell me something more about the blessed Mother of God."

When he fell into any fault, it was enough to say to him, "What you have done has displeased the Mother of God," and he took care never to do it again; and if his mother, in asking him to do something, said, "If you do this, you will please Our Lady," he did it at once with the greatest joy."

NESTORIUS THE HERETIC.

The first heretic who dared to refuse to give Our Lady this title was Nestorius, who preached that Mary was indeed the Mother of Jesus Christ as man, but nothing more.

The whole Catholic world rose up in indignation at this insult offered to Mary. A general council was held at Ephesus to protest against this heresy. The Bishops met in the church, and the people assembled in the great square of the city. During the whole day they remained there, awaiting the decision of the assembly; and in the evening, as soon as the Bishops came forth and declared that Nestorius was condemned, and that the glorious title of Mother of God, by which they had always honored Our Lady, was still to be given her, their joy and enthusiasm knew no bounds.

During all that night they ceased not to cry out: "Mary is truly

Mother of God. O Holy Mary, Mother of God, pray for us sinners now and at the hour of our death."

A magnificent procession was formed in the streets; the city was illuminated; the men carried lighted torches, and the women scattered sweet-smelling perfumes, to testify their great joy.

My child, every time you say the "Hail Mary" say these words with the utmost fervor, and Mary will show you that she is not only the Mother of God, but your own sweet Mother too.

ST. ODILIO CURED BY OUR LADY.

When St. Odilio of Cluny was a little child he lost the use of his limbs, so that he could not walk, and had to be carried from place to place in the arms of his nurse.

One day she laid him on the ground, not far from the door of a church which was dedicated to the most holy Mother of God, whilst she went to a little distance on some business of her master. The child, thus left alone, and seeing the door of the church open, dragged himself along the ground towards it. He crept in, and after some time reached the altar. Then, taking hold of the cloths that covered it, he raised himself on his feet; it was the first time he had ever stood erect: the Blessed Mother of God had cured him. When the nurse returned to the place where she had left him, and did not see him, she became alarmed, and began immediately to search everywhere for him. As she entered the church to look for him, Odilio saw her, and leaving the altar, to the surprise of all who were present, ran forward to meet her.

The news of the child's miraculous cure soon spread throughout the city, and the people with one accord went to the church to thank their heavenly patroness for this manifestation of her love and power.

81

"HOLY MARY, MOTHER OF GOD"— WE ARE ALSO HER CHILDREN

We have already seen that Mary, the Mother of God, is our Mother also; let us now read some examples of how tenderly she watches over her children, obtaining for them many temporal and spiritual graces.

ST. PHILIP NERI MIRACULOUSLY CURED.

St. Philip Neri was one time so ill that no one thought he could recover.

While the brethren were standing around him weeping, they suddenly heard him exclaim: "O my most sweet Lady! O Lady full of bounty, be thou a thousand times blessed!" These words he repeated many times, to the astonishment of those who were present in the room.

But greater still was their amazement when they saw him raised above the bed, and stretching out his hands towards some object invisible to them, and exclaiming: "Oh, I am not worthy! I am not worthy!"

And when they asked him what had happened, he answered: "Do you not see the Blessed Virgin, my Mother Mary, who has come from

Heaven to cure me?" Then, perceiving that the room was full of people, he covered his head with the bedclothes, being ashamed in his humility of their being witnesses of his ecstasy. It was with difficulty that they could persuade him to remove them; and when the physicians had examined him, they found that he had been restored to perfect health.

Life of St. Philip Neri.

THE VISION OF BLESSED MARY OF THE ANGELS.

"On the Festival of Our Lady's Assumption," related Blessed Mary of the Angels, "as I was approaching the altar to receive Holy Communion, I felt myself so filled with heavenly sweetness that I thought I was already in Heaven.

"At the same time the Blessed Virgin appeared to me; she was so beautiful, and shone with so much splendor, that I could not look on her, for my eyes were dazzled with the light that surrounded her. She held in her hand a white robe, but the whiteness was quite different from any earthly whiteness. I said to her: 'O my Lady, for whom is that beautiful robe prepared?'

"She replied: 'It is for yourself; I will give it to you when you have reached the end of your trial on earth. You have still some time to live and much to endure before you receive it. Have frequent recourse to me, therefore, and say to me: "At thy feet, O Sovereign Lady, I wish to live and to die."'"

ST. STANISLAUS' LOVE FOR MARY.

One day St. Stanislaus Kostka was preaching on the glories of Mary before the Fathers and Brothers of his Order.

One of his Superiors who was present during the sermon was amazed at the fervor and eloquence with which he spoke.

When the sermon was done, he took him aside and said to him; "Stanislaus, do you love Mary?"

"Love her!" he replied. "How can you ask me such a question? Is she not my Mother?" And as he spoke tears of affection burst from his eyes.

From his Life.

ST. IGNATIUS CONSECRATES HIMSELF TO MARY.

From the moment of his conversion, St. Ignatius became one of Our Lady's most devoted children. He had taken the firm resolution of serving God faithfully to the end of his life; but, knowing the many difficulties and dangers he would meet with in fulfilling it, he placed it under the protection of the most holy Mother of God. He humbly knelt down before her image, and solemnly consecrated himself to her forever.

The Blessed Virgin was pleased to show him how agreeable to her was this offering. A few days after he had made it he was assailed by a great temptation. "O Mary, my Mother, help me, your child," he cried.

In an instant Our Lady appeared to him in the midst of great brightness. The Child Jesus was in her arms, and He looked on the servant of His Mother with eyes full of love. At the same moment the temptation disappeared, and he felt in his heart a joy and peace which ever afterwards remained there.

Our Lady may not appear visibly to you as she did to that great Saint, but if you are as faithful as he was to call upon her in your temptations, and say as he did, "O Mary, my Mother, help me, for I am your child," she will at once come to your assistance, and drive the temptation away.

OUR LADY'S ANSWER TO ST. ALPHONSUS.

About the middle of the fifteenth century, there lived at Segoria a pious child named Alphonsus Rodriguez. His mother had instilled into his soul from his childhood a great love for the most holy

Mother of God, so that when he grew up to manhood this affection for her preserved him from sin in the midst of many temptations.

Every time he saw a picture or image of the Blessed Virgin he saluted it with some loving salutation, and begged of her whom it represented to pray for him and to keep him from sin.

One day, as he was gazing with affection on an image of Mary, he said: "O my Lady, if you only knew how much I love you! I love you so much, that it would be quite impossible even for yourself to love me more than I love you."

To reward these tender words the Queen of Heaven was pleased to appear to him in a visible manner. "O my child," she said, "you are wrong in thinking that your love for me is greater than my love for you; for I love you far more than it is possible for you to love me."

OUR LADY AND ST. ELIZABETH OF HUNGARY.

One day as St. Elizabeth of Hungary was meditating on the life of Our Divine Lord, and was anxious to know more deeply the mystery of that love that brought Him down from Heaven for our salvation, the most holy Mother of God appeared to her, and said: "If thou wilt be my pupil, I will be thy teacher; if thou wilt be my servant, I will be thy mistress."

Elizabeth, not daring to think herself worthy of such an honor, said: "Who art thou who dost ask me to be thy pupil and thy servant?"

Our Lady immediately replied: "I am the Mother of the living God, and I will be better able to instruct thee in these things than anyone else."

At these words Elizabeth extended her hands towards the Mother of Mercy, who took them in hers, and said: "If thou wilt be my child, I will be thy mother."

These words filled the Saint's heart with unbounded joy. The thought that she was now in such a special manner the child of Mary made her more happy than if the whole world had been given to her. Yet she was afraid that she might not show herself so loving towards her as she ought to be; and though she tried to avoid everything that she thought would displease her, she felt that her love for her was still very imperfect.

One day she had been guilty of a slight fault, and when she saw what she had done she wept very bitterly, because she knew that it would so much displease Our Lady. While she was thus weeping over it, the Blessed Virgin suddenly appeared to her, and said: "My child, why are you weeping? I did not choose you to be my child that you should be unhappy. Take courage, then, and, although you have not been entirely obedient to me, try to be better for the time to come; say one 'Hail Mary' in my honor, and this fault will be forgiven you."

Mary is your mother also, my child, and loves you with a mother's love. She knows how weak you are, and has pity on you when you have fallen into some fault, if only you are sorry for it, and resolved to do better for the time to come. In all your trials and sorrows, therefore, have recourse to her with confidence, and she will show you that she is really your mother

BLESSSED STANISLAUS OF CASMIR CONSOLED.

Our Blessed Lady appeared to Blessed Stanislaus of Casmir, who loved her exceedingly, and said to him: "My son Stanislaus, be full of joy because of your love for me. Continue to love and serve me to the end of your life as you are doing now, and a great reward will be given you with my Saints in Paradise."

When he was at the point of death, Jesus Himself appeared to him, accompanied by His Blessed Mother, and, calling on him in tones of heavenly sweetness, said to him: "My son Stanislaus, arise in haste and come, for to-day thou shalt be with Me in Paradise."

Such is the holy end of those who love and serve Mary.

"I AM GOING TO HEAVEN."

Blessed Alphonsus Salmeron never allowed a day to pass without offering to the most holy Mother of God some tribute of homage and love.

Whenever he was in trouble it was to Mary he had recourse, and if he was in any difficulty, it was to her he went for assistance. In all his sermons he spoke of her, and during the whole course of his life he tried to inflame the hearts of all who came to hear him with a great devotion towards her.

To excite in their hearts a still greater desire of honoring her, he used often to tell them of the special protection she would give them at the moment of their death, if they did as he recommended. When his own last hour had come, as if to reward him for all he had done for her, she took away from him the terrors of death.

When he saw himself near his end, he cried out: "I am going to Heaven! I am going to Heaven! Oh, blessed is my life, O Mary, that I spent in honoring thee! Blessed are those sermons in which I extolled thy greatness and thy mercy for poor sinners. Blessed are those labors I endured for thee, and blessed is all I have done and suffered and written in thine honor, O my Mother."

Then, turning towards those who were kneeling round his bed, he said: "O my brethren, how sweet it is to die when one has during life honored and loved Mary!"

These were his last words.

From his Life.

ST. ALPHONSUS RODRIGUEZ AND OUR LADY.

One year, on August 15, the Festival of Our Lady's Assumption into Heaven, St. Alphonsus Rodriguez went very early to the church to prepare for Holy Communion. After he had received his Divine Master in His most Holy Sacrament, and while he But our Divine Savior consoled her by a vision. She saw Our Lady standing at the

Judgment-seat of her Son Jesus. Charles stood there to be judged. Satan also was there to claim his soul, but found that the Judge had, through Mary's intercession, passed on him the happy sentence of the just.

Satan complained to God in these words: "Your Mother has done me two wrongs here. Before he died, she went into the place where he lay, and protected him in his last struggle, and did not permit me to tempt him. Then, instead of allowing me to bring him to be judged, she herself took him in her arms and carried him here. These are the two great wrongs she has done me; so, Just Judge, give orders now that the soul of Charles return to his body, that I may be able to tempt him."

But Our Lady here interrupted him. "Although you are the father of lies, you have here spoken the truth: I did assist Charles in a most special manner when he was dying, and also here at the Judgment-seat, because he served me well during life, and at the moment of his death gave his life in honor of me."

Jesus turned towards Satan, and said: "My Mother has a right to command here, because she is a Queen and a Sovereign in My Kingdom, and can do in these things whatever she wills. In this matter she has done well."

By these words Jesus imposed silence on Satan, and St. Bridget knew that her beloved child was safe.

Revelations of St. Bridget. were, to the feet of His heavenly throne, and procure for him whatever he asked.

One day, while lying on a bed of sickness, and so ill that the physicians themselves thought he would never rise again, he was suddenly heard to exclaim: "O my most holy Mother, my most beauteous and blessed Mother!"

The physicians and the priests present hastened to his side, and beheld him raised in the air more than a foot above his bed, his arms stretched out as if he wished to embrace someone; at the same time they heard him exclaim: "Dearest Lady, I am not worthy of this favor. I do not deserve that thou shouldst come to visit and heal me. What return shall I make to thee if thou restoreth me to health—I, who have never done any good?"

To the surprise of the bystanders, he arose from his bed perfectly cured. Our Blessed Lady had healed him.

Like St. Philip, my child, when you are anxious to approach Jesus in Holy Communion, go in company with Our Lady, and she will procure for you from Him a loving welcome.

THE SON OF ST. BRIDGET.

St. Bridget had a son called Charles who was a soldier. One day he was fighting in a great battle, and was wounded. The wound proved fatal. He was taken off the field, and soon afterwards breathed his last. His mother, knowing how seldom those who are soldiers live good lives, was filled with grief when she heard of her son's death, because she was afraid lest he might have died in sin, and so be lost.

But our Divine Savior consoled her by a vision. She saw Our Lady standing at the Judgment-seat of her Son Jesus. Charles stood there to be judged. Satan also was there, to claim his soul, but found that the Judge had, through Mary's intercession, passed on him the happy sentence of the just.

Satan complained to God in these words: "Your Mother has done me two wrongs here. Before he died, she went into the place where he lay, and protected him in his last struggle, and did not permit me to tempt him. Then, instead of allowing me to bring him to be judged, she herself took him in her arms and carried him here. These are the two great wrongs she has done me; so, Just Judge, give orders now that the soul of Charles return to his body, that I may be able to tempt him."

But Our Lady here interrupted him. "Although you are the father of lies, you have here spoken the truth: I did assist Charles in a most special manner when he was dying, and also here at the Judgment-seat, because he served me well during life, and at the moment of his death gave his life in honor of me."

Jesus turned towards Satan, and said: "My Mother has a right to command here, because she is a Queen and a Sovereign in My King-dom, and can do in these things whatever she wills. In this matter she has done well."

By these words Jesus imposed silence on Satan, and St. Bridget knew that her beloved child was safe.

Revelations of St. Bridget.

BLESSSED HERMANN JOSEPH, OUR LADY'S CHILD.

One of the most favored of Our Lady's children was, without doubt, the blessed Hermann Joseph. From his very childhood he belonged to her, and was never so happy as when kneeling at the foot of her image and speaking familiarly with her.

In the church of the village to which he belonged there was a beautiful image of the Divine Mother, carrying in her arms the holy Child Jesus. It was the boy's delight to go thither, where, kneeling at the foot of the altar, and keeping his eyes fixed on the image before him, he would talk sometimes to the Mother, and sometimes to the Child, of all his boyish troubles and the hardships he had already to endure, on account of the poverty of his parents.

"My dear little Jesus," he used to say, "I had nothing for breakfast this morning but a piece of dry bread, so that I am still very hungry. Yet I am not going to complain, for You Yourself, although You are the Son of God, did often suffer hunger like me."

Then he would tell the holy Child all that he had learned since the night before, and all that he intended to do during that day. He used to say before leaving the chapel: "I would much rather stay here with You and Your dear Mother, but I must go to school; give me, then, Your blessing, and sometimes think of me till I come back again to see You."

The most holy Mother of God loved the little boy because of his simplicity. One day when the child came to make his usual visit, he brought with him a beautiful apple which someone had given him. "My dear holy mother," he said, "I have brought this beautiful apple;

take it as a mark of the great love I have for you and for your holy Son Jesus."

"Wonderful to relate," says the historian, "the Queen of Angels, that she might not seem to disregard the child's offering, caused the arm of the statue to bend down towards the child and receive the apple."

Another time, when he was in the same church, he saw in a vision, far above his head, the most holy Mother of God with the Divine Child and St. John the Evangelist. As he was gazing on this vision, he heard them speaking in so heavenly a manner that his whole heart seemed to be inflamed with the desire of being up beside them.

And as he was thinking of this, suddenly he heard the sweet voice of Our Lady saying to him: "Hermann, come up to us."

"O my Mother, I cannot reach you," he said, "for I have no ladder, and you are so high up."

The Blessed Mother, then stretching out her hand, took him up, and placed him by the side of her Divine Son, and there he spent many hours in sweet conversation with Him.

Another time, in the middle of winter, Hermann came to the church without any shoes on his feet. The Blessed Virgin again appeared to him, and asked him why he had come barefooted in such cold weather.

"O my dear Lady," he answered, "you know that my parents are so poor that they cannot give me any shoes."

She told him to go to a certain spot, where he would get as much money as would buy for him that of which he stood so much in need. Hermann went to the place, and found the money as Our Lady had told him. He then went back to thank her for her kindness. Our Lady embraced him, and promised that she would provide for him the things he needed, because he had so great an affection for her.

Thus the pious child of Mary grew up, and each day became more and more fervent. Over and over again did Our Blessed Lady appear to him in all her loveliness to console him and to comfort him.

But a day came when this fervor came to an end. Hermann began to grow very careless in all his spiritual duties. He did not now say his prayers with the same devotion; he became less patient in his trials, and allowed the spirit of sloth to take possession of his heart. In punishment of this he was no longer favored by the visits of Our Lady which had hitherto been his greatest consolation.

One day as he was grieving over this, he saw walking along the corridor of the monastery where he dwelt a lady of majestic appearance, clothed in rich garments, but with a countenance that seemed to have once been very beautiful, but which had now lost all its beauty.

Hermann, seeing a lady within the walls of the monastery, was very much astonished, and, going up to her, was about to ask her who she was and whence she came.

But, as he was approaching, she said to him: "Hermann, you do not seem to know me."

Hermann at once knew the voice; it was one he had so often heard before—the voice of the most holy Mother of God.

"O my own most sweet Mother," he cried out, "is it you? But oh, how changed you are! What has become of that beautiful countenance which I used to look upon with so much joy?"

"And you, my child," she answered, "what has become of your former fervor, your former generosity, your former great love for me? When you were fervent and pious, and when your soul was adorned with heavenly beauty, I appeared to you under a celestial likeness. Today I appear to you in a very different manner, to show you how displeased I am with you, and what unkindness you have shown me by your ungrateful conduct.

While Our Lady was saying these words of reproach, Hermann had cast himself on the ground at her feet, and broke forth in sighs and tears.

But the heart of Our Lady seemed to be melted to tenderness as she saw the sorrow of her dear child. "Rise up, my dear Hermann," she said to him; "if you begin to be fervent again as you used to be, you will be my own dear child, as you were before."

Hermann Joseph rose up from his knees consoled and comforted. It was a lesson for him which he never afterwards forgot. From this example you also, my child, will learn how ungrateful it would be in you, and how much you would grieve the most holy Mother of God if, like Hermann, you should ever grow cold in your devotions towards her.

From the Life of Blessed Hermann Joseph.

OUR LADY'S LITTLE ORPHAN.

There was once a little girl who had just lost her mother. She was left alone in the world, with no one to care for her, no one to love her.

People came to the house where the dead body of her mother lay, and carried it away and laid it deep down in the cold grave.

"Oh, my mother! my mother!" cried out the little child, "what will now become of me? Who will give me something to eat, or who will protect me?" And the tears fell from her eyes upon her mother's grave, as she knelt there, forsaken and alone.

When the night came on, she rose from the ground to go away. But whither was she to go? She had no home now. She suddenly remembered that at the entrance to the neighboring forest stood a little chapel dedicated to Mary, the Mother of God; so she went towards it.

Going in, she knelt down before Our Lady's image, which stood upon the altar, and with eyes filled with tears, she thus began to pray: "O my most sweet, heavenly Mother Mary, my poor dear mother on earth is dead, and I have no one to take pity on me. I am a poor orphan child left alone in this weary world. Ah! my own dear Mother Mary, do not forsake your lonely child in her afflictions."

And as she was thus praying, a sudden and dazzling light began to fill the chapel, and she heard the strains of the most ravishing music that ever fell on mortal ears. The chapel was at the same time filled with a most sweet perfume. In the midst of the brightness there appeared a most beautiful lady, clad in a raiment whiter than snow.

On her head was a crown of the purest gold, and she was accompanied by a choir of the heavenly host singing joyously.

The lady, smiling sweetly on the child, said to her: "My daughter, I am Mary, the Mother of God. I have heard your prayer, and for the time to come I will be your mother, and you shall be my child."

When she had said this, she placed her holy hand upon the forehead of the little girl, as a sign of her adoption, and then disappeared.

The child's heart was now filled with joy and consolation. She arose from her knees to face the storms and tempests of a wicked world. She now feared nothing, because she knew that under the protection of her Mother in Heaven she would be safe from every danger.

When the time of her exile was ended, Mary was again by the side of her child to help her to die well; and when the end came she carried her happy soul to Heaven to rejoice forever in the presence of God.

Legends of Albert Weijer.

MUSA'S VISION OF OUR LADY.

St. Gregory the Great tells us that one night the most holy Mother of God appeared to a young girl called Musa, accompanied by a large company of girls like herself, clad in beautiful white garments.

Musa was filled with admiration at the beautiful vision, and would willingly have joined herself to them, but she was afraid to do so.

Then Our Lady asked her: "Would you not like to come and join this happy company of my favored children?"

Musa answered: "My Lady, with all my heart I desire it. That was just the thought that was in my mind when you asked me, but I was afraid to go."

Then Our Lady said to her: "You also shall join them, but not today. You must become a little more serious than you are accustomed to be, and, above all, you must not give so much time to play and amusements as you have hitherto done, and more time to prayer. If you do this I will come back again in thirty days, and I will take you with me to join them."

Musa promised to do what Our Lady asked. She became more serious, and gave up all thoughts of vanity, dress, and play, which had till then so much occupied her mind, so that her parents were astonished and pleased at the change that had come over her.

On the thirtieth day she died. At the moment of her death the Blessed Virgin returned according to her promise, accompanied, as before, by the company of white-clad children.

"Musa, my child," said Our Lady, "come, now, and join the company of my good children, who, when on earth, were so faithful to me."

Musa answered: "O my Queen, I am ready; let me go at once." Saying this, she died.

Dialogues of St. Gregory.

82

"HOLY MARY, MOTHER OF GOD"—" PRAY FOR US SINNERS NOW."

It is especially when you are troubled with temptations to do things that are very wrong that you ought to have instant recourse to Mary. Those who fly to her protection in those moments never fall into sin.

"O MARY, HELP ME, FOR I AM THINE."

A young man who had many times fallen into grievous mortal sins went to Confession to a certain priest. The good priest was greatly afflicted on learning that he had fallen so often; but, to encourage him, he said: "My child, I will tell you an easy means of overcoming the temptations to which you have so often yielded. If you do what I tell you, you will never fall again."

"O my Father," he replied, "tell me what it is, for with my whole heart do I desire to overcome these evil habits."

"Place yourself entirely under the protection of the Blessed Virgin," said the priest. "Say a 'Hail Mary' every morning and evening in honor of her immaculate purity; and whenever you are tempted to do evil, say to her at once, 'O Mary, help me, for I am thine.'"

The young man followed this advice, and in a short time was entirely delivered from his evil habits.

Now, it happened some time afterwards that he was relating this to some of his acquaintances whom he had formerly scandalized by his bad conduct. He told them of his having placed himself entirely under the protection of her who is called the Refuge of Sinners, and of the prayer he always said when tempted.

Amongst those who were listening to him was a young officer, who, like himself, had fallen into many sins, because he went willfully with bad companions.

As soon as he heard the young man's story he resolved in his own mind to follow his example. He at once prepared himself for Confession, and continued afterwards to lead a pious life under the protection of the Immaculate Mother of God. Her holy name was continually on his lips, and that devout prayer, "O Mary, help me, for I am thine," was his watchword whenever any temptation assailed him.

Some months after his conversion he had the imprudence to go again to visit those companions who had formerly led him into sin; he wished to see if they had imitated his example and begun a new life as he himself had done, or were still following the path of evil.

But no sooner had he reached the place where they dwelt than a strange feeling of terror came over him, and he cried out: "O Mary, help me, for I am thine."

That very instant he felt himself thrust back by an invisible hand, and found himself at a distance from the house. He immediately saw the danger in which he had been, and returned his most heartfelt thanks to God and to his holy Mother Mary for having thus preserved him.

AN UNEXPECTED GRACE.

St. Alphonsus Liguori tells us the following incident:

"One of my priests was in a certain church hearing confessions. A young man came into the church and began to look around him.

There was something in his countenance that told the priest that he was not happy. So he went up to him and said: 'My friend, are you going to Confession?'

'Yes, I want to go; but I am afraid I will take a long time. Could you take me to a very retired place, as I would like to tell you something before I begin my confession?'

"When they were alone, the young man told the priest his past history, as follows:

'I am a stranger in this place. I have done so much evil that I cannot expect to obtain God's pardon. I have even committed murder, and detestable sins of all kinds. I did all these things not so much to gratify my passions as to show my hatred for God. I used to have a crucifix about me, but I long ago threw it away, also through hatred.

'This morning,' he continued, 'I went to Communion for the purpose of committing a sacrilege, but since then I have found no rest. In going past this church a little time ago, something seemed to force me to enter. I could not resist it. As soon as I came in, remorse of conscience filled me with terrible fear. I felt within me at the same time a vague desire of going to Confession. I went up to the place where you were sitting, but I could not make up my mind to enter. I thought that God could not pardon my terrible sins, so I turned away to go out.

"'Still something, I know not what it was, made me remain.

"'At that moment, Father, you came up to me, and here I am at your feet ready to begin my Confession.'

"The priest then asked him if he had the practice of doing any good work, even a little one, or if he had the habit of saying any little prayer. 'Perhaps,' he said, 'you may have had the custom of performing some devotion in honor of Mary, the Mother of God, for such conversions are generally the effect of Mary's prayers?'

"'No, Father, nothing,' he replied.

"'Think again,' said the priest. 'What is this you have around your neck? A scapular? Ah! I see what has brought you this grace.'

"The poor sinner replied: 'It is true I was long ago enrolled in the scapular, but I had forgotten all about it; I have not for many years said any prayer to the Blessed Virgin, although I was at one time very devout to her.'

"'Well, my child,' said the priest, 'you may have forgotten Mary, but she has not forgotten you, and she has obtained for you the grace of conversion because you have not taken off her holy scapular. And you must also know that this church is under her special protection.'

"The young man burst into tears and made his Confession. Soon afterwards he was admitted to Holy Communion, which he received with great devotion.

"He told the priest to publish everywhere the great grace Mary had obtained for him because he wore her scapular."

St. Alphonsus Liguori.

THE EIGHTH SWORD.

There was once a young man who had a great devotion to Our Lady. Every day he went to a chapel not far from his home, and kneeling there before her altar, would say his prayers with great fervor.

The image on this altar represented Our Lady of the Seven Dolors. There was on the breast of the image a heart which was pierced with seven swords. The sight of this image used to fill him with great compassion for the most sorrowful Virgin, and he sometimes shed tears when he thought of the cruelty of the Jews in persecuting her Divine Son.

One night a terrible temptation assailed him, and he had the misfortune of yielding to it and committing a mortal sin. On the following day he went as usual to the chapel to say his prayers before Our Lady's altar.

He was afraid to look up to the face of the holy image, because he remembered the sin he had committed. But when he took courage and did so, he was surprised to see Our Lady's heart pierced with eight swords instead of seven.

"Ah! wretch that I am!" he exclaimed. "It is my sin that has driven this sword into the heart of my good Mother," and tears of heartfelt sorrow flowed down his cheeks.

He immediately rose from his knees and went to find his confessor. He confessed his sin with the greatest compunction, and took the firm resolution never again to grieve his Mother in Heaven by offending her Son Jesus.

On his return to the altar of the Blessed Virgin, he once more looked up to the holy image, and to his great joy he no longer saw the eighth sword: it had disappeared the moment his sin had been cancelled in the tribunal of penance.

In his after-life, when Satan came to tempt him, he would at once call to mind the vision he had seen in the chapel; and thinking of the sufferings of Jesus and the sorrows of Mary, he would say, "Jesus and Mary, I love you; Jesus and Mary I give you my heart;" and in this way he overcame every temptation.

Ann. de la Comp. de Jesus.

83

"HOLY MARY, MOTHER OF GOD"—" PRAY FOR US AT THE HOUR OF OUR DEATH."

"HOLY MARY, PRAY FOR HIM."

In the city of Reisberg lived a holy priest named Arnold, who was exceedingly devout to Our Lady. When he saw that his end was near, he received the last Sacraments with edifying piety. He also asked the religious who were praying at his bedside not to leave him, but to pray earnestly to God to give him a happy death.

He had scarcely made this request, when a sudden and terrible fear came over him, and he trembled from head to foot. A cold sweat also covered his face, and his eyes, glazed with the approach of death, rolled wildly in his head.

"O my brethren," he cried out in a voice of agony, "do you not see the evil spirits around me, waiting to carry me to Hell? Oh, ask my heavenly Mother Mary to help me, for in her do I trust in this hour of deep distress."

Immediately the religious began to recite the Litany of the Blessed Virgin. When they came to these words, "Holy Mary, pray for him," he cried out: "My brethren, say those words again; say again the name of Mary, for I am already standing at God's Judgment-seat."

It seemed as if he saw the wicked spirits standing there to accuse him, and as if he heard their words, for he said, as if answering some question: "Yes, but I did penance for that."

Then, as if speaking to the Blessed Virgin, he said, "O my Mother Mary, I will overcome all these enemies if you will only help me."

The night advanced, and terrible must have been the temptations he had to endure; but he constantly pressed the crucifix to his lips, and continued without ceasing to whisper the holy name of Mary.

As the morning dawned, the dying man became calm, and on his countenance there beamed signs of joy which showed the peace that was in his soul. Mary, his Refuge, had obtained for him the final victory.

Suddenly he turned towards a certain spot in the room, as if he saw something. It was the Immaculate Mother of God herself who was there, and who had come to conduct him into Paradise.

"I come, my Lady, I come!" he exclaimed, and while saying these words he tried to raise himself in his bed; but in doing so he calmly expired, and went to follow Mary, as we may fondly hope, into the kingdom of eternal happiness.

St. Alphonsus Liguori.

ADOLPHUS, THE PIOUS NOBLEMAN.

In the chronicles of St. Francis we read the following example:

There was in the territory of Alsace a young nobleman called Adolphus, who, in his youth, had renounced his rich inheritance and become a religious, that he might serve God better.

Even when a child he had a great devotion to the Blessed Virgin, and as he grew up this devotion increased with his years.

When the hour of his death drew near, he became sad, and seemed to be full of fear. His brethren asked him what caused him so much trouble.

He replied: "I am so soon to be judged, and I know not what that judgment will be."

They tried to console him by speaking to him of God's mercy to poor sinners, but their words seemed to give him no comfort.

In the midst of his affliction Our Merciful Lady appeared to him. Along with her there was a company of happy souls, her servants, who, when on earth, had been most devout to her.

"Adolphus, my son," she said to him, "why do you tremble, and what is it that fills you with so much fear? Were you not all your lifetime my dutiful child, and have you not always served my Divine Son faithfully? Did you not renounce all your earthly possessions for His sake? Ah! my child, rather rejoice now that your labors are over, for He will so soon reward you in Heaven."

These consoling words took away from him all fear of death, and he died, as the faithful servants of Mary always die, a holy and a happy death.

Chronicles of St. Francis.

A CONVERSION AT THE ELEVENTH HOUR.

The following is a letter from the island of Cyprus, dated May 25, 1864:

"We have just been witnesses of a great wonder, the recital of which, I am sure, will fill the servants of Mary with great joy.

"There was a man here who was very rich, and who held a very important position in our island. He died about six weeks ago in sentiments of the greatest piety. Everyone was astonished at his conversion, for from the time of his daughter's death, many years ago, he had never gone to the Sacraments. Almost all his children were dead, and, strange to say, most of them had died without the priest.

"When the priest learned that he was so ill, he went to see him, to try if he could induce him to prepare himself for death; but to all his exhortations he always got the same answer: 'Father, there is plenty of time for that; we will think about it afterwards.'

"But as each day passed by the man became worse; it was evident to all about him that the end was not far off. The priest called one day and found him sinking fast; his feet and hands were already cold. 'My dear sir,' he said to him again, 'it is now time to make your Confession, and to receive the last Sacraments.' But he received the same answer as before: 'There is yet plenty of time; we shall think about it in a few days.'

"The priest gave him a little medal of the Immaculate Conception, and asked him to put it on. He took it into his hands, not through any affection for it, but because he was too weak to refuse it. Next day we heard that he was dead. We met the priest as he was coming from the house of the deceased, and we asked him how he had died.

"'Oh, thanks be to God and to His most holy Mother, he died a happy death. Yesterday, as I was sitting by his bedside praying for him, a thought came into my mind to interest the Blessed Virgin in his behalf. I had with me a medal of the Blessed Virgin, but at first I was afraid to let him see it, since he showed no signs of piety, and seemed to have lost his faith altogether. I fervently prayed to her who is the Refuge of sinners to come to his assistance. While these thoughts were passing through my mind, I slipped the medal into his hands and continued to pray for him. Not many minutes afterwards I was astonished to hear him say to me: 'Well, Father, when are you going to begin?'

"'Begin what?' I asked.

"'Begin to hear my Confession. I don't want to put off a moment longer, for we do not know what may happen.'

"He began immediately to make his Confession, and I gave him the last Sacraments. He raised the medal with his dying hands to his lips and kissed it fervently; then I hung it round his neck. From time to time I heard him utter these words: 'O my God, my God! have pity on me, a poor sinner, and pardon me.' Then, having the medal on his heart, and with the names of Jesus and Mary on his lips, he calmly breathed his last.

"This took place on the morning of April 11, 1864."

Huguet: Dev. à Marie.

Mary delights to receive the homage of our prayers and praises, but only when we love her Divine Son. To offer them with a heart defiled with sin would be to insult her.

DELICIOUS FOOD ON A FILTHY PLATE.

There was once a young man who had the bad habit of committing sins against holy purity. From the days of his childhood he had always honored the most holy Mother of God as his pious mother had taught him to do; and although he was living in the state of sin, he every day said some prayers in her honor.

One night he had a strange dream. He dreamed that he had gone out to walk in a forest, and that he had lost his way. He wandered about for a long time looking for the path, but in vain. Soon he began to feel the pangs of hunger, and he looked on all sides for something to eat, but found nothing.

Suddenly there appeared before him a beautiful lady surrounded with a heavenly light, and accompanied by an escort of virgins clad in white.

This lady went up to him and placed before him the most delicious food that he had ever seen, but on a dish which was exceedingly filthy, and covered with worms. The sight of the dish filled him with disgust, and although he was almost dying of hunger, he could not bring himself to taste the tempting food which was upon the plate.

The lady said to him: "Take and eat this delicious food I have brought to you."

"Oh, how willingly would I eat of it!" he answered, "because I am so hungry and the food is so tempting, but I cannot eat it out of that loathsome dish!"

The lady (it was the Blessed Virgin herself) then said: "The prayers which you say in my honor every day are indeed beautiful in themselves, but your heart is so impure. How can you expect that I can receive with love prayers from a soul that is steeped in the filth of sin?"

Having said these words, she disappeared, and the young man awoke.

"Ah!" he said, "my soul is indeed black and filthy on account of the sins I have committed, but from this hour I will change my life and never sin again."

He kept his word. Having washed away his sins in the Sacrament of Penance, he began a new life, and persevered in it till he died. During his whole life he was ever grateful to his Mother in Heaven for the timely warning she had given him.

Rep. du Catéchiste, iii. 413.

84

"HOLY MARY, MOTHER OF GOD"—" AMEN."

When the time of your trial is ended, if, my child, you have loved and served Mary faithfully on earth, great will be your joy in Heaven. May such be the happy lot of everyone who reads this little book.

THE MUSIC OF HEAVEN.

There lived, many years ago, a pious monk named Thomas, who loved Our Lady with all his heart. Day after day he besought his blessed Queen to be pleased to visit him even during his mortal pilgrimage.

One night he went out into the garden of the monastery, and, looking up to Heaven, asked Our Lady again, with sighs and tears, to grant his prayer.

On a sudden he saw a brilliant light shoot down from Heaven like a star, and a beautiful and radiant virgin stood before him.

The virgin called him by name, and said: "Thomas, would you wish to hear me sing?"

"Oh, most certainly, my lady," replied the religious.

Then the virgin sang, and sang so sweetly that Thomas thought he was in Paradise. But suddenly the singing ceased, and the vision disappeared.

The heart of the good monk was burning with desire to hear more of this heavenly music, when another beautiful virgin appeared, and sang to him with the same celestial sweetness.

When the virgin had ended her heavenly strain, she said to the pious monk: "The virgin whom you saw a little while ago was St. Catherine, and I am Agnes. We have been sent by Our Lady to console you. Give thanks, then, to Jesus and Mary, and prepare to receive a still greater favor."

She immediately vanished from his sight, and the heart of the good monk beat high with hope and love, for he was now at last to behold the object of all his desires—the Immaculate Mother of God. Looking up, he beheld a brilliant light, and his heart was filled with unspeakable joy. There in the midst of the dazzling light he beheld Our Lady; surrounded by a multitude of angels, and radiant with celestial beauty.

She smiled upon the happy religious. "My dear son," she said, "your devotion is pleasing to me; you have long desired to see me. Look on me now, and I, too, will sing to you."

And now the Blessed Virgin sang. Never before did such entrancing melody charm a mortal ear. The pious monk was ravished out of his senses, and sank on the ground as dead; and, in truth, he would have died had not God given him strength to bear that excessive joy.

After remaining long in this trance he came to himself again, but he could never forget the sweetness of that heavenly song. He slowly pined away, and soon died of sheer desire to hear in the Kingdom of Heaven the rapturous canticles of the blessed.

Fr. Müller: The Prodigal Son, p. 566.

FATHER EUSEBIUS.

In the year 1846 there died in the monastery of La Trappe a holy religious called Father M. Eusebius.

When he was a boy at school, he felt within him a great desire of leading a perfect life. Therefore, as soon as it was possible for him, he left his father's house and retired into the monastery.

The rules of this institution imposed on him many and strict obligations, but he fulfilled them all with scrupulous exactness. Although of feeble health, he mortified himself with as much energy as if he had been of a strong constitution, and when some persons suggested to him that he should ask a dispensation from some of the more difficult points, because of his infirmities, he answered them: "I did not forsake the world and become a religious that I might obtain rest and comfort; no, I did so that I might obtain the Kingdom of Heaven. It matters not how much I suffer here below, provided that is secured."

When he was near the moment of his death, and the Fathers around him had finished reading the prayers for the dying, he cried out in a transport of joy, and, raising his hands to Heaven: "They are coming!"

"Who are coming?" they asked.

"The angels!"

"How are they coming?"

"They are all in procession."

"And what are they doing?"

"They are singing, oh, so beautifully! Do you not hear them?" The Father Abbot asked him if Our Blessed Lady was there.

"No, Father," he replied, with a little sadness. "She has not come yet."

In a little, his eyes sparkling with joy, he exclaimed: "Father, she has come now; she is here." Then, as if addressing her, he said: "Ave Maria." Then he was silent for some time, as if wrapped in an ecstasy.

"Oh, how beautiful it is! Oh, how beautiful is Mary! How beautiful, how lovely!" he cried out. Then, speaking to the Fathers, kneeling in silence at his bedside, he said: "O my Fathers and Brothers, how sweet it is to die and to go to Heaven in Mary's company!"

A few moments afterwards he raised his head from the pillow and sighed. Thinking he might be wanting something, they asked him if there was anything he would like.

"Oh no, nothing," he replied. "I want nothing now but my Jesus and Heaven!"

And when he had uttered these words he expired.

Look up to heaven now while you are in the world, and when the hour of death comes you will have the happiness of entering into it.

OUR LADY INVITES HER CLIENT TO HEAVEN.

A certain pious religious called Leonard, who had the custom to recommend himself two hundred times a day to the Mother of Mercy, was lying at the point of death.

Our Lady appeared to him, and said: "Leonard, will you die and come to Heaven, to live with Jesus and me?"

Leonard answered: "And who art thou, Lady?"

Mary answered: "I am the Mother of Mercy whom you called upon so often. I am come now to receive your soul. Come, let us go together into Heaven."

That same hour the good religious died, and, let us hope, is now possessing the joys of Paradise in the company of Our Lady whom he loved so much.

www.ingramcontent.com/pod-product-compliance
Lightning Source LLC
Chambersburg PA
CBHW070859120626
46546CB00001B/57